A New Kind of Life is a l[...] the reader from World War I Glasgow, through New York in the 1940s and 50s to modern day Washington DC. On the way Helen Lillie's life has mirrored the march of women's self-direction from domestic appendage to independent citizen.

Born into a respectable if repressed Scottish middle class family, she resolved early on not to emulate her female role models who, if not 'rescued' by marriage, spent their time looking after elderly relatives and going on long country walks. Having battled the regime at the Edinburgh's St. Trinnean's School in the 1920s, followed by Glasgow University and the Yale Drama School, she tried against the odds to establish herself in the world of work as a writer.

Written with frankness and humour, and sparing few details in experience of life and love, she takes the reader on an insightful journey through her fascinating experience of the twentieth century.

Helen Lillie has worked as a journalist, columnist and author. She lives in Washington DC.

previous books by the same author:

The Listening Silence (Hurst & Blackett/Arrow/Hawthorne Dell)
Call Down the Sky (Hurst & Blackett/Arrow)
Home to Strathblane (Argyll)
Strathblane and Away (Argyll)
The Rocky Island (Argyll)

A New Kind of Life

an informal autobiography

Helen Lillie

Argyll
publishing

First published 1999
Argyll Publishing
Glendaruel
Argyll PA22 3AE
Scotland

British Library Cataloguing-in-Publication Data.
A catalogue record for this book is available from the
British Library.

ISBN 1 902831 06 3

Origination
Cordfall Ltd, Glasgow

Printing
Caledonian International
Book Manufacturing, Glasgow

I am a part of all that I have met;
Yet all experience is an arch where thro'
Gleams that untravelled world, whose margin fades
For ever and for ever when I move.
How dull it is to pause, to make an end,
To rust unburnished, not to shine in use!
As though to breathe were life. Life piled on life
Were all too little, and of one to me
Little remains; but every hour is saved
A bringer of new things; and vile it were
For some three suns to store and hoard myself.

Ulysses
Alfred, Lord Tennyson

Foreword

Many people have influenced my life, including some I don't even know.

Those whose contribution I acknowledge most gratefully include my mother Helen Barbara Lillie; my professional role model Dr. Catherine Gavin; my "second cousin" Dr. Morag L. Insley; my father image and best boss "Cappy" Capotosto; and above all my husband for over forty years, Charles Robert Scott Marwick, my dearest Charlie.

I appreciate the faith in this chronicle shown by my agent Cathie Thomson and my publisher Derek Rodger.

I also remember with appreciation Sandy, our Cairn terrier when I was growing up in Strathblane, as well as Victoria Regina ("Vicky-My-Pet") and Ah So the Second ("Mr. So-So"), both long gone to the Celestial Cattery.

Helen Lillie
Washington DC
June 1999

Contents

One Hundred Per Cent a Lillie

As hostilities in World War I really got going, I was born in Scotland on September 13, 1915 in a nursing home in Glasgow's Blythswood Square, then as now a fine example of Victorian architecture, and the location, sixty years earlier, of a shocking deed.

Murder aficionados will recall it was at a house in Blythswood Square, that in 1857, 21-year-old Madeleine Smith, from a respectable Glasgow middle class family, served cocoa through a basement window to a young Frenchman, Emille L'Engelier. She had had a passionate affair with him but was trying to break it off to marry a richer, more conventional suitor.

Shortly after he drank Madeleine's proferred refreshment, L'Engelier died in agony from arsenic poisoning. When his friends found a collection of explicitly passionate letters from her among his possessions she was arrested and tried for his murder.

But the Victorian male jury couldn't accept that a girl who might have been their own daughter had enjoyed and then poisoned her lover, even though he was a foreigner. So they brought in that indigenously Scottish verdict "Not Proven", meaning, "We suspect you did it but we don't want to see you hang."

I've often wondered whether being born so close to the scene of Madeleine's activities acted subconsciously on me. According to the Chaos theory of the 1990s, it's possible. I never considered her a role model, but our lives did have certain similarities. We both grew up in comfortable middle class Scottish families. We were both extremely curious about life beyond the confines of Glasgow. In our twenties, for different reasons, Fate helped us leave the city. We also lived the latter part of our long lives in the United States of America.

That I never poisoned anyone, at least to my knowledge, is

not from lack of a killer instinct but because such extreme measures weren't necessary by the time my generation of Scottish girls replaced Madeleine Smith's. World War II gave us a legitimate way to seek a life beyond the city of our birth.

Which brings me to the reason for this memoir. Many people have suggested that I've had "such a fascinating life" I should write about it but my own motivation is to offer some perspective on the changing options women have achieved in my own lifetime, i.e. during the twentieth century.

Today, in most developed countries, girls have the right to control their output of offspring, the right to vote, and the right to keep the money they earn. None of these three major liberators were in existence when I was born in 1915. There have been other important developments, like the discovery of antibiotics, but for us females birth control, financial independence and the political clout that comes with money have been the greatest aids to women in the past eighty years.

Marriage is now an option rather than, as in the past, a survival strategy. Nor is it a way to help families financially and socially, or like the ill-fated union of Lady Diana Spencer and Charles, Prince of Wales, to assure heirs. Despite the outcome of that marriage, as the twentieth century ends, the divorce rate is levelling off, in the USA at least. There's more equality in marriage and more role reversal with house husbands now accepted.

The negative side of women's progress is that we are experiencing a strong though subtle male backlash.

My generation was probably the last in which upper and middle class girls expected to stay at home unless they married and repeated their mothers' pattern of running households and raising children. There were exceptions, but that was the norm. We were given better education than our mothers and aunts but got little or no guidance on how to make use of it.

When you had a talent for painting or playing some instrument you could study art or music. If, like me, your aptitude was for words, maybe you went to college and then presumably you'd know how to write books. If you had no special aptitudes, you took courses in cookery at "the Dough (short for Domestic Science) School," or you stayed home arranging the flowers, doing volunteer work, like collecting for charities or running the Girl Guides.

It wasn't taken for granted, as it is today, that the objective of an education, for girls as well as for boys, is the independence gained by a paying job.

If a girl didn't attract or have a chance to meet eligible men, or if her family wasn't "working class" but hadn't much money, she trained as a school teacher or a social worker. Most of my female friends at Glasgow University aimed for those two professions even when they had little or no interest in them. Neither attracted me. Once I asked a history lecturer about the academic life, but when he outlined the long years of study towards a PhD, I lost interest.

The few girls motivated to study law or medicine weren't usually the marrying kind and their role models were single too. The average career woman was a spinster or a widow.

Raised on a literary diet of Jane Austen and the Victorian novelists, I determined at an early age to find a husband. Otherwise, I believed I'd be a failure as a female. Vanity had a good deal to do with it and what is today known as peer pressure.

Why I desired so strongly to be married I don't know because, though they generated enough love to stay together until death parted them after forty-some years, my parents were an ill-matched couple. They were not, as the saying goes, comfortable with each other though they came from similar backgrounds. They were first cousins and both their fathers were bankers.

My brilliant beautiful mother, Helen Barbara Lillie, known as Nellie, was born in the late nineteenth century when women's suffrage and feminism were already in the air. Her fate was possibly typical for a girl with her middle class background. She was sent to a boarding school in England where she became, as she loved to recall, The Head Girl. She was also a talented pianist, and a compulsive reader as I am too.

After she died in 1970, I found a fragment of autobiography she'd written describing her longing for a career, like two spinster friends who ran a pioneer club for girls in Aberdeen. But my mother was the eldest in a family of four, with two brothers and a mentally defective sister whose existence I discovered later

11

by chance. When I was little, my grandaunt loved to show me family photographs, and there were several of a childish girl in a pram-like bathchair, dressed in layers of Edwardian clothes. "That's Margey!" Auntie would say, but never identified her any further. From an undocumented (and questioningly accurate!) family history compiled by Mummy's brother Jack in his old age, I learned that Margey was stone deaf and had survived into her twenties.

By the time I was born, Mummy's father, a bank agent, had retired to a house on Greenbank Crescent in Edinburgh's fashionable Morningside. These grandparents died when I was too young to have many memories of them although those I do have are vivid. "Gan," my grandmother, *nee* Ellen Tait, was a handsome stormy-looking lady who always wore round gold earrings, which I now enjoy.

Grandpa, after whom my father was named Thomas Lillie, wrote sentimental poetry which he had privately printed. The most embarrassing to me was written ostensibly in my name and described how as a baby I'd slept through the only World War I air raid on Edinburgh. Grandpa also played the piano badly. After a long, healthy life, he developed what may have been a hiatal hernia and used to have scary fits of gagging during meals. When I was about five we were on holiday in England, and upon returning to our hotel, the porter said to my mother, "Tell Mr. Lillie he had a phone call from Edinburgh to say his uncle died." This could only have been my mother's father as she immediately figured out. But you didn't give women bad news directly in those days.

Soon after, when our home phone rang, Mummy answered it, then rushed into my room crying incredulously, "Gan's DEAD!" My father commented to me, later, that my grandmother "made Uncle Tom's life miserable then died of remorse after he died. I don't want your mother to do the same." He also told me that when he asked for Mummy's hand, Grandpa warned him that she was "a very queer girl. Sometimes she bursts into tears and locks herself in the bathroom."

No wonder, thought I, by then a teenager.

Of my mother's two brothers, John Adam Lillie, QC, LLD, my

Uncle Jack, later Sheriff of Fife and Kinross, was a wonderful crochety bachelor who lived to be nearly one hundred years old. He left home early but lived all his life in Edinburgh and took care never to marry. I was his residuary legatee and I believe we respected each other. In old age I look rather like him.

My Uncle Bertie, Robert Alexander Lillie, who had a PhD in Philosophy and was therefore known as Doctor Lillie, was a brilliant charmer. When he was eighteen his appendix ruptured and was removed on the proverbial kitchen table. During a lengthy convalescence, his mother so spoilt him he grew neurotically self-centered and, as the saying goes,'enjoyed' ill-health until he died in 1977 at the age of eighty-seven, prematurely according to Uncle Jack who complained to me over the transatlantic phone that "Bertie's death was so *unnecessary*. He went into town without his top coat and caught cold."

My grandmother's brother Adam Tait, known as Uncle Ned, was a handsome "lad of parts" from the Borders, who joined the Royal Bank of Scotland and wound up as its General Manager in Edinburgh. He settled money on the young invalid "so he would never have to worry about the future." So, at his leisure, Uncle Bertie attended Edinburgh University and earned his impressive degree writing a dissertation on Emmanuel Kant. He never worked for a salary, save for a brief stint as a bank clerk during World War I.

Uncle Bertie was a Renaissance man in his interests. He shared quarters briefly with Uncle Jack at 85 Great King Street in Edinburgh after their parents died, then he moved into a small comfortable house on Braid Road near the Mortonhall golf course, with a series of hopeful housekeepers to care for him. He played the piano and the organ, went to music festivals, met stimulating, creative people, and reviewed unreadable philosophical tomes for the *Scotsman*.

He had a talent for appreciation and told me many times how much he enjoyed my weekly Washington Letter in the *Glasgow Herald*. His many friendships with women never endangered his comfortable bachelor life style. In his later years he invested his money creatively in contemporary Scottish works of art, particularly those of Sir William G. Gillies, who became a close friend. These pictures Uncle Bertie donated to the nation and got an MBE for it. This infuriated my mother. "Why didn't the painters get the honour?" she complained to me. "They did the work!"

Her feelings for her brothers were ambivalent. She admired their achievements but deplored their 'selfishness.' In her brief memoir, she told how, though she was smarter than they were, she had had to abandon all hope of college when Bertie took ill because she was needed at home. I suspect Margey was still alive then, and unable to be left alone. An old Edinburgh lady told me, many years later, that she saw my grandparents in the Greenbank Church each Sunday "and they always had the little girl with them in her go-cart."

So the only way my mother could get away from home was to marry. She had two suitors, one an extemely dull banker, and the other her cousin Thomas Lillie, the second son in the large tightly knit family of another Glasgow bank agent who died relatively young leaving a formidable widow to bring up eight children.

My father's mother I called "Granny-in-Milngavie". She lived in that pleasant Glasgow suburb in a house called Sprouston which overlooked little Loch Tannoch. Granny – Mary Stroyan Lillie – came from farming stock in Galloway. She liked her children to come home every night and sit around the fireside. So engrained was this habit, four of them were still doing it when they died of old age in the 1960s. I later described this household as I remember it in my novel *The Listening Silence*.

All the Lillies were hard of hearing in later life. My father's elder brother Robert, whom I called Uncle BoBo, wanted to be a painter but was firmly steered into banking to provide for his siblings. However he spent his evenings and weekends studying art and when his deafness allowed him to retire with a good pension, he put commerce behind him, grew a well-trimmed white goatee beard and evolved himself into "Mr. Lillie the Artist." He painted prolifically, sometimes well enough to be accepted for inclusion in major exhibitions. My cousin George Laird who was an architect, told me the buildings Uncle BoBo drew would have fallen down.

But of all that talented, frustrated family, Uncle Bobo's face was the happiest, and when he died, in his eighties, he left his money to found the charming Lillie Art Gallery in Milngavie. His self-portrait hangs in the lobby, and his old friend Mary Armour, a fine Scottish painter, contributed a beautiful flower picture for the poster advertising the gallery's twenty-fifth birthday.

Odd that both the Roberts in the family – first cousins – should have become identified with art, Uncle Bobo as a painter and Uncle Bertie as a collector.

Of my father's other siblings, beautiful talented Mary Jessie "threw herself away" happily on an architect called John Laird and produced my glamorous cousin George. Agnes, my Auntie Nanny, had a romance that came to nought and spent the rest of her life doing beautiful embroidery and making dolls. Auntie Jane, the baby of the family, never succeeded in marrying, she was probably too sharp-tongued. She was good at extracting information out of people and would have been an excellent investigative journalist had she been born fifty years later. James Samuel – Uncle Jamie – and Uncle Allan, both handsome and intelligent, never amounted to anything.

Uncle Willie was the "black sheep" due to some character weaknesses attributed by his wife to his experiences in World War I. He sired an admirable, successful son, James Mitchell Lillie, my cousin "Hamish," who had the good sense to emigrate to the USA and settled the next generation of Lillies in Texas. It's a logical place, if it's true that the family is descended from French Hugenots from Lille, i.e. they tended to be "agin the government." Like the common ancestor of the Glasgow and Edinburgh branches of the family, my great-grandfather "the Dominie" from Duns who "went out in the Disruption" of 1834 and eventually moved to the West of Scotland from the Borders. As a child, I remember seeing Lillie gravestones going back to the 1600s in the churchyard of Sprouston in Berwickshire.

The Tait family, into which my grandfather Thomas Lillie married, is buried in Melrose Abbey, and illustrates Scottish upward mobility. The first of the three Tait gravestones, dated 1744, is modest and describes those buried there as "probaiers" of Darnick, an adjacent village. The second stone, bigger and handsomer, commemorates ancestors who are now "feuers" or middle class. The final stone lists my granduncle as "Adam Tait of Wooplaw" – in other words, he was a man of property, a gentleman referred to by the name of his country estate. When my mother died in 1970, I had her ashes interred in Melrose Abbey beside Uncle Ned's because he appreciated her ability far more than her parents or her husband and she loved him accordingly. He appointed her executrix on his sizable estate, thumbing his nose from beyond the grave at his nephew the QC who was so irked he contested the will and had himself declared Uncle Ned's heir. This gave him Wooplaw House and its adjacent farming land, though not the money.

So I grew up with two distinct sets of relatives, one in Glasgow and one in Edinburgh, all named Lillie except my granduncle, Adam Tait and his sister Margaret, known simply as Auntie. The Lillies all had blue-green eyes and fair reddish hair. The Tait descendants were dark-haired and brown-eyed, with the exception of Uncle Jack, the QC, who resembled his cousins in the West.

"You look just like your father!" people told me for years and it infuriated me. It shouldn't for he was tall, fair-haired and handsome. To get him out of his stultifying home, Uncle Ned transferred him to the Royal Bank's head office in Edinburgh. There, in his free time, the ambitious young man studied law although he never took a degree. He also fell in love with my mother and married her in 1912 when, in his early thirties, he was appointed Manager of the Bank's Exchange Square office in Glasgow which handled more business that either the Edinburgh or London offices though it lacked their prestige. My father stayed in that same job until he retired during World War II, a disappointed man because he had never been offered the General Managership or the knighthood which, by then, went with it.

I was an only child, ostensibly because three months after my birth, Mummy had scarlet fever. This left her with a damaged heart and she was told she must have no more children. Birth control methods were unreliable in those days and seldom attempted by respectable people. My mother resolved her problem like many other women of the pre-Pill era by slamming the bedroom door on my father.

What this did to her own emotional health no-one will ever know. For him the consequences were disastrous and all too evident. Today the couple would probably have sought counselling but I question whether the marriage would have worked out much differently. They were emotionally and intellectually incompatible – he was an Aries and she was a Scorpio – but in a curious way they loved each other.

Mummy did once walk out on her marriage. I was too young to understand the acrid arguments she had with my father. She kept saying, "I am in Hell" which I thought was some contraction of Helen. My father was very cold, made notes on a scrap of paper, remarking, "'Hell.' A very good word." Then Mummy and I went to Edinburgh, and she had long talks with Uncle Bertie. After we returned home she directed her emotional energy into bringing me up, turning her house into a showplace, working in volunteer projects, and reading constantly. Today, she would probably have found herself a job.

For some forgotten reason, I never called my father "Daddy", I named him "Littie" and briefly called myself "Lottie." As a small child I admired him, he was so big and handsome, though I never liked his nicknaming me "Kipper" and "Ginger". A gap started early between us as he grew increasingly frustrated both as a husband and later professionally. In the early days of World War I, he was an enthusiastic member of the Territorial Army, but never saw any fighting because the Bank vetoed his being called up for active duty. Evidently corporations could do that in those days.

By the Armistice in 1918 nearly every man in his regiment had been killed. Moreover, his handsome young nephew, George Laird, who had given a false age and enlisted, came back from France a hero and remained a prominent Territorial officer, eventually becoming a colonel in World War II. All this gave my father a guilt complex and the feeling that he'd missed something. I became so tired of hearing about how he hadn't died in the Great War that I became an ardent pacifist and remain one to this day.

2

Country Life between World Wars

When they were first married, my parents lived on Cecil Street in the West End of Glasgow which I know my mother hated. I remember nothing of that period because as soon as she could, she bought, with Uncle Ned's help, a modest house called Bluerisk in Strathblane, a country parish at the base of the beautiful Campsie Fells only twelve miles from town and so, even in those days, within commuting distance of my father's office. Although it was never mentioned that the house belonged to his wife, my father was so proud of it, he delighted to show it off to guests.

Strathblane in 1916 was "real country" in contrast to Milngavie and Bearsden, and Bluerisk, though not large, was big enough to employ two maids and a chauffeur-gardener. In my novel *Home to Strathblane*, set in 1792-3, I described the original house, named Blaeresk, and in it I house a brilliant ornery young physician from Edinburgh, Doctor Douglas Elliot Stewart who becomes the hero of *Strathblane and Away* and its sequel *The Rocky Island*.

I grew up creating imaginary characters and devoted to dolls because, perforce, I was a rather lonely child. There were not many households close by with young families. Indeed, there were not many houses and whenever one went up, people worried about being "overlooked" and losing privacy. Then of course they became friendly with the newcomers who joined their ranks and feared about the effect on the neighbourhood of the next home to be built.

In the early decades of the twentieth century the Blane Valley had two churches with two ageing ministers. The Strathblane Parish Church was run by the Reverend William Begbie Moyes, a charming, cultivated man whose rich English wife didn't fraternise with the villagers.

A few years after her death, when he was in his seventies, he had a heart attack while preaching, fell from the pulpit and broke his ankle. He was much loved but as a widower he had become a recluse, so instead of phoning him people went around asking each other in hushed tones, "And how is Poor Mr. Moyes?"

Then the astonishing news broke that he was doing so well he was getting married again! And to a pretty nurse ten years younger than his daughter. The agency which had sent her to care for him didn't permit her to remain beyond a certain time. "And when that came, we couldn't bear to part!" she told Mummy.

Catherine Moyes was tiny and fragile-looking with prematurely white hair and a delicate pink and white complexion. But behind this dainty exterior was a formidable personality. She made no secret of her professional disagreements with the local doctor and she also well knew the things being said about her marriage so she took the initiative and made herself known. With her husband's guidance, she called on people throughout the parish and charmed them, even the sceptics. The day she had tea with Mummy and me, we all became friends.

She brought Mr. Moyes back into circulation and he gave me enormous help when I was researching the development of the parish for Scottish history assignments at Glasgow University. I won a prize for those essays even excluding some of his favourite stories.

He had come to Strathblane as a young man at the turn of the century and instituted the first Christmas Day service there. It was thinly attended and as he walked home afterwards, he encountered one of his elders, a roadman who was digging away as usual.

"Geordie," said the young minister, bracing himself, "I didn't see you at the Christmas Day worship."

"Naw!" was the scornful reply. "Ye'll be haein' candles next."

"In other words," Mr. Moyes explained to me, "Next step Popery!"

An elderly female parishioner remarked to him on his first pastoral visit, "I hear your sermons are never more than thirty minutes long. Your predecessor aye preached for an hour or more. It's no' worth puttin' on ma Sunday clothes to come out and hear *you*."

This lady was a relative of the celebrated writer Andrew Lang, and when he published a biography of Mary Queen of Scots, she asked him what he thought of her?

"Read my book and find out," he replied, author-like.

"I'm no' wastin' my time on what you wrote, Andrew. I want your own honest opinion of Mary."

Lang thought, then delivered judgement, "I think she was a bad one. But a good sort."

The Moyes' difference in age didn't matter intellectually. Nursing had matured Catherine and "William Begbie" as she always called him was extremely youthful in his point of view. In *Home to Strathblane* I based my fictitious minister of Baldernock and his wife on this couple.

Mr. Moyes and the United Free Church minister, the Reverend Theodore Johnston, retired at the same time and their two congregations were united under the Reverend Frederick Kennedy, who was young and newly married to a university-educated woman. The village wasn't sure about her at first for she was seen in Glasgow lunching by herself in an Italian restaurant and ordering wine. But people eventually grew fond of her. This couple were good friends to me when I was in college. My parents, who had been attending a church in Milngavie, moved their "lines" to Strathblane and from then on we were all more involved in the life of the parish.

My father became Church Treasurer, my mother worked hard and without fanfare on many local projects, and when someone thought up a Girl Guide Troop, I became Tawny Owl of the Brownies. Our Brown Owl (or leader) was a pretty young married woman called Eba Haddow. Years later, when I revisited Strathblane in 1946 I asked her about our troop and was somewhat horrified to find that quite a number of them had strayed from virtue during World War II.

"What on earth did we teach these kids?" I asked.

"You didn't teach them enough," said Eba's handsome husband, Archie.

3

Women of their Time

In my teens I had a memorable friendship with two contemporaries who lived in Mugdock House near Milngavie, Heather and Hazel Muir-Simpson. Their father owned a furniture emporium in Glasgow and their mother had hearing problems.

These two girls and I shared a passion for drama, read and wrote plays and acted them out. Once when I arrived for tea, Hazel met me at the door with the news that "Heather's in her room crying her eyes out."

"What's the matter?" I asked.

"Jo didn't marry Laurie! Amy did!" Heather sobbed as she joined us, clutching a damp copy of *Little Women*. Her tears made sense to me, in a way they wouldn't today. Jo March's union with a professor led to an unglamorous future, teaching. Amy never did do much with her talent for painting, but she had a rich, handsome husband and travelled abroad. The real life Jo, Louisa Mae Alcott, never wed. There was a message in this, somewhere.

The older people living in the Blane Valley between the wars usually had unmarried daughters at home. And these middle class, middle-aged women spent their days taking care of their mothers' households – i.e. managing the maid or maids, and for relaxation taking long country walks, sometimes accompanied by a dog or female relative.

At Milndavie House, along the road from Bluerisk, two talented spinsters, Minnie and Alice Young, lived with their mother and found an artistic outlet decorating their home and making beautiful, fashionable clothes for themselves. They had a married sister who lived in the Channel Islands.

When old Mrs. Young died the house was sold to a retired newspaperman, James Davidson, the first managing editor of a now defunct Glasgow tabloid called the *Bulletin*. A heavy-set elderly man with a voice throaty from smoking, he passed his time exercising two Scotty dogs, up and down past our house. He looked so lonely Mummy and I often went out and visited with him. I was then a teenager and he was very fond of me, talked to me about the newspaper business and writing in general, and I credit him with steering me towards journalism.

He had two daughters. One was married, and the other, Mary, a big stout woman, found an outlet exhibiting her pedigree wolfhound, Katinka. Once when in heat Katinka disappeared and Mary drove many miles around the valley before finding her. When the next dog show fell due, Katinka was found to be pregnant!

"And we've no idea what breed the father is," Mr. Davidson told Mummy, adding darkly, "It's probably that Ricky," meaning an adored, adorable Dalmatian owned by the Kirsops, mother, son Jack, and unmarried daughter Violet, who lived next door.

Fortunately for community relations, the puppies were black Labradors obviously sired at an outlying farm, but this ended Katinka's show career and soon after, Mary got rid of her to a family who wanted a pet for their children. When Mr. Davidson died some years later Mary left the Valley. She had shown no evidence of marketable skills or any desire to find an outlet in work.

The Kirsops were, as the saying goes, in trade. Jack managed the family business, a menswear store in Glasgow, but his real interest was fishing on Loch Lomond. Mrs. Kirsop was a dear gossipy old lady lovingly cared for by her nice, homely, capable daughter Violet who stayed on in the little house after her mother and brother died, and, I'm told, eventually had a male lodger! She did some volunteer work in later life, and was interested in the theatre. She'd have been a good career woman if she'd had to be one.

Up the Glasgow Road in Ardunan House lived Mrs. Moncrieff, another widow with two unmarried daughters. Their sister was a doctor in England and also single. These spinsters' most visible occupation was walking purposefully around the Strathblane roads. One dabbled in the stock market and frequently phoned my father for tips, usually at our dinner hour. These two ladies were handsome and well-dressed and I don't know why they never married.

The unmarried daughter who made the strongest impression on me was Sheena Pirie, whose father, an elderly charmer, was the famous painter Sir George Pirie who lived in a beautiful house in Torrance where he painted scruffy fowls and barnyard animals. His wife was dainty and white-haired and had a will of iron. She allegedly had forced her two sons to achieve. One took his artistic talents into the film industry. The younger, Norman, despite a nervous stutter, became a famous research scientist.

But Sheena, the daughter, could only use her administrative ability as a volunteer in the Girl Guides. She looked great in uniform which transformed her from a dowdy, rather snide spinster into an outgoing, handsome woman. When I was the Tawny Owl of the Strathblane Brownies we met at church parades as well as over tea with our families. I admired Sheena though I was slightly in awe of her and, somehow, sorry for her too when she started to have illnesses that even in those days seemed psychosomatic.

Next door to Bluerisk, in Napier Lodge, lived two elderly maiden ladies. Their brother W.P. Ker was an Oxford professor, but I doubt if he was any cleverer than his elder sister Caroline, known as "Miss Carrie." My dentist in Glasgow once asked me if I knew his patient "a Miss Ker from Strathblane." When I asked "Which one?" he replied, "She described herself as 'the wicked one'." "That," said I, "is Miss Carrie."

Though she lived a blameless life she called a spade a spade. The parish church had a dreadful organist, a woman with an invalid husband who held the job to pay for a car. Her voluntaries

> "These unmarried, middle class, middle-aged women spent their days taking care of their mothers' households – managing the maids, and for relaxation taking long country walks, sometimes accompanied by a dog or female relative"

were so appalling, Mummy called them "Mendelsohn's Songs Without Music." One wintry Sunday the organ was frozen and inoperable. "So nice without the music, wasn't it!" fluted Miss Carrie Ker as she emerged shivering, from her morning worship. She stated this fact entirely without malice.

Her sister Miss Penelope was a beautiful, fey, white-haired lady who always wore thin Madonna blue dresses with white organdy at the neck and matching wool capes that did little to protect her from cold winds. She devoted herself to Good Works and constantly fluttered past our house en route to a Children's Hospital close by. Miss Penelope brought her neighbours flowers and little gifts but it was difficult to talk with her, she was so hard of hearing. She used an ear trumpet and I'm sure heard no evil through it. Once my mother borrowed a biography of the pioneer nurse Florence Nightingale from Miss Carrie and when she returned it, commented that "the 'Angel of the Crimea' must have been difficult to live with."

"Oh, saints are like that," said Miss Carrie. "I live with one myself."

Rumour had it that the money these ladies had inherited originated in the slave trade and Miss Penelope's preoccupation with charities came from a sense of guilt. Both sisters lived to a great age. The saintly Miss Pen died of agonising cancer. The "wicked" Miss Carrie, who loved her flowers, sat down in her garden one sunny morning and Hannah the housemaid found her there peacefully dead when she came to tell her lunch was ready.

I doubt if either of them seriously considered either marriage or a career. Miss Carrie once told me how some man in the parish had expressed curiosity as to why she hadn't a husband? "If he ever asks me directly," said she, "I'm going to burst into tears and sob that my fiancee was 'Drowned Before My Eyes!'"

They would have felt at home in Jane Austen's society. They had many friends, and entertained intellectual, academic people I was always invited to meet. They were happy and well-occupied, Miss Carrie with reading and elegant embroidery, and Miss Penelope through her interest in the Children's Hospital.

The younger generation of spinsters were different. In my

teenage opinion, they hadn't much fun other than going to plays or concerts with their parents, as I did too. Their uniform was a raincoat over a good tweed suit, usually brown, with a woolly twinset which they had probably knitted while listening to the wireless in the long evenings. They wore solid footwear, felt hats, and if their walking sticks were for protection, I doubt if they were needed to fend off predatory males.

This apparently was how women lived if they didn't get away from home, and I could see myself stepping into their sensible shoes. I already took long walks with my dog Sandy and was involved with the Brownies on Saturdays. I also grew up close to my brilliant mother with no outlet for her abilities other than the house and garden, which she was constantly re-arranging. This meant workmen and mess underfoot, which I hated but presumably it gave her an interest besides reading interminably.

On a small estate called Ardoch, farther up the Valley, lived a lively old couple called James and Ruby McClellan. They had turned to landscape gardening for income after losing James's family fortune, made in whisky which, the Scots claim, never lasts through the third generation.

In palmier days, the McClellans had lived in Europe and known celebrities like Anna Pavlova. James reminded me of Beatrix Potter's foxy Mr. Todd. He had a reddish moustache, wore brown tweedy jackets, plusfours, leggings and a beret, and was redolent of Gaulois cigarettes. White-haired Ruby wore voluminous blue denim skirts to grub around in rock gardens since ladies didn't wear pants in those days.

The McClellans were popular, and when they opened their own spectacular garden to the public each spring, Ruby's women friends served tea while their husbands directed the traffic. As a teenager, I escorted guided tours up to the top of a hillside covered with flowering shrubs.

Worn out by hard work, the McClellans retired to Hyère in France in the 1930s. When World War II began to wind down, my mother got a letter from James who was hard pressed to keep his now bedridden wife warm and nourished. Mummy forwarded this sad communication to me in New York and I sent them a "Care" package. I also met James in the winter of

1947 when he brought Ruby's ashes to the Blane Valley. He still wore his beret and stylishy shabby clothes smelling of French tobacco.

Ruby McClellan, who in poverty teamed up with her husband and maintained their lifestyle through work they both loved, i.e. creating beautiful gardens, stands out in my memory as much happier than the aimless though better-heeled spinsters who were her neighbours.

And another country wife – whose maiden name was Beatrix Potter – profoundly affected my decision to become a writer. When I had just learned to read, we went to the Lake District on holiday and in our tiny Morris Cowley car drove through Sawrey, the locale of my favorite books about Peter Rabbit and his friends.

Hill Top Farm, where their author lived, was surrounded by a tall hedge but my father lifted me up so that I could see over it. Just then a large stout lady in a shapeless brown hat and suit emerged from the front door carrying a basket and marched down the path to the gate. She gave me a lovely smile.

Mummy, greatly daring for her, asked, "Are you Beatrix Potter?"

"Yes," said the lady. "I am."

I've since read that she was usually short with snoopers but that wasn't our experience. I don't remember her exact words but I think she asked me my name. I told her and added breathlessly that I'd read all her books.

"Would you," she asked, "like an egg that Sally Henny Penny laid this morning?" When I nodded, she took it from her basket and handed it to me. With its innards blown out, I treasured it until eventually it fell off a shelf and broke.

So I learned that behind the books I enjoyed were real people. And though I have since met many authors, if you asked me off the top of my head to describe "a writer" I'd say unhesitatingly, "She's a big stout lady in a brown hat and tweeds and lives in the country." But, like Ruby McClellan, a far cry from those spinsters in their aimless peregrinations.

Among our relatives was a family of cousins, poor relations known as The Camerons. All female, two got married, three worked and two stayed at home in Edinburgh. One moved to Canada after marriage, taking a sister along, a teacher who never married but had a lot of fun, according to her niece, Nancy Donaldson, my contemporary and lifelong friend. Nancy became a succesful dietician then made a happy marriage and could only work part-time to avoid paying additional taxes. Thumbing through her photograph albums after her death, I found that while growing up, she was always surrounded by young people. I, on the other hand, was always pictured alone or with a parent or elderly relative.

The other married Cameron also had a daughter, my second cousin Lillie Gibson, who had an impressive career as a banker in Glasgow. Had she been born a generation later, she might well have made it into top management.

Of the other working Camerons, Mary was a nurse who had a legendary career during World War I then became director of a hospital. She was always smiling. Lillie, another sister, lived at home and had a high-level secretarial job. She played golf and seemed to enjoy life. Of the two who didn't have jobs Kate was "delicate" and presumably unable to work although she had a lively mind. Maggie, overweight and loving food, kept house.

Another cousin – Agnes Adams later Mrs. Rolf Henderson – to whom my mother was close, married and did much volunteer work in local dramatics. Cousin Aggie, as I called her, indicated that if she'd been able to go into the theatre professionally, she'd have done well. Her daughter, my second cousin Dr. Morag Lillie Insley, is, like me, a dedicated careerist – as a gerontologist, in public health and, in retirement, UK representative for the African Gerontological Society. She also married and raised three children, the eldest my godchild, Jane.

So, growing up, I absorbed the information that to work outside one's home led to a more satisfying life. Certainly my mother enouraged this idea and my father gave it a certain lip service, once suggesting that I become a minister so I could spend my time writing sermons, an idea typical of his concept of what women did if they left home to have careers.

4

Growing up Without Antibiotics

There were also, in those days, other factors affecting a girl's future at least from her parents' point of view.

I was considered "delicate". Although I breathed fresh country air and had little contact with other children, I was always catching colds which turned into bronchitis. "Helen had it nine times in one winter," Mummy would tell her friends.

The local doctor recommended that I spend a winter in a milder climate. So my mother took me to Torquay where I could enjoy the warmer temperatures and the nourishing Devonshire cream. It made me sicker than ever, so she insisted on a test for food allergies, then a new procedure involving a lot of little scratches down the arm. If any of these swelled it indicated sensitivity to something edible.

"I hope it's not roast beef," I remarked. It wasn't. It was the casein of milk. So I could eat butter but not cheese and no longer had to imbibe horrid white stuff or eat a slimy pudding called junket.

"Just don't let her eat those things and she'll be all right," said the local medico. But I wasn't, and after some fruitless consulting with paediatricians, one a woman, Mummy turned to what is today known as complementary medicine. She took me to Dr. William E. Boyd, an eminent homœopath who was "on call" when the Royal Family came north to Scotland.

He was a nice, unassuming, unfrightening physician who lived and practised at 17 Sandyford Place, another one of those respectable Glasgow buildings which had been the site of a spectacular murder in Victorian days. I found this out when I discovered William Roughhead's books on Scottish crime.

Dr. Boyd's sensible diagnosis was that my resistance to disease needed building up. This he did by giving me little white pills and prescribing "sunbaths" i.e. stretching naked under an ultraviolet lamp with my eyes goggled against its rays. He also suggested we holiday in warm, sunny places, like France instead of the Scottish Highlands.

As I grew stronger I gained faith in homœopathy. "Helen uses Dr. Boyd like a medicine man," Mummy remarked. Once, as a student, I started a cold just before the opening of a play in which I had a leading part. I phoned him and informed him in no uncertain terms that he had to get me well! He did. Though I coughed and snuffled, to the distress of the student director, throughout the dress rehearsal, I was well by the opening night!

Years later, in 1936, not even Dr. Boyd could control a horrendous ear infection probably the result of overtaxing my energies. By then I had achieved a lively social life and was studying hard at Glasgow University. I was also acting in two plays with the Dramatic Club. These had been planned to open several months apart, but King George V died and rescheduling pushed them into opening within a week and uncomfortably close to degree exams. I played the female lead in one play – Anne Whitefield in Shaw's *Man and Superman* – and had an important scene in *Children in Uniform* as a Grand Duchess. I wasn't bad in either.

But, exhausted after the plays closed, I wakened one morning with a high temperature and painful swelling on the right side of my face. Today, I'd probably have been given an antibiotic – even by a homœopath! Prior to penicillin it took surgery to drain the poison.

After the operation, my appetite bounced back. But Dr. Boyd took the opportunity to test my sensitivity to certain foods and put me on such a bland diet I was served nothing, it seemed, but boiled chicken and stewed apples!

I complained loudly to the surgeon.

"Well, what would you really like to eat?" he demanded. He was my youthful idea of an attractive male.

"Something with a taste!" said I. "Like sardines!"

"Give her a sardine!" he ordered the grinning nurse, and I fell in love with him. Until the day I left the nursing home, when I discovered he was a male chauvinist. "What are you going to read after you go home?" he'd asked on the morning he discharged me.

"Moral Philosophy," said I. "My degree exam's only a week away. Then I have to read up on European History. That's coming up next."

He frowned and turned authoritarian. "I'd rather you read Agatha Christie. You can't possibly sit these exams."

"Why not?" I asked. "I'll be reading something anyway. What's wrong with Plato's *Republic*?"

"It's heavy going. It'd be a strain. Can't you sit those exams in September?" His tone implied it shouldn't matter much anyway. Why did I, a girl from a well-to-do family, need a degree?

"The subject's fresh in my mind now so I'm pretty sure I'd pass Moral Phil. And I don't want exams hanging over me all summer."

"But you've just been very ill!"

At this point, in walked Dr. Boyd and we both converged on him for reinforcement. He just shrugged well-tailored shoulders. "I've known Helen a long time," he told his colleague. "If she says she's going to do something, she means it. If she wants to sit her exams, I'm just going to do everything I can to help her."

That ended my crush on the surgeon. I sat both papers and passed, my energy sustained by homœopathic remedies.

Ill health in childhood doesn't only affect growing bodies. It establishes patterns. Like Uncle Bertie, I found I could use sickness to advantage. In my teens, when I wanted to avoid my father's dinner table diatribes on how You Women Simply Can't Imagine the Weight of Responsibility I Carry and the Amount of Work I Do, I'd claim I had a sore throat and go off to bed. Annie the table maid would bring my dinner up to me on a tray and I'd eat it in peace, enjoying a book.

Mummy, inadvertently through her concern, made me a hypochondriac and if I'm apprehensive about some coming event I develop symptoms of sickness. In youth it was the ubiquitous Scottish cold. Nowadays, tension or anger or even the anticipation of some activity like a trip brings on backaches.

When I left home and was among people who didn't expect me to come down with sniffles whenever I got my feet wet I grew healthy. Once a New York friend who met my parents in Scotland remarked to me, "They told me you were delicate as a child. I couldn't believe it. You're seldom sick nowadays, even in a heavy, stressful job and busy after work."

> "Ill health in childhood doesn't only affect growing bodies. It establishes patterns."

Will we ever find out how much of physical illness is generated in the mind? After undergoing a modified radical mastectomy for breast cancer back in 1981, I found myself purged of a lot of the anger which had built up in me both from professional frustration and problems with my father. I once tried to discuss these with Dr. Boyd and got nowhere. "Children always love their parents," he told me, in essence, and from then on would drop into his conversation what "a fine man" my father was. Indeed he was, but not always as a husband or father.

After the mastectomy, the medical school where it was performed, prescribed a year of adjuvant chemotherapy. My husband Charles Marwick, by then an experienced science writer, saved me from that by taking me to another cancer research centre where the authorities assured us I needed only three months and maybe not at all so if I didn't like it I could quit. This I did and, knock wood, have had no recurrence to date.

A few years later, the *Glasgow Herald* asked me to write a piece about this experience which I did, emphasising that women should demand second opinions before obediently accepting their physicians' recommendations. There was a huge reader response followed by an indignant Letter to the Editor from the cancer department of a prestigious Glasgow hospital complaining that I was undermining their patients' confidence! Women were calling up wanting to know the reason for their treatments – exactly as I'd hoped! – and also asking for sources of impartial advice.

If I'd been male and had prostate cancer, I suspect the

reaction of the medical establishment would have been that to request different points of view on treatment was only sensible.

My cousin Morag's daughter Fiona, also a careerist, had a series of operations for cancer. Her mother says the results were always better when the surgeon treated the young woman as an intelligent person and omitted the old authoritarian "Doctor knows best" approach.

I consider it progress that sexist attitudes on health care and research are now out of the closet, having been exposed by many extremely well qualified women doctors!

And if you're deaf, blind, "delicate" or in a wheelchair, today you can train for professions that will bring satisfaction and money.

5

Going to School

When I was five, I was sent to a little school in Milngavie called Heatherbank run by two maiden ladies known as the Miss Taylors. My chief recollection is wearing a little white rabbit fur coat in the playground and going for lunch with my aunties at Sprouston on Tannoch Drive.

Their mother was an imposing old lady dressed, like Queen Victoria, in black with a white lacy cap trimmed with velvet ribbons. She always sat by the fire in the living room. "I sit here all day," she'd sigh to me. "And I'm always tired. Tired from doing nothing." Well, she'd brought up eight children and now her two spinster daughters took care of her and kept house for the brothers they'd prevented from marrying. (Though my father and Uncle Willie escaped, Uncle Bobo the artist once mailed a proposal to a young lady he met on holiday, then told his sister Jane who talked him into sending a telegram saying "Disregard contents of letter!")

My parents' generation were much concerned about who their children were educated with. "Where did he go to school?" always seemed to be the first question Mummy asked about my college boyfriends.This started with Heatherbank. Years later Eba Haddow said to me, "Your mother tells me you went to nursery school with (Someone-or-other, I forget the name) who has a programme on the BBC. What was he like?"

"Look," I confessed, "Mummy mentioned that to me too but frankly all I remember of him is a big burly boy in a kilt who used to pinch little girls' bottoms."

Said she, "He's still a big burly boy in a kilt who pinches little girls' bottoms."

I didn't last long at Heatherbank, probably because I caught too many colds. Then I had a governess called Miss Anderson who came out from Glasgow on the bus and instructed me in arithmetic, history, piano and French conversation. She even tried to teach me drawing but hadn't much luck.

Once, when I was very young and lying in the double bed I shared with my mother, she picked up Shakespeare's plays and started reading me *A Midsummer Night's Dream*. I'd just seen it on the stage and I followed every word on the page. That and probably similar, now forgotten sessions motivated me to learn to read. It was, I remember, a difficult skill to acquire, but suddenly I grasped the principle of it, something called phonetics or the sound of each letter, and instantly I had a lifelong addiction. Discussing the drug culture of a later generation, a woman friend remarked to me, "I always mainlined books." So did I, and the habit grows stronger with the years.

After Miss Anderson came Miss Dunlop, who as 'Loppe' remained a friend until her death in the 1960s. Good-looking and sociable, she attributed her spinsterhood to World War I, hinting about a fiancee killed in action. She had no formal academic qualifications because as the daughter of an impecunious alcoholic doctor, her brother got all the educational opportunities. But she, not her brother, had to support their widowed mother and Loppe had a gift for and love of teaching. She and Mummy became lifelong friends. They were in agreement on the deficiences of men and both tried subtly to pass their opinions on to me.

Pretty soon, probably with Mummy's financial help, the daily 'lessons' I and two other children shared with Loppe developed into a small school in a West End Glasgow house on Athole Gardens. Out of my eight or ten classmates there, four became lifelong friends.

From Loppe, until I was in my early teens, I got an education that stimulated my imagination and my literary creativity though it left me with a lifelong incapacity to grasp the simplest mathematics. I also learned how to play the piano, more or less. And I have abominable handwriting, which a boyfriend once compared to unravelled knitting or a Russian code. I share this affliction with the two friends who were the nucleus of that first school, Christine and Jessie Watt, otherwise known as The Twins.

They were dainty little blondes, always elegantly dressed in identical outfits. Their mother, an old friend of Mummy's, had made an injudicious marriage to get away from home and gone to Canada. "After the twins, she was told never to have any more children, but she was pregnant when she died the following year," I overheard Mummy confide to Loppe. Christine and Jessie were shipped back to Glasgow to live with their grandparents. They had nurses and governesses and went to see all the musical comedies with their grandmother as soon as they were old enough. This, together with their extensive matching wardrobes, gave them great glamour in my eyes.

When they were around twenty, their grandfather died and the beautiful Christine found a job modelling wedding gowns until she herself married and moved to London and went to work to support herself and also her husband, a clever but eccentric man. The equally lovely Jessie was a ballet dancer before she wed an artist and raised a large family, all of them professional achievers.

For years, the twins and I were inseparable and remained emotionally close in old age. Once, after World War II had caused a long hiatus in foregathering, we were reunited in London and within five minutes were giggling and making childish private jokes as though we had never been parted! We suffered through measles together. It left Jessie with a lifelong tendency to stutter. Once Christine developed some nasty spots on her face. No one thought much about them until her twin came down with chickenpox. I presume I must have had a mild case, too, since we shared the soap and towels at Loppe's. Nor did I succumb to an epidemic of the disease a few years later at my next school, St. Trinnean's in Edinburgh.

St.Trinnean's? Yes indeed. It existed and Ronald Searle got the name, which he spelled a little differently, from some former pupils. The exploits of his monstrous little "Belles" in his cartoons and later in the movies, were sheer wish-fulfilment for me and, I'm sure, for many others. The school is long gone, but some of its "old girls" held a reunion in 1985 and again in 1998 to which the artist contributed champagne.

Why was I sent to an Edinburgh school? It wasn't simply that, as Mummy put it, she didn't want me growing up with a Glasgow accent. The twins and I were out-distancing Loppe's scholastic capabilities. We needed more formal instruction to achieve Leaving Certificates or to pass "The Prelim", the Scottish college entrance examination.

I could, of course, have been boarded at St. Trinnean's but my health was still chancy enough to provide Mummy with an excuse to keep me under her eye. Besides, she had other reasons for being in Edinburgh.

Perhaps this is as good a place as any to explain that, with exceptions, I don't much like old people, and now I'm one of them, I don't much like myself. I relate better to people in their thirties, forties and fifties, although I have friends even older than I am who will never be elderly in their attitudes.

I deplore my aversion to senior citizens. My second cousin Dr. Morag Insley grew up as an only child around elderly people and went on to become a pioneer gerontologist while I fled to America, the Land of the Free where the accent has always been on youth.

I'm not simply turned off by the physical aspects of ageing like wrinkles, arthritis, deafness and blindness. I'm repelled by how advancing years bring out the worst in people and seems to stimulate their selfish instincts. I developed this reaction during my adolescence in Edinburgh, and some of it came from observing how Mummy was stuck with the responsibility of caring for elderly relatives.

After her parents, Grandpa and Gan, died close together, Uncle Ned and Auntie had become Mummy's extended family. Neither had ever married. Uncle Ned was, I believe, more of a father figure to my mother than Grandpa for the eminent banker recognised and appreciated her qualities – her intelligence and her knowledgability, as well as her capacity for unselfish love and loyalty. In his old age he shamelessly exploited this.

Many people, starting with her husband, considered Mummy unsociable. She wasn't. She was, however, extremely reserved and being married to a handsome public charmer didn't help. Moreover, she didn't relate to Littie's business acquaintances or the sonsy Glesca "boaddies" who were their wives. With

Edinburgh snobbishness, she refused to cultivate these people, although she did, when required to do so, entertain them graciously at Bluerisk.

She was friendly with a couple of women neighbours in Strathblane, but she was a lonely person until World War II gave her the opportunity to demonstrate her ability in the kind of career she'd always wanted.

During the 1920s, my parents' marital problems had settled into a pattern. Littie directed his emotional energy into the Bank. Mummy centred hers on me and on the man who most appreciated her, Uncle Ned. To a lesser extent, she was also devoted to his sister, Margaret Christie Tait.

"Auntie," who was my grandaunt, was a sweet, somewhat scatterbrained lady who had been a beauty in her youth. Someone, a missionary I believe, did propose to her but she couldn't face leaving home where she kept house for her working mother. My great-grandmother had been left a widow in middle life and become the Curator of Melrose Abbey, in the Borders. A cottage came with the job.

Later, Auntie kept house for her successful brother in Edinburgh. By then Manager of the Royal Bank, he had built an imposing red sandstone mansion called Darnick at 22 Braid Avenue in Morningside. It was – and is – so enormous that after his death, it was divided into three residences, one of them purchased by Lord Thomson, the Canadian entrepreneur who, when he added the *Scotsman* to his chain of newspapers, came to live in Edinburgh and wanted a home with central heating. This was hard to find in those days, but Darnick had it.

As a child, I loved visiting Darnick. It was comfortably warm and contained a fascinating proliferation of family photos, knicknacks, and wardrobes filled with antique clothes I could dress up in. My only problem was getting to sleep at night. Every hour on the hour – and sometimes in between – at least three clocks would strike, and never at exactly the same time. The final one also girded its loins for the toll with an unnerving whirring. Years later, when my husband Charlie wanted to buy a nautical clock with striking bells for our boat, I vetoed it!

I also had plenty of company in that house. Auntie, in later life, had a series of 'companions', indigent ladies with no commercial skills who needed jobs. They were usually the unwed daughters of old family friends. Some were pathetic, others were quite lively and went on to better things, one even married a widower!

When his eyesight failed, Uncle Ned hired a secretary in addition to the last 'companion' who by then had graduated to housekeeper. In the kitchen were three maids – a cook, a house-tablemaid and a 'between' maid, whom my father described as "being between the De'il and the Deep Blue Sea." Outdoors, the garden and the ancient Daimler were cared for by Mackenzie, an old retainer who wound up as Mummy's master of works when she and Littie were restoring a small Edinburgh house which they moved into during 1947.

Throughout my childhood, Mummy, from her own home in the West of Scotland, had to ensure the smooth running of Darnick by resolving innumerable problems generated by the clash of prickly egos among the 'companions' and the kitchen staff. And, in spite of having five women working for them, if Auntie or Uncle Ned as much as sneezed, Mummy was summoned from Strathblane to cope with the crisis. Her two brothers, Jack and Bertie, both lived in Edinburgh but confined their involvement with Darnick to going there for an enomous midday dinner every Sunday after church.

Whenever Mummy and Littie planned a holiday, particularly if this meant going abroad, there was a cliffhanger about "when we should tell Uncle Ned" whose invariable reaction was to come down with either pneumonia or acute stomach problems. Sometimes we went away anyhow, but it was never very relaxing.

In her eighties Auntie grew blind and 'frail' as the Scots call it. And with ill-health her dependence on Mummy increased. This coincided with my outgrowing Loppe's school.

I don't know how Mummy persuaded my father to let her rent a house in Edinburgh, so that I could go to St. Trinnean's and she could cope on the spot with Darnick's problems. Perhaps she simply told him what she planned to do. On weekends, we either drove through to Strathblane, or he joined us in Morningside. I don't remember any major rows between them and we lived this way for three years. But I developed a nervous rash on both hands which greatly embarrassed me, so there must have been tension in the family, although I forget the form it took.

I had always loved Edinburgh. Now I discovered that city living freed one from dependence on the increasingly ubiquitous automobile. In Glasgow, I'd felt odd because I didn't make my own way to Loppe's school, and my life was organised around being picked up by a car. Now I had the privilege of walking to and from St. Trinnean's unless I took trams. On these, I usually met two kids from the class immediately below mine, Margaret Glass and Lucie Schache, who is now Mrs. Stewart, a retired teacher and still a valued friend. Her correspondence is as salty as her youthful conversation. These two kids' clear-eyed evaluation and verbal dissection of everyone in the school from the Headmistress down taught me never to underestimate children's observation and understanding.

Every Saturday morning, unless we went to Strathblane, I'd shed my school uniform, dress myself up, and go downtown where the highpoint of my morning was an "elevens" at McVitie's Restaurant on Princes Street. I didn't know any such snack bar in Glasgow and I developed such a fondness for Scotch Eggs, I went to great trouble to learn how to make them after I settled in America, where they are hard to find.

After eating my Scotch Egg, I'd parade up and down Princes Street, window shopping and looking across to the magnificent Castle which always stimulated my teenage imagination about Scotland's past. Edinburgh was so beautiful, so much more colourful than grey Glasgow which had not yet cleaned up its handsome Victorian architecture or developed the variety which it has in more recent years.

I'd also people-watch and often met schoolmates similarly occupied. I doubt if we'd have had this shared, though essentially private, Saturday ritual in Glasgow where there is no central thoroughfare comparable to Princes Street. The other St. Trinneans' pupils and I would nod to each other, but seldom joined forces, though sometimes on Mondays we'd compare notes on the fashionable clothes in Jenners' store windows.

There was far more sunshine in Edinburgh than in the West. Less rain, too, and the air was invigorating though chilly. I still had colds but not as many as before, and when, one freezing November, St. Trinnean's Headmistress announced that we mustn't put on our woollen pullovers "because we don't really have winter yet," Mummy bought me 'Chilpruf' vests to wear under the tussore silk blouses we wore with our navy blue gym tunics.

The school occupied a former stately home called St. Leonard's off Dalkeith Road on the edge of the King's Park. I have mixed feelings about St. Trinnean's. I think I agree with another pupil who started there on the same day I did. From time to time, I'd ask her how she liked the place and her invariable reply was, "I don't approve of schools but if we have to go to them, I suppose this one's as good as any."

Looking back I think I profited most from the English teacher, Olive Christian Sampson. Her father was the Astronomer Royal so maybe that was why she so often seemed to be in the clouds. She was shortsighted, dumpy, wore red skirts with black tops, less smart than they were supposed to be, and she was erudite, intellectual, and managed to pass on to us her love of the classics. We read Shakespeare's plays aloud in class, taking the different parts as though in a theatre. She gave us stimulating assignments like book reviewing. On one of mine she wrote, "The words I've circled are journalese, which you should avoid. Ask me if you don't know what it means." I didn't but I was too shy to inquire. She always encouraged me, gave me good marks, and took seriously my ambition to be a writer.

But Sammy got a better job in a prestigious English school. Maybe she too wanted to get away from home. Anyway, she left and her successor was a poseur called Dorothy Q. Magill, who had no sense of humour and disliked me after I wrote a poem about her in Chaucerian English which my classmates greatly enjoyed. In it, I had referred to her large engagement ring and commented that "she shall not go single all her life."

The History teacher, whom I admired, was a gravel-voiced lady called Miss Frances Kennedy whose family were big enough wheels in the Edinburgh legal profession to impress Uncle Jack.

Once, when I tried in an essay to cover up a lack of information with fancy verbiage, she wrote tersely, "Facts wanted! Not Words!" I learned from that criticism.

Our education was organised on something called "the Dalton System" which allegedly trained us to manage our workload by doing homework assignments on a weekly basis rather than every-night-for-a-class-tomorrow. We were assigned a chart showing how much time we should spend on each subject over a week and our housemistress would regularly review what we marked off. This provided good practical experience in 'padding' and manipulating records which I later found useful in making up business expense accounts.

In the 1930s the Europeans were learning to survive dictators, and we were living under the iron heel of our Headmistress, Miss Catherine Fraser Lee, who also fed us the myth that we were a democracy, or as she put it "a self-governing school". However, if she caught any of us doing something forbidden, liking running in the corridors, she never gave us a chance to explain why. She would just hand out judgments and refer us for punishment to our housemistresses.

Miss Lee was a big woman, probably in her sixties, with a mass of thick frizzy grey hair and a long nose scarred by white pockmarks. She dressed well, but walked so fast she always seemed hunched over. She had a younger sister, Miss Mamie, a skittery physical parody of her who taught piano and trilled with laugher, up and down in scales. "She ruined your touch," Mummy said to me later. "Spoilt your love of playing, too." It was one the few criticisms she expressed to me about the school.

I was scared of the Headmistress and just kept out of her way. Then something happened which matured me, though not through the methods outlined in the school curriculum.

At the end of every summer term we had exams to evaluate our academic progress. If you were graded a One in any subject, you were in the clear. A Two was good. A Three meant you were in trouble. My weakest areas were Arithmetic and Latin. The Maths teacher was a motherly widow who loved teaching and had endless patience with her pupils. The Latin teacher, Mrs. Rose Phillips, was a brilliant woman who didn't suffer fools

41

gladly. Her husband was a rabbi which intrigued us. There weren't many Jews in Edinburgh and we didn't know what he did, except that he was some kind of clergyman. Mrs. Phillips wore much smarter suits than the other teachers. She also used perfume, Coty according to some teenage sophisticate, and she was always tastefully made up, with lightly tinted fingernails. I admired her chic but dreaded her sarcastic tongue. She gave us Latin names, and I was "Helena" with an emphasis on the "ah."

Tests always challenged me and I was good at them. So at the end of my second year at St. Trinnean's, I achieved a Two grade in both Maths and Latin and Mrs. Phillips actually complimented me! I took off for my summer holidays with an easy mind and in September expressed the opinion to my parents that I was looking forward to going back to school. At that my father muttered something about not raising my hopes too high, but as usual I paid no attention to him. My mother kept silent.

So I was totally unprepared for what happened on the first day of the autumn term.

Every morning, we would assemble at our "house" then have two classes one after the other, followed by a break for Prayers – i.e. we processed into the biggest room of the building singing a hymn and Miss Lee, in an impressive academic gown, delivered a brief sermon. Her father had been a minister and if she had been born at a later date she probably would have gone into the Church. She always wound up her homily by announcing the names of girls she wanted to talk to, and they stayed behind while the rest of us returned to classrooms for another session before lunch. Usually when Miss Lee summoned a pupil it was to deplore some peccadillo or to deliver a lecture on failure to concentrate on a weak or uncongenial subject.

I had, several times, been warned off writing too much fiction in my spare time. In those days, the *Queen* magazine had a marvellous young people's feature run by a gifted columnist called Levana. She offered literary competitions, with subjects like a poem written by anyone under ten or an essay or short story for contestants up to sixteen. And periodically each age group had a "Do As You Like" contest and I of course, submitted short romantic suspense novels! There was always a small cash reward, about ten shillings, and I won a lot of these.

But far more valuable that pocket money was Levana's critique of whatever you submitted, and this appeared in the magazine even when you didn't win a prize. You saw your name in print, and absorbed the need to be professional by using the appropriate format and technique if you wanted to be paid for your work. I wonder why no other adult magazine ever offered such a useful juvenile feature. It created new generations of devoted readers for the magazine. But when Levana retired or left in the mid-1930s, the contests disappeared from the *Queen* and with them went constructive criticism and some nice small change for me. Other children's publications, like *Little Folks*, ran literary competitions, but they weren't stimulating, and there were none of Levana's valuable suggestions. For example, she once told me, "You show considerable aptitude for dialogue and see that it does its work effectively." This started me writing plays.

Loppe, with her genuine interest in developing individualism, encouraged me to enter these contests, but Miss Lee didn't approve of them, since they were an activity outside her control. She told Mummy my writing fiction and verse took time and energy away from my school work. My mother listened, passed the comments on to me, but did nothing to stop me scribbling. She even bought me a terrible old typewriter with a heavy touch and helped me transcribe my manuscripts using the time-honoured hunt and peck system.

When St. Trinnean's staged a post-summer exhibition of what we'd done during our holidays, my schoolmates brought in photos, artwork, knitting and embroidery, and I contributed historical romances. So, when told to stay behind to talk to the Headmistress, on that first day of school, I assumed she was going to lecture me on my latest literary effort. To my teenage mind it was pretty racy.

Not so. "Helen," said Miss Lee. "This term you will not continue in your present class. You are going to stay behind for a year to strengthen your Latin and Maths."

I was stunned. At fifteen everyone in a class below is a kid. And I was shocked by the injustice of holding me back when I had been rated so well at the end of the previous year.

"Miss Lee!" I protested. "I got a Two in both those subjects in the summer exams!"

"Yes, but it was a strain on you. Your health must be considered."

"But . . . Miss Lee . . ."

"Your Mother and I have decided you are to stay behind. Now run along! Go and change your textbooks in the library. Return the new ones you took out this morning, and take back what you used last year."

I intended to do nothing of the sort but at least this let me escape from her presence. I had to think about what to do, and since the only place offering privacy was the lavatory, I headed for the nearest one, and shut myself in there.

After I stopped crying, my devious young mind went to work on the problem. The first necessity was to find out from Mummy what exactly had happened. But it was midmorning. She'd be up at Darnick and would probably stay for lunch with Auntie.

Besides, there was a roll call during our midday meal and if I didn't answer "Present!" I'd be in more trouble.

But what to do in the meantime? I couldn't join my own class or face the one I was now supposed to be in, so I headed for the Free Study room where we went if we had an unassigned period. There I sat, with a book open in front of me, until the bell rang to announce our midday dinner.

Still in deep shock, I've no recollection of what I talked about with my table companions. I'd already learned to hide my feelings from them. During my first days at St. Trinnean's, I'd spoken up freely at lunch, as I'd done at Loppe's, talking about my writing, my reading, my love of acting. I'd even quoted Shakespeare, but I'd soon learned this wasn't acceptable. You were supposed to discuss games, in which I had little interest because I was very bad at all of them and wasn't allowed to play outdoor ones in winter for fear I caught cold.

I did have a few pals, but none I could then confide in and my "best friend," Cicely Crewe, went home for her midday meal. She wrote poetry and was in the class above me. How could we continue to fraternize if I was kept back among the kids?

So I just sat pushing an unappetizing mush of mince and soggy vegetables around my plate, and answering "Present!" loud and clear when Miss Lee took the roll call. We were then supposed to get some fresh air to jumpstart our minds for afternoon classes. If the weather was too wet for lacrosse or tennis practice, or you didn't go because it was "that time of the month," you put on your hat and coat and walked "up the Hill" towards Arthur's Seat. That day I simply strolled through the school gates onto Dalkeith Road and headed for home.

"Are ye sick?" exclaimed the maid as she opened the front door, always locked even in those days.

"No!" said I. "But is my mother home yet?"

She was having her rest but I rushed in on her, bursting into furious tears and announcing that I was never, ever, going back to that school!

After I'd calmed down, she told me Miss Lee had indeed "discussed" the situation with her – i.e. there had been a meeting and the Headmistress had done all the talking. "She thinks it would be best for you to have another term to consolidate what you've learned," Mummy explained.

"She just wants to keep me for an extra year and get the fees!" I replied.

Mummy didn't argue with this, and since, like Dr. Boyd, she knew I always meant what I said, I think it was partly her idea that I ring up some of my teachers and get their opinion on my work. I reached the Maths instructor at home and she agreed I should move on with my group. So did a funny, wonderful, homely, intellectual little woman, a Russian refugee called Anna Semyonov, known as "Madame Sem" who did special coaching. She took my side vehemently, and since she'd helped me with my Latin, I didn't try to get in touch with Mrs. Philips.

It was a Friday so Mummy and I took off in the car for Strathblane. There Littie admitted he too had known all about the situation, and reminded me he'd tried to give me "a hint."

"Why didn't you tell me outright?" I demanded to know.

"Because Miss Lee thought it would be better if she told you herself and explained why," said Mummy.

"She didn't." I retorted. "She just announced what she'd decided."

That weekend, as never before, I outpacked my furious heart in words. I wrote to every sympathetic teacher, stating my case. "They're very good letters too," said my father. "But hold them until you've seen Miss Lee again."

For by now I had got it across to both my parents that no way would I return to St. Trinnean's if I didn't continue in my regular class. I didn't care if they'd paid substantial fees for the new term. I wasn't going to sacrifice a whole year of my life and lose face with my peers just to satisfy an old woman who knew nothing about what made me tick. I pointed out that if I was forced to rehash stuff I'd already learned, I'd be so bored, I wouldn't apply myself and both Mummy and Littie recognised that. Probably they also wanted to avoid my becoming a problem and aggravating the strain between them.

Mummy composed a letter to Miss Lee, which I read. It stated unequivocally that I was not to be demoted and added that my father agreed with this decision. The latter point was something of a clincher, since as the male of the family he presumably paid the fees.

Monday morning, I arrived at school early and dropped this communication off in the Headmistress's box. Then I went to the Free Study room and stayed there incommunicado until Prayers. I didn't bother to check what classes I should have been attending, either with my regular group or the other one.

When at the end of her sermon Miss Lee announced that I was to stay behind, I wasn't surprised. Her reaction came to me as a complete shock. Without preamble, she started scolding me furiously for not going to a pre-Prayers session of the junior class!

"But, Miss Lee, I'm not going to be with that group this year! Didn't you read my mother's letter?"

She said, "You Had No Right To Cut That Class! It Was Very Rude! It Was Mrs. Phillips' Class and What Will She Think?" Whereupon, she grabbed my arm in a strong claw-like hand and hauled me down to the classroom where, as it happened, the group I was now to remain with were being introduced to their new Latin assignments.

Storming in, Miss Lee interupted whatever Mrs. Phillips was saying with a tirade about how Helen had come to apologise for her bad behaviour in not showing up at the ten o'clock instruction period. As she ranted on, I raised my eyes and met those of the Latin teacher. For once we were in accord. We were both embarrassed by the Head's temper tantrum.

"Well!" said Mrs. Phillips, interupting the torrent of words at the earliest possible moment. "Thank you, Miss Lee. And, Helena, go to your desk and open Caesar's *Gallic War* to Page Two. That's as far as we've gone this morning."

I never did develop any fondness for Mrs. Phillips but I respected her after that. For by the time I'd slipped thankfully into my usual chair, the Head had departed.

"What was all the row about?" my classmates wanted to know, at the end of the period.

I shrugged it off. "Just a mix-up about where I was supposed to be this morning."

I never delivered the letters I'd composed for the other teachers, but I'm still glad I wrote them. They were good practice in presenting an argument, a skill I found in later years more marketable than Latin.

Once, in New York, I consulted a psychiatrist. When he asked me to describe some events in my early life which I considered traumatic I told him about this incident. "But why should it bother you?" he asked. "You handled it well. And you came out on top."

"But it destroyed a lot of my trust in my parents. I felt they'd deliberately mislead me. And that holier-than-thou Headmistress was such a hypocrite! Talking about my health when I'm sure she just wanted an extra year's tuition. Also, when her precious authority was challenged, she couldn't take it, and poured her anger out on ME. It was disillusioning to find that trying hard to do good work wasn't enough without discovering that a person of authority and respect could be so petty and dishonest, disregarding facts when these didn't suit her own agenda."

He shrugged. "So what else is new? Didn't this wise you up to what happens all the time in the real world?"

It did, and when I once tried to turn the experience into a short story, I entitled it "Education for Life."

According to psychological testing, I have a 'conflict with authority.' I'm not surprised.

6

Some Real Education

The showdown with Miss Lee was the start of my last year at St. Trinnean's, though my classmates returned for another nine months. During the remainder of my time there the Headmistress left me alone, and later that winter Auntie died.

There had been so many false alarms about her health, it was a shock when the pneumonia actually carried her off. This was still the pre-antibiotic era, and the year before, she'd been very ill. Mummy told me how she'd gone into the room, sat by the bedside, and tried to talk of this and that but to no avail.

When she got up to leave, however, Auntie had opened her eyes and croaked, "Nellie! Come back. I must speak to you."

"I thought," Mummy said, "that she had some 'last words' for me. But what she gasped out was, 'I've been wondering about what colour would be best for a new winter coat. I Haven't A Thing To Wear!' She's got so many clothes she doesn't know what to do with them! I didn't know whether to laugh or cry."

Instead, she took Auntie, when convalescent, to her favourite store, Wilkie's on Shandwick Place, where the old lady ordered a beautiful dark blue coat trimmed in black Persian lamb, and with a suit to match. I doubt if she wore it more than once, but I inherited it and, after some alterations, it was my 'best' outfit throughout my college career.

But with Auntie gone, Mummy lost a reason for staying in Edinburgh and Littie was pressuring her to come home. "People in Glasgow are saying my wife's left me," he told me during one of those long country walks in which he confided many things about his marriage that no parent should have passed on to a teenage daughter. But I suppose he had to talk to someone and I was available.

Mummy was also disillusioned about St. Trinnean's. She was

afraid the school wasn't preparing me to pass the university entrance examinations. She had really investigated those, because she was determined I'd go to college whether I wanted to or not. Though what form my future would take was still embryonic, she meant me to have the career opportunities she herself had missed.

So I spent the winter of 1933 at home in Strathblane and went to a tutor in Glasgow, a wonderful spinster called Miss Christine Renton. She had been a successful instructor in a school run by an elder sister until hearing problems made it impossible for her to conduct classes. But on a one-to-one basis, probably by lip reading, she could still teach, and she had researched the University entrance exams with such a gimlet eye she could get almost anyone through them and with the least possible effort.

"Lumber in the brain!" she would say, crossing out whole chapters in textbooks. "You don't need to bother with all that stuff!" She had an endearing way of referring to the powers-that-be who graded the papers as "That Man" and if there were two possible answers to any question she'd recommend, "Give The Man both!"

Darling Miss Christine demanded hard work but she also appreciated application and she tried to get to know her pupils and understand them. "Helen can take a bad lesson well," she once wrote in a progress report and she never scolded or tried to interfere with one's real interests. She encouraged me to keep writing fiction and lent me many fascinating books that weren't required reading. It was too bad the *Queen* had given up its competitions by then.

In this warm intellectual atmosphere (though her flat was perishing cold) I overcame some of my inability to comprehend algebra and trigonometry to say nothing of my extreme boredom with Julius Caesar's invasion of Britain in 55BC and after six months, I knew enough to persuade "The Man" that I was qualified for admission to a Scottish university. "We knew you'd pass English and History with ease and probably Latin too but that Maths exam was your greatest achievement!" said Mummy, when we got the good news.

I also had singing lessons with the delightful Mrs. A.M.

Henderson, whose husband was the university organist. Mummy by then had given up on trying to make me a pianist. With hindsight, I don't think my failure was all due to Miss Mamie Lee. I have little manual dexterity and my fingers on the keyboard didn't obey me any better than they ever did on a typewriter.

I never had much voice, but to this day I love to sing and find enormous pleasure learning new music in church choirs. Mrs. Henderson also encouraged my histrionic ability and gave me an insight into the kind of life artistes led. She knew people like Sir Edward Elgar. She was full of stories about Ellen Terry. She and her husband were fun to be around.

Nevertheless, I remember that winter as one of the lowest points in my life. Each day started with a chilly scramble to wash, dress and drink a cup of tea in time for a trying drive into town with Littie. He was a morning person, bright-eyed and bushy-tailed while I was still trying to wake up.

"Why won't you talk to me? Tell what you're going to do today?" he'd grumble.

"I don't know yet," I'd answer sullenly. "Leave me alone." But he never did.

I'd spend a couple of hours with Miss Renton, then, unless I went on to Mrs. Henderson's, I'd take a bus home, consume some soup and a soggy salad, and Have A Rest Until Teatime. This my mother considered a necessity to conserve energy. She shut herself up in her bedroom every afternoon ostensibly to lie down and rest her heart, more likely to enjoy the latest from Boots' Library.

I'd sit in "the Den" and browse through a variety of books which had nothing to do with my studies. Or else I'd take Sandy the Cairn terrier for a walk. Sometimes I'd meet up with our neighbour Mr. Davidson, the retired journalist, and pass the time of day with him. Otherwise I would have to be satisfied with my own company and the dog's.

Between 4.30 and our dinner at 7.00, I'd study. After that meal, my parents and I would spend an uncomfortable hour sitting in the drawing room listening to the radio, reading, or occasionally playing cards, trying to learn whist and bridge. After we'd heard the BBC's 9 o'clock news, we'd go to our three separate rooms where I and, I suspect, Mummy read in bed.

We went to a concert once a week and sometimes to theatres but I don't remember much socialising other than Sunday tea parties with people like the Piries during that grey-skied, lonely, interminable winter. What I do remember is my well-concealed but overpowering depression, something in those days people didn't realise could afflict teenagers. Needless to say, it showed itself in a lot of coughs and colds.

"My mother announced that I was going to spend the summer in a Swiss boarding school – Europe in 1934 was a revelation to me"

My mother did realise I was unhappy, but probably thought I was worrying about my exams. In Spring, as soon as I was assured of admission to Glasgow University the following September, she announced that I was going to spend the summer in a Swiss boarding school. There I would brush up on my French and also learn *Ecole Menagere* (i.e. domestic science), for, although most of my companionship, apart from my mother, was in the Bluerisk kitchen with the cook and Annie the housemaid, no-one ever taught me how to prepare meals. These were always set before me until, at the age of around twenty-three when I was at Yale University, I moved from the New Haven YWCA into my very first apartment.

Knowing I'd passed the Prelim exam for university, we went off for an Easter holiday at Grange-over-Sands in the Lake District. There I developed a fever and acute pain in my right side. Remembering Uncle Bertie's trauma, Mummy slapped cold compresses on me, then loaded me into the car and drove me home where Dr. Boyd confirmed her diagnosis of appendicitis and recommended surgery but not until the inflammation had died down.

Catherine Moyes, the nurse who had married our parish minister, was my moral support through that ordeal. When she heard I was to have the operation, she showed up on the doorstep in sensible shoes and announced that we were going out for a good walk every day until I went into the nursing home. We had some grand talks, and on the last excursion, she gripped my arm firmly and said, "Now I'm going to tell you everything that's going to happen to you tomorrow."

I wasn't sure I wanted to know, but I had to listen and it was powerful therapy. I lost much of my fear, and in the post-operative period, mentally ticked off every medical procedure from the list Catherine had given me. Years later, when I had the first of several ear operations and was more scared that I'd ever been in my life, I re-read a book called *Cotton in My Ears* by Frances Warfield and memorised the chapter in which the author underwent the stapes mobilisation surgery I was about to undergo. It reassured me mightily.

I had an uneventful convalescence from the appendectomy, encouraged by the prospect of spending the summer at the Swiss boarding school. Mummy was going with me at least as far as Lausanne and we'd have a few days together before the term started. Littie worried that I'd be homesick. He claimed that emotion always engulfed him on the few occasions when he'd gone abroad on business.

"Then she'll just have to get over it," said Mummy crisply.

I was never homesick. I was too enthralled by being on my own. Moreover I was entranced by the lovely school, a converted chalet, formerly a hotel overlooking Lac Leman. The doors to the bathrooms still bore the words *Mesdames* and *Monsieurs* which amused Mummy. All our rooms were designed for comfort unlike the spartan St. Trinnean's, where coldness was considered an aid to learning.

I also had no difficulty making friends with the other pupils who came from a variety of countries. There were some half-dozen English girls, one American, a couple of French and Austrians and innumerable Swiss Germans whom no-one liked. For the first time, I became aware of Jews in society and often wonder how some of my schoolmates fared a few years later when Hitler overran their home countries. We had one probable Nazi, a German girl I didn't like. She wanted to correspond with me after the term was over, but I didn't give her my address or take hers.

"Parlez francais tous les temps!" we were told but of course we didn't. It was also *"absolument défendu de fumer"* so that was where I smoked my first cigarette. In the evenings, we'd gather on our little balconies and puff away, then throw the butts down into the garden where Monsieur and Madame, who owned the school, would find them during their evening strolls. Periodically, Monsieur would deliver a homily on the evils of tobacco and also advise us to *"Restez les jeunes filles simples!"* which none of us intended to do.

On weekends, we'd go to a beach, an excursion that quickly took the place in my life of eating a Scotch Egg at McVitie's in Edinburgh. One Saturday, with her husband away at an education convention, Madame rose at the end of the lunch period and announced tersely that the following girls, whose names she read off, had been smoking and would be punished by staying at the chalet instead of going swimming! This action, I noted, had a good deal more effect on us than all Monsieur's homilies. At least, we took more care not to be caught.

I didn't like the cookery classes because our schoolmates ate the meals we prepared and I believed that if I botched something, everyone would go hungry and I'd never hear the end of it. So I worried, needlessly because our teacher kept everything well in control and I don't remember as much as a burnt potato being served. Actually, I didn't learn much about cooking, I'm not sure why. We prepared meat, vegetables and dessert, also baking, and I still have, in my little textbook, *Nos Bonnes Recettes* an incomprehensible assemblage of yellow papers which we pasted inside the back cover to remind us of the technique involved in preparing *la pate feuilleté* i.e. puff pastry, which we never made. Mummy was greatly entertained when I wrote to her and said I'd been preparing prunes soaked in red wine.

"They're pretty good on psychology in this school," an English girl called Daphne confided in me. "I had a terrible inferiority complex when I first came here." For myself, I lost much of my hypochondria once I found I wasn't automatically expected to get a cold after some chilly Alpine excursion. No one paid any attention or even cared. I did succumb briefly to *"une petite gripe de l'ete"* but did so largely because everyone else had it and the symptoms got me excused from a cooking class.

I also learned to use lipstick and experimented with other make-up and different hair styles. Individualism was encouraged at *L'Institut Prealpine pour Jeunes Filles à Vevey*. I had enjoyable piano lessons from Madame. She loved Mozart and told me no-one took him seriously as a composer who plumbed the depth of sorrow and compassion. In Scotland I'd never even heard of his *Requiem*. It is my all time favourite piece of music. And I had singing lessons from a *cantatrice*.

To demonstrate my acting ability to Daphne and others, I simulated a "pash" on one of the more stuck-up senior girls, a beautiful half-Russian who fell for it completely and basked in my apparent admiration while those in the know giggled! Her first name was pronounced "Cheez-Anne" and she intrigued us. Her mother had left instructions with Madame that every Saturday her daughter was to go to a special *coiffeusse* in Lausanne. So when we went to the beach, Chesanne would board a local train and return with her hair duly done. But somehow we discovered that upon arrival at the station in the big city, she was always picked up by a handsome young gent in a sports car.

Nothing like that had ever happened at St. Trinnean's.

Europe in 1934 was a revelation to me. I had been to Mont St. Michel and Dinard on holidays with my parents, but passed most of my time with fellow Brits, in particular a boy called Brian who had a pawky sense of humour. So I didn't meet many French and when I did their speech wasn't anything like what I'd learned from a Mademoiselle at Loppe's. When Mummy and I arrived in Vevey I was astonished to find that even the maids in the hotel spoke good English as well as French, German and sometimes Italian.

At the end of that glorious summer, a turning point in my life, I took a train to Paris where Mummy met me, and we spent a marvellous week. Our sightseeing included a packaged tour of night clubs which we couldn't have gone to without a male escort. At Glasgow University, students who'd never been abroad could write French correctly but they were afraid to voice the simplest phrase in the language. I, on the other hand, had no problem answering questions fired at me by a lecturer who spoke it in all his seminars. He asked me if I'd lived in France? No, said I, but I'd spent time in Switzerland and visited Paris. He suggested I describe some of the places I'd seen there, so I rattled off the Louvre, Napoleon's tomb, etc. etc.

"Et des autres environs, Mademoiselle, un peu moines austeres?"

"Mais naturellement, Monsieur," said I, and added the Moulin Rouge and the other night-clubs. This motivated a male student to ask me out for coffee. He must have been disappointed to find I wasn't as hot stuff as he'd hoped. In the movie *Born Yesterday* Judy Holliday, as the uneducated but smart blonde, interrupts her tutor, played by William Holden, to ask, "Are you the kind that talks or the kind that acts?"

I was definitely the kind who talked. It was all I knew how to do.

7

Brief Innocent Encounters

The twins and I had the usual adolescent curiosity about sex.
When I was ten I asked Loppe straight out, "How are babies
born?" She looked embarrassed, hedged, said she'd rather not
go into it, I'd learn about it in due course, adding, "It's a matter
of love, largely." With hindsight, she was probably a virgin.

One morning Christine stayed off school, and Mummy, that
afternoon, explained to me that my contemporary had started
"a monthly haemorrhage, something that happens to girls." I
was fascinated because it meant I was no longer a child and it
also explained some brown stains I'd just discovered in my
knickers. Why we suffered this inconvenience Mummy didn't
say. She just produced some sanitary napkins, known as "pads",
and showed me how to put them on. Subsequent discussion
with Christine didn't enlighten me any further. But when I went
to St. Trinnean's I found that "the curse" was a useful excuse for
missing gym and other miseries. "She's not going to games just
now," was how my friend Cicely once described her dog's being
in heat.

By way of sex education, Miss Lee organised one lecture,
with slides, which parents were invited to attend. It had diagrams
of pregnant animals and there was some talk about "tired
mothers" but no practical information. Nor did the earthier
passages in Shakespeare enlighten us on how to do it.

The Prime of Miss Jean Brodie, Muriel Spark's inimitable
depiction of Edinburgh school life in the 1930s, catches the
ignorance and innocence my generation of teenage girls had
about "sexual intercourse," a term I never heard at St. Trinnean's.
We didn't have any male teachers either.

Littie, in his usual heavy-handed way, once tried to make me
aware of the differences between the sexes. Uncle Bertie had

given me a subscription to a lovely magazine with some title like An Outline of History and Art. Thumbing through it, Littie came upon a photo of an ancient statue captioned Torso of a Boy. He stuck this under my adolescent nose and said, "That's what the Greeks called it." I was completely mystified as to what he was trying to get across because I knew what men looked like. I'd found out long before I could appreciate the implications.

When I was five, a little boy called Ramsay had come to tea with his parents and he and I were sent outside to play in the garden. He felt a call of nature, unbuttoned his pants, and relieved himself without apology. I was so impressed by the easy way he could do this, I later demonstrated it to Annie, crushing my dress into the shape of a penis. I couldn't understand why she laughed so hard or why she warned me not to tell Mummy.

In line with my determination to avoid spinsterhood, I cultivated every boy I met on holiday although what transpired was extremely innocent. There was, for instance, Henry with whom I shared long walks around the corridors of some hydro talking, talking, talking. We wrote letters to each other for several years but never met again.

When I was fourteen, the same age as Juliet, I met the first and longest-lasting romantic involvement of my life, Philip Anthony Spalding, a writer with whom I corresponded, off and on, until he died in the early 1990s. In his last letter to me, he said he was glad I'd told him he was the inspiration for Walter Paterson, my hero in *Home to Strathblane*, who was tall, blond and handsome and wrote essays and poetry.

I met Anthony in Strathpeffer where he was holidaying with his father, an Oxford professor, his mother, and his sister who was a heavy-set dark haired girl with the romantic name of Ione. To add to his glamour, Anthony was an older man – i.e. he had just left school and was about to go to Oxford where he joined in all those famous anti-war debates, thereby reinforcing my pacifism.

He must also have had some physical problems, which we never discussed, for he was not called up in World War II. After he graduated from Oxford, he went to London and eked out a living in vague literary jobs until some relative left him a small legacy and he bought a cottage called appropriately "Inner Meadow" in Farnham, Surrey. There he lived for the rest of his long life, writing off and on. He published several collections of essays and married a doctor whom I never wanted to meet nor was such a meeting ever suggested.

Indeed, I only saw Anthony twice after that brief Highland holiday. He and his family visited us in Strathblane on their way home from Strathpeffer, and a few years later, when I was in London, we went out to dinner then back to his flat where he read poetry aloud to me and we stared into the fire all evening, not even holding hands.

Our long relationship, which meant a great deal to me, was the epitome of a platonic love affair, but it was love nonetheless. In the beginning, we may have had other ideas – at least I had – and maybe Anthony shared them. He wrote a poem entitled *Helen* about our meeting in Strathpeffer.

> She came from out the South lands
> On dainty feet she came,
> Clad in a gown of yellow
> That set my heart aflame;
> Over the dim blue mountains,
> Before the dawn of day,
> With morning in her happy eyes,
> And stole my heart away.
>
> A-down the dusty highroad,
> Beyond the haunts of men,
> I followed where she led me,
> Over mountain, moor and glen;
> By where the red-tressed rowan
> Nods to the brimming fall,
> Into the mist of mountain
> I followed at her call.
>
> Into the dim blue mountains,
> Far on and out of sight,
> Passed she and I together,

Under the vault of night;
And on her lips the laughter
The song all youth has sung,
That none has sung more sweetly –
That night the hills were young.

She's gone! On wings of morning
Back to the South went she –
She of the gown of yellow
Who stole my heart from me.
I cannot breathe the sweet air now,
Nor hear the pine-trees stir,
Nor see the dim blue mountain
But comes the thought of her.

The "gown of yellow" was a taffeta creation with a skirt short in front and dipping in the rear. The poem was printed in a "slim volume" privately published during Anthony's Oxford days. When I showed it to Mr. Davidson, his comment was, "He's not a poet."

Maybe not, but Anthony was a fine prose writer, the first I communicated with on a regular basis. He gave me a feeling for good style, and encouraged me to read the Russian novelists. I never got to the end of *The Brothers Karamazov* even after repeated attempts but I didn't admit this in my letters. I confided in him all my literary aspirations. He always encouraged me and sent me copies of his own collected essays.

But I soon sensed this epistolic friendship was all we'd ever have. My first husband once went to England and met Anthony, whom he described to me as looking like "a young W. B. Yeats." They got along well, which wasn't surprising as they both wrote beautifully but non-commercially and neither ever got the critical acclaim they deserved. To love and be loved by a poet was wonderful, but it wasn't the answer to the sex situation.

One summer, while I was in Glasgow University, my parents and I went to Mallaig and stayed at the little Station Hotel then run by a French family who served excellent food.

There were about a dozen guests besides Mummy, Littie and

me and among them were two young men. Nigel, who had flowing locks, wore sandals and was known in those days as "a pansy," was with his mother and father.

His companion, Percy, had literally come along for the ride. He was good-looking and thoroughly heterosexual, short and fine-boned, darkish-skinned with lively brown eyes and a small moustache. He had grown up in India with an English father and an Indian mother. She had been a nurse and had motivated him to study medicine in London.

That summer, not having any money but curious to see Scotland, Percy had hitched a ride to the North with Nigel and another student. Somewhere in the Midlands, they were involved in a traffic accident and the car, as the Americans say, was totalled.

During the crash, Nigel was thrown clear, Percy dislocated his shoulder, and the third youth, the driver, was badly hurt. Said Percy laconically, "Blood was spurting from an artery. I got my thumb on it, plugged it. Had to push my shoulder back in place first. I told Nigel to go and get help – we were on the edge of a town – but he just fell apart. Sat down on the roadside and cried. I spotted a public telephone about a quarter mile ahead, and Iliterally dragged that wounded fellow up there, hanging onto his neck to stop him bleeding to death, and I dialed the police. They got him to hospital in time and he's still there. He won't forget that trip in a hurry!"

"You saved his life!" I breathed, all starry-eyed.

"Look, that's what you study medicine to do. It was lucky I knew how." We were sitting outside the hotel, looking over to Skye. "I came on up here with Nigel as we'd planned. He wanted company. I can't stand him but I'll have to stay with him until he goes back to London because I haven't enough money to pay my own way. His parents have been really nice to me. They think I'm a good influence on him or something. . ." He stared out at the magnificent view. "But Gawd! I was bored until you turned up!"

"How could you be bored, looking out on all this magnificent scenery!"

"I'd rather watch a good operation," said Percy, who I

discovered wasn't really interested in anything except medicine, unless it was girls.

He, and to a lesser extent Nigel, sought my company every minute of the day. I loved it. I was halfheartedly studying for a certificate in elocution and singing and asked Percy for some good medical words to show I understood anatomy. He did better than that. He dictated to me whole paragraphs on the subject of breath control. Then he pulled up his shirt and told me to place my hands on his diaphram while he breathed. I thought this was very risque behaviour. "It's the only way to learn," he told me severely.

> "Romantic involvement in those days didn't go beyond a squeeze and kiss. I suspect it was all most of the boys knew about sex too."

I saw him on my next trip to London. He hadn't time for letters even to his mother. "When I left India," he said, "she gave me a package of postcards, and made me promise to send her one every week so she wouldn't worry. All I had to say was, 'I am well. Love, Percy.' I do try to let her know what I'm doing, but lots of times I've been so busy with classes and hospital work, I've fallen back on those cards."

Soon after this reunion – and he kissed me! – I went to America, then World War II got under way and we lost touch. In a book about one European campaign, I came on a medical officer with a name much like his. I'm sure he was in the thick of things. I wish I did know what happened to him because, years later, he created for me Doctor Douglas Elliot Stewart in *Home to Strathblane*, who didn't look like him and had a different background with different hangups, but was the same kind of man. Thank you, Percy, wherever you are, for giving me my best fictional character.

Romantic involvement in those days didn't go beyond a squeeze and kiss. I suspect it was all most of the boys knew about sex too. A London medical student like Percy would have had more experience but he wouldn't have "tried anything" with a "nice girl" like me, even though physically attracted as he was.

It seems incredible, looking back on it in the 1990s. Of course, in those days "the Pill" was unknown. Other methods of contraception were chancy to say the least and I didn't find out about them until I got married in America and lost my virginity on my wedding night at the age of twenty-four. That I'd held onto it so long was, I think, a bad idea. Chastity is all very well, but a woman ought to know what she's getting into, physically, before she promises to live with a man until death do them part.

I was never a *femme fatale* but I had lots of dates at Glasgow University. One chap, an engineering student I met in my first year, was a reasonably good dancer and looked so handsome in his dress kilt, I loved going to college hops with him even though his chief interest was the behaviour of steam-propelled wheels. He had a roommate who had more general conversation, which helped between foxtrots, but periodically they'd check their watches and remind one another that there was just time to reach Central Station to see such-and-such an engine pull out! Trainspotting isn't new to Scotland.

Then I met Ian Godfrey Neilson, who became my "steady" throughout my college career. He had gone to a good school, the Glasgow Academy. He was handsome, charming and excellent company. Although by modern standards we never "went very far" beyond a lot of kissing and cuddling, always fully clothed, we were compatible physically. We danced. We hiked around the Strathblane roads. One of my Brownies once informed Eba Haddow who ran the troop that "I seen Tawny cleekin' a lad!"

Ian's mother and mine became friends. They had many interests and acquaintances in common. Mummy couldn't fault his gentlemanly manners and he was smart enough to act interested when Littie dominated the conversation at the Sunday tea table with reminiscences of his own outstanding performance in Edinburgh legal classes. Ian planned to go into law.

He liked to visit Bluerisk which, I suspect, represented to him the kind of home he'd have had if his father hadn't died prematurely leaving his mother to bring up two sons in a Glasgow flat.

At the university, we were part of a small group that did many things together. Ian played football and one of the highlights of the social season was the Rugger Dance where we knew nearly everyone. Once I wore to it a dramatic flame red taffeta dress with a big waistbuckle in the form of a Greek actor's mask. I – or rather, Mummy – found this stunning creation at Forsythe's in London, a Bond Street store which sold off clothes worn in fashion shows. Although Glasgow was an extremely dressy city, this ballgown stood out. It was even written up in one of the evening papers by a student who earned extra money for her tuition covering social events.

"If my highest ambition had been a nice country house and a family, Ian and I might have made out all right"

I don't know what Littie thought of that dress. He didn't like me wearing clothes that, to his way of it, were "conspicuous." Nor did Ian, although he appreciated being the escort of someone who made the fashion pages of the local press. Ian also tolerated my time-consuming activities with the Drama Club. But I did sense conflict between us when we talked about the future and I made no secret of my ambition to be a novelist and a playwright, who, of course, would be away from home a lot on her own.

If my highest ambition had been a nice country house and a family, Ian and I might have made out all right, we were so compatible in many ways. But after leaving Strathblane and living among creative people in a city, I knew I couldn't return to the suburbs and business-oriented neighbours. How and why Ian and I went our separate ways comes later. Sufficient to say that due to a breakdown in communication he felt I jilted him, and I've always been sorry about that.

Nevertheless, as time passed, we re-established contact, exchanged Christmas greetings and met each other's spouses. Once during a visit to London, he entertained me to lunch at his club, the Atheneum. I restrained myself from arriving laden with bags from Marks and Spencer, spending the morning instead at the Victoria and Albert Museum. We had a delightful meal and talked about the past with, of course, special references to our own achievements which we both contrived to work into the conversation. I also drank enough wine to inspire me to say, as he was taking me back to my hotel in a taxi, "Ian, I think it's just as well you and I never married."

He burst out laughing and the reaction was so spontaneous, I knew he was in agreement with me although, as a successful public relations man, he didn't say so.

From then on we became real friends again. By the end of the War, he was a colonel, decorated for bravery, and married to the sister of one of my friends at Glasgow University. They eventually lived outside London, had a son and daughter and several grandchildren. I include this brief biography because as a reader I like to know what happens to people. Ian and I, incidentally, continue to correspond. Like me, he sings in a choir and loves music.

8

How do Women Dress?

How women dress is an indication of how independent they are.

Pictures of the writer Edith Wharton and her friends when on display at Washington's National Portrait Gallery illustrated the dramatic watershed in fashion from tight-fitting velvet gowns to blouses and skirts around the time of World War I. It recalls the equally striking change to loose, simple, comfortable dresses which liberated women from hoops and huge head-dresses during the French Revolution a hundred years earlier.

The fashion clock turned back during the Industrial Revolution and the Victorian era when men began spending their business time in offices and factories leaving women at home, their virtue protected by voluminous clothes. Edwardian ladies who were having affairs prefered to enjoy these in late afternoon when their maids were around to remove corsets.

Sexual chastity in young girls growing up between the two world wars was encouraged by unaesthetic underpinnings.

Until I went to America in my twenties, I always wore next to my skin, a horrible garment called a "combination". It covered the body completely with a slit between the thighs to expedite natural functions. In winter it was made of wool jersey, and in summer of cotton or, occasionally, silk. "Combies" were plain and ugly, less stimulating to male lust than today's bra and pants.

Prior to puberty girls of my generation also wore a Liberty Bodice, a boneless corset worn over one's combinations. When breasts developed, a brassiere and a corset replaced this unaesthetic garment.

World War I liberated women from long, multiple petticoats but the short skirts of the "flapper" generation made pants a necessity. I remember heavy textured knickers reaching almost to my knees that I wore through school and college and how I only changed these a couple of times a week. I shudder to think how I must have smelled for I never used deodorants. These were available in chemists' shops but few girls considered them necessary.

My mother's generation, according to their photographs, bicycled and played games in long wide skirts, but mine didn't. Our tennis dresses were brief and quickly evolved into shorts.

In the early 30s came another major breakthrough – trousers for women! In my teens we went to France one summer, and before we left, with Mummy's connivance, I snitched a pyjama bottom from Littie. He usually wore a night shirt but at some point he'd acquired a set of more modern sleeping garments, all in white. I remember pinning the fly shut and hiding the drawstrings at the waist under a wide belt and strolling along the Dinard beach feeling chic and trendy.

Mummy also let me buy wool slacks which, she emphasised, must be well cut. I only wore them in the country, even in the coldest weather. And the first time I put them on for a visit to my aunties in Milngavie they hustled me indoors fast in case the neighbours saw me!

If she'd lived a generation later, I feel sure tiny, skinny Auntie Jane would have enjoyed wearing slacks and she'd have looked good in them. Nowadays, pants are the norm for clothes-conscious old ladies, and as one of them, I approve.

Before World War II, hats for women were socially obligatory rather than for warmth or shade as they are today. No one, not even a little girl, went to church without something on her head. That, according to Mummy, was "all the fault of that anti-feminist Saint Paul." Gloves were as necessary as hats to show one was a lady. To have bare hands outdoors, even in summer, was considered low class.

Stockings weren't so different, though. For school ours were black and heavy in texture and we considered them unsexy. When Eba Haddow and I foregathered at her house in Strathblane on Saturday mornings all tricked out in our smart Brownie officers' uniforms, her husband, Archie, would deflate our egos by calling us "the girls in the black cotton stockings."

The discovery of nylon and other synthetics liberated women from constantly darning hose and also ironing underwear. "I gave up ironing in 1953," a co-worker once informed me, "after I noticed I was staying home on Saturdays to press my clothes while my friends were going out to the beach. I went through my wardrobe and I discarded everything that wasn't drip dry." Although a washerwoman took care of the bedding and table linen at Bluerisk and the tablemaid did the ironing, I was brought up to launder my own smalls, blouses and summer dresses, the only real domestic skill apart from sewing that I was taught at home.

I also made a lot of my own clothes as did my friends. It was more fun than embroidering tea cloths like the aunties. I knitted too, but had to give it up after my ear surgery when I developed a pinched nerve in my neck.

"I snitched a white pyjama bottom from Littie – I remember pinning the fly shut and hiding the drawstrings at the waist under a wide belt and strolling along the Dinard beach feeling chic and trendy."

Even before the two Wars, female work clothes had improved. My great-grandmother, Mrs. Alexander Tait *née* Barbara Black, was left a widow with three children in 1844, when career options for a respectable woman must have been almost non-existent. But great-granny found herself a good job as Custodian of Melrose Abbey. One of its impressive archways is the backdrop for many of the carefully posed family photos fashionable in her day. One, taken in 1866 and now in the National Monuments Record of Scotland, shows a young and demure Auntie in a light-coloured dress, the bodice embellished by dark braid and buttons, the ground-sweeping skirts protected by a token apron. She wouldn't have done any cooking in that outfit.

Several other photographic portraits have the same background but taken some years later because Auntie now has her hair braided round her head as she wore it throughout her life. Great-granny wears what looks like black taffeta and a cap composed of white muslin entwined by black velvet ribbons. She is surrounded by several young women in elegant skirts fringed with ruffles. Their tiny pillbox hats are perched on heavily braided hair.

But in *Borderland*, a collection of rare Victorian and Edwardian photos compiled by Peter Adamson and R. Lamont-Brown, (Alvie Publications, St. Andrews 1981), there's a less formal snapshot of great-granny standing outside the now demolished custodian's cottage at Melrose Abbey. She's chatting with a bearded white-haired man who might be her son-in-law, Mummy's father. Great-granny is in her working clothes – a plain black skirt over a small hoop and a black top decorated by a large brooch, possibly a badge to identify her as Custodian. She has a plain white cap over her hair, and around her shoulders lies a light-coloured knitted shawl. Today in a similar job she'd be in a jacket and pants.

In winter, in Scotland, we wore layers of scratchy jerseys and cardigans and still shivered indoors. Desire for more comfortable temperatures was considered slightly decadent.

"I wonder why the British are so resistant to central heating?" I once remarked to an American who had an English wife.

"It's because if their houses were warm, people might take their clothes off," he explained, deadpan.

I loved perfume and from time to time Mummy gave me a bottle but never showed me how to use it. Once I dowsed myself before going to a concert with my parents and later on Littie complained about "an awful smell" which had interfered with his musical appreciation. His suggestive form of instruction was memorable though extremely annoying to the youthful recipient. I know I never used that particular scent again.

As for make-up, it wasn't allowed at St. Trinnean's, and Mummy never used any, so my first experiments were made in Switzerland. After that summer, I used lipstick and experimented on my eyes. Once I went to a dance with a lot of Pond's Cold Cream slathered over the lids, a hint I'd culled from some magazine. I'd also just had a cold. "And look at your eyes! You're still full of it!" remarked Eba Haddow. I disappeared into a ladies room and wiped most of it off.

Uncle Jack, who liked to ride, invited me during my college years, to a Hunt Ball at Lauder Castle. When I told him I'd invested in a new lipstick for this occasion, he gave me a fatherly talk about how the kind of people I would be meeting didn't paint their faces.

"Every girl does," I informed him. "And after it's over, I'll tell you what cosmetics the ones in our party used."

He considered this fair enough and luck was with me. One of the girls was a judge's daughter and therefore considered respectable but she was going on the stage and when we collected her at the Lauder Hotel, she took me upstairs to freshen up and commented as we entered the bedroom, "Isn't this impossible lighting for putting on false eyelashes?!"

" 'I wonder why the British are so resistant to central heating?' I once remarked to an American who had an English wife.

'It's because if their houses were warm, people might take their clothes off,' he explained, deadpan."

We had a glorious evening, and the other female member of the party, a minister's daughter, wore lipstick and powder, like me.

Next morning, going back to Edinburgh with Uncle Jack, he nearly drove the car into a ditch when I said, "Sonya was wearing false eyelashes."

"She was NOT," he stated with all the authority of an Edinburgh advocate. "I danced with her and I didn't see them."

"She told me herself," said I, and repeated verbatim what she'd said to me. I always enjoyed conversations with Uncle Jack. We'd slap contradictory statements back and forth but there were no hard feelings. However, he did check up on me about the eyelashes. He went to our Cameron cousins, and cross-questioned one of them discreetly. Since she'd just had a good laugh with me about the incident, she knew what to tell him.

9

Gilmore Hill

I spent the happiest years of my youth at Glasgow University between 1934 and 1938, on the eve of World War II.

I took four years rather than three to complete my degree because I signed on for only one class in my first year. Mummy wanted to avoid my overstraining myself. I didn't argue because I wanted to have fun and meet young men.

There were no departments of drama or journalism in those days and little career guidance beyond private talks with instructors. After completing what would be called a liberal arts MA, both sexes might go 'up to Jordanhill' and study teachering, or, if female, go 'down to the Western' and become a hospital almoner (i.e. social worker). There were far more men than women in the Law and Medicine departments and I suspect Engineering was all male.

Psychologically, I was ready for college. Miss Christine Renton had trained my ability to learn. The Swiss school had shown me how to be part of a group and make friends. I no longer felt I was an 'odd man out' among my peers, and didn't need to hide my precocious intelligence or my interests. The Dramatic Club was eager to use my acting ability. And, in my first experience since the Heatherbank kindergarten of being among contemporary males, I discovered I wasn't as unattractive as I'd often feared.

In those days, students could wear red gowns and many of us did. They were comfortably warm and saved wear and tear on our clothes. My memory is of milling around the quadrangles between lectures, giggling and gossiping with classmates, reading many books in the Mitchell Library or the University's libraries, and finding out the hard way that it was a good idea to follow the advice of other female students and avoid being alone in the Geography lab with the professor who, today, would certainly have been accused of sexual harassment. All he did was pull our hair, attempt a little fondling, and make salacious comments in class, but it was unnerving. What if he refused to provide a class attendance ticket for the year because his advances had been spurned? Would that mean repeating the whole performance?

I had, during my grim winter at home, achieved a small measure of independence, though my Milngavie aunties were still asking Littie if I really travelled on the bus by myself? My biggest problem with the public transport was that to arrive in Strathblane in time for our 7 o'clock dinner I had to miss the last reel of many films and this was in the era of Fred Astaire and Ginger Rogers, Ronald Coleman in *A Tale of Two Cities* and other classics! On free afternoons Ian and I would have a cuppa at one of Glasgow's numerous tearooms, like The Green Twig on Sauchiehall Street, then we'd hold hands in the movies until I had to sneak out and rush to the bus station to catch the 6.10 to Strathblane.

Just once I stayed until the end of the picture and didn't arrive home in time to eat dinner with my parents. My dinner had been kept hot and was served to me on the dining room table by the disapproving cook, Mrs. Thom, who stood over me while I ate, muttering, "It's a' wasted. . . a' wasted."

But usually, since I'd survived a summer abroad, my parents didn't worry about my going to and from Glasgow. With hindsight, I'm amazed by their trustfulness. Women students could join the Queen Margaret College Union, a building offering not only a cafeteria and rooms for study between classes, but overnight accommodation, plain but adequate. The manageress was a distant cousin by marriage, a smart spinster called Miss Mary Laird. Presumably her being in charge set Mummy's mind at rest when, as often happened, I spent the night at the Union after university dances.

My parents didn't seemed to realise that I was simply given a key to admit me during the wee sma' hours when Miss Laird was sleeping soundly in her private premises. If I'd stayed out till dawn, she'd have been none the wiser. That I never did so is an another example of my naiveté and probably that of the young men who delivered me to the doorstep after the parties, and left me with ae fond kiss.

We didn't drink much, either. Some social affairs served claret cup, a mild concoction with a sticky sweet taste, and beer was available or at least some of one's less desirable dance partners had it on their breath. Once, my engineering friends, who had a car, took me and another girl to a bar after a dance and we consumed several rounds of sherry. I'd tasted it before, and when Mummy had a dinner party, she served white wine, but that was the extent of my experience with alcoholic beverages.

When I told Mummy about our "going downtown for a drink," she said firmly, "You mustn't do that again." And I don't think I ever did.

Until then, my mingling with society had consisted of an occasional evening function in Glasgow like the annual Royal Bank Dance where I was chaperoned by my parents and always supplied with a suitable escort, usually some dull young man whose father was an agent. Or, until he got married, my dashing cousin George Laird, my senior by sixteen years.

George spotted the wolves and kept them at bay! He was also a good dancer and his presence made me the envy of all the other girls. Once he came through to Edinburgh and squired me to a dance at St. Trinnean's, my finest hour there! And on our way back to the house Mummy and I were then renting, he stopped the car and in the nicest way introduced me to some agreeable but unthreatening necking!

My father's one veto during my college years was that I mustn't dress up and go out on the streets rattling a collection box on Charities Day. "I've seen too much of What Goes On," he said darkly. So I confined myself to going into town that day, usually with Mummy who enjoyed the fun.

On my first day at Glasgow University, I met three girls – and a woman lecturer – with whom I remained friends until geography, death, and disease started separating us. How little our actual studies affected our later lives is probably typical of that generation of women students.

One of these girls I'd already met at Saturday morning

Dalcroze Eurythmics classes in Glasgow. Emilie Coats was a big pleasant-looking girl, easy to get on with and so intelligent she was starting work on an Honours Degree. We met in the Modern European History class conducted by a young Unionist (i.e. Tory) Party politician, Dr. Catherine Gavin, who had already made some history herself running for Parliament, unsuccessfully, in the toughest slums of Glasgow challenging the great Jimmy Maxton, the Socialist. She was also then married to a well-known local actor. I had heard her make speeches to political groups Mummy belonged to.

"My father's one veto during my college years was that I mustn't dress up and go out on the streets rattling a collection box on Charities Day. 'I've seen too much of What Goes On,' he said darkly."

Catherine played an important part in my life and was my matron of honour when I married Charles Marwick. By that time she was living in America with her second husband, John Ashcraft, an advertising man. Before she became an enormously successful historical novelist, she contributed a weekly column on American life to the *Bulletin*, a tabloid which later merged with the *Glasgow Herald*. When she quit that job, I applied for it at her suggestion and got it. She and her husband moved to California and in her eighties she signed a contract for three novels about Napoleon all duly completed and published. The second she dedicated to me.

In 1934, Catherine was in her twenties, stocky and good-looking with shingled dark hair. When she marched in to take that first class the boys started whistling and making cat calls. She paid not the slightest attention, calmly arranged her papers on the podium, hitched her academic gown into line over her smart suit, and then looked over her audience. Her sharp brown eyes travelled around the lecture hall, missing no one. She said nothing and by the time she had completed her survey, you could hear the proverbial pin drop. It was a tour de force that made a lifelong impression on me.

After grading our term reports, she would ask those whom

she considered had done especially well to stay behind after class and she'd return our papers individually. Emilie and I were among the chosen, and I preceded her into Dr. Gavin's office. She liked the way I presented my material, she said. "But your spelling, Miss Lillie," she added, "is hellish. Now send in Miss Coats."

I waited for Emilie, who came out giggling. "What did she say to you about your spelling?"

"She said it was hellish. Why?"

"Because after she'd complimented me on my paper she grinned and said 'But your spelling is the same as Miss Lillie's!'"

I still can't spell and "Teach" in her nineties continued to point this out to me!

Emilie sat her final exam the day war was declared. She passed, then promptly enlisted in the Land Army. When she ran into one of her professors shortly thereafter, he expressed the hope that her Honours in History was helpful in milking cows!

Like me, she was active in the Dramatic Club and she wanted to get married but she was the kind of girl the boys considered good company but didn't get romantic about. However, towards the end of the War a distant male cousin from New Zealand turned up on her parents' doorstep in Glasgow. He had been disfiguringly wounded and before commencing plastic surgery the Army doctors had told him to take some leave. Since he had been a farmer, Mr. and Mrs. Coats suggested to him that he might enjoy visiting their daughter on the estate where she worked. It was love at first sight on both sides. So, in due course, Emilie moved to New Zealand and lived there on a farm. Now a widow, she revisits Scotland from time to time, usually accompanied by one of her sons and we keep in touch.

Our mutual friend, Jean Morrison, came from Paisley and was taking a degree so that she could be a teacher. The prospect didn't thrill her and if some different career had presented itself, she'd probably have changed direction. Small, dark-haired and attractive, with a good fashion sense, she and I kept in touch through thick and thin until her death in 1992. She taught for many years, married Duncan Whyte, an engineer, and raised a son and daughter. He also kept in touch until his death.

In 1936, people kept up with the news by listening to the radio or reading the hand-written posters displayed on the sidewalks. Looking out of a tram window en route to the University one afternoon, Jean and I read the announcement, KING ABDICATES.

"That's History!" Jean exclaimed to me. "We're living History!"

She was one of my most valuable sounding boards when I was writing my columns for the *Glasgow Herald*, warning me I should curb my love of statistics and offer a more personal reaction to the news. I listened to her suggestions because she was the kind of reader I wanted. Jean and Duncan appreciated books, including novels, went to the theatre, were active in volunteer groups, travelled in Europe and always found interesting people for me to meet when I visited Scotland. Jean probably made more direct use of what she studied at Glasgow University than any of my other girl friends.

Completing our quartet was Euphemia Margaret Cameron, better known as Fay. Her father was a Highland minister and she had gone to school in Oban. Fay was studying social work but she loved the good things in life. She had fine long straight golden hair pulled up and away from a sonsy pink and white face dominated by clear smiling blue eyes. She looked a little like the young Queen Victoria and was just as self-assured. Fay drove the boys crazy, she was so unattainable. Once a besotted suitor phoned her in the student residence where she lived. "He got me out of the bathtub!" she complained to me. "There I was standing in the corridor, dripping wet, with only a towel around me, and I told him I couldn't talk but he kept on about how much he loved me and wanted to marry me . . . I just hung up on him."

Then she met Turner McLardy a medical student who was, literally, tall, dark, handsome and a good dancer. He was also brilliant and had a private income, and graduated just as war was declared. He was sent to North Africa. Fay found a family going to Alexandria who needed a nanny for their children. When there were problems about her leaving Britain due to the War, she went down to London and charmed her local Member of Parliament into expediting the trip.

In Egypt, Fay and Turner contrived to meet and, as she put it, "staged a whirlwind romance" and got married. While she was pregnant with the first of their three children, Turner applied for a transfer back to Britain. This the Army granted, but suggested that he get some experience of desert warfare first and sent him to Tobruk. Just as his position fell to the Germans, Fay in Alexandria gave birth and was evacuated across what she described as "the Red Hot Sea." She contacted the Red Cross and told them to inform her husband he had a son. "But Major McLardy is missing in action!" she was warned. "He'll turn up." said Fay.

Eventually he did, in an Italian prison camp where, somehow, he had got the news about his heir.

Fay and her baby made their way back to Scotland, travelling halfway round the world. Communication with Turner broke down after the Allies invaded Europe until she got a telegram to meet him Glasgow at short notice.

"How did she react?" I asked Jean, who'd been with her at the time.

"Just said, 'I've got to wash my hair!' Then started ironing all the silk underwear she'd bought in Alexandria."

By the late 1950s Turner, a neurologist, felt he had gone as far as he could go within the British medical establishment, so moved to America. He and Fay had been living in London where she did make use of her training in social work and had two more children.

In the USA, the family lived in Boston then on Cape Cod. Charles and I visited them several times in their beautiful house. Turner, still associated with a local hospital, had a Sailfish. Fay collected antiques, grew herbs and lectured on them to women's groups. She always looked the same, though a little heavier, and her hair turned from pale gold to white. She loved to entertain and knew many well-known people. Like me, she loved good mystery novels.

In his seventies, Turner succumbed to a fatal heart attack while shovelling snow. Soon after, I became aware that something was wrong in Fay's mind. One of her sons took her back to Scotland and put her in a mental hospital near where'd she grown up and there she died.

10

Glasgow University before World War II

Professor Archibald Allan Bowman, the head of the Moral Philosophy Department at Glasgow University in my day, impressed upon us that one of the highest and most important things in life was the communication of spirit with spirit. Bowman practised what he preached and someone quoted him in every student debate regardless of the subject under discussion and it always clinched the argument.

Stooped and balding, he was physically unimpressive but had hypnotic dark eyes. He was interested in Mesmerism and I think sometimes he hypnotised his class, time passed so quickly. He spent the better part of a year discussing Plato's *Republic* which I enjoyed not just for its ideas but for the beautiful clear way these were expressed. W. Somerset Maughan in an essay on style recommends reading the great philosophers and points out that their prose grows muddy only when their thoughts aren't clear.

Bowman was also a considerate man. I met him socially a few times but the gap between professors and their many students was wide so I didn't expect him to know who I was. But when I was felled by the ear infection, he wrote to me saying I mustn't worry about his signing my class ticket which meant that if I failed in my degree examination, I wouldn't need to attend his lectures the following year in order to sit the exam again.

That I did pass was partly due to another of his thoughtful gestures. This was the year the dates of the Dramatic Club's two plays ran into problems when King George V died. The second play, *Children in Uniform*, had been staged as a protest by the aspiring actresses because *Man and Superman* had so few female parts. I had one of them but I had also joined my friends in the second play.

The women's drama group had had the foresight to enlist Professor Bowman's wife as a patron for our show, ostensibly staged in aid of a charity. When we found that our performances would coincide with the next-to-the-last Moral Phil. class examination, we appealed to her. Mrs. Bowman pointed out to her husband that it was easier to find an empty room for a test within the University than to change the rental date on a downtown theatre, so he gave us a week's grace! At every performance, the cast's backstage reading was Plato or John Stuart Mill.

Professor Bowman had spent World War I in a prison camp which undermined his health. Soon after my graduation, he went to a funeral service for Principal Sir Robert Raitt in freezing weather and caught a chill which developed into pneumonia and killed him.

His lectures had the most lasting influence on my thinking of any professors. In a healthy Republic, according to Plato, everyone feels responsible for their own occupation and Justice means minding your own business, keeping yourself out of other people's affairs. Constantly running to lawyers and invoking the letter rather than the spirit of the law is a sign that something is wrong with the social structure. Both the modern UK and USA are classic examples.

I took no English Literature classes at Glasgow University since, through friends who did, I found I'd studied most of the classics already with dear Sammy at St. Trinnean's. The only exception was Richardson's *Pamela or Virtue Rewarded*, which Fay lent me. I wrote a dramatization of it and was interested to find that, stripped of her long outbursts of moralising, the poor but honest heroine was a tough, salty, practical little broad. Her only negotiable asset was her virginity and that she sold to the highest bidder in return for a wedding ring and financial security.

Instead of taking the freshman English class, I attended two in European History, one being Catherine Gavin's, and two in Scottish History. Professor J.D. Mackie, then head of that department, had a stimulating way of discussing long-dead kings and nobles as though he'd known them personally. Once, while talking about the disasters which followed the murder of King

James I, he mentioned "the injudicious remarriage of the Queen." Then he paused, thought about this phrase, and remarked, "Oh, he was a decent enough chap but he couldn't handle the situation."

Professor Mackie instructed us up to the Union of the Parliaments in 1707. After that, we were in the hands of Dr. George S. Pryde, who succeeded Mackie as head of the department. Dear Dr. Pryde (I always called him that in my thoughts!) was young, with a handsome brown beard and a sonorous voice which was relaxing after the Geography class with its oversexed and quirky professor.

A fellow student once remarked that Dr. Pryde must be colour blind because he invariably wore Wednesday's tie with Tuesday's tweeds but he was as easy to look at as he was to hear. He also had the considerate habit of pausing in his lecture periodically, then raising his voice slightly to say, "Now we'll just write some of this down." Whereupon we'd reach for our pencils and he'd dictate a succinct precis of the information he'd just given us.

For class exercises, he had us research the political and social evolution of where we lived. This, of course, must have supplied him with excellent material for his own books, but it was also valuable experience for his students in finding primary sources. What I uncovered so stimulated my imagination I used the social history I learned working on Dr. Pryde's assignments in my Strathblane novels. I won the second prize in his 1938 class.

Dear Dr. Pryde had been a Fulbright Fellow in the United States and had an American wife. When I discussed with him the possibility of spending a year on the other side of the Atlantic after I graduated, he strongly approved and wrote the letter that got me into Yale. He died relatively young but left a wonderful collection of definitive Scottish history books, as did Professor Mackie.

Pryde's classes stimulated my interest in Scottish Nationalism which was enjoying an upbeat period while I was at Glasgow University. One weekend, someone removed the Wallace Sword from his memorial in Stirlingshire. The following Monday, a male student who was involved in the nationalist movement appeared in class with an interesting bandage around one hand! He was so cagey about how he'd injured himself we all suspected him of liberating the Sword, though this later turned out not to be so. It turned up again, anyway.

I hope I live to see my country enjoy more independence from the London government, but as a student of history, I "hae ma doots" that there will ever be sufficient consensus of opinion to achieve a genuinely effective Scottish Parliament with Highlanders, Lowlanders, Borderers, Glaswegians and "men of all sorts that have been bred in Edinburgh" who, as Benjamin Franklin pointed out "fall into the disputatious form" even when they are "persons of good sense."

Although I did attend an occasional political gathering, my chief outlet beyond my studies was the Dramatic Club. Until the year I'd gone to the Swiss school and on to the university my closest companions had been my beloved dolls. As a lonely only child, I'd developed a habit of talking to them and making up dramas in which I was far more assertive, attractive and popular than in real life.

I longed to be an actress and spent hours before the full length mirror in my bedroom practising gestures and trying on costumes. "But you aren't goodlooking enough for the stage," a St. Trinnean's classmate once warned me. I had straight mousy hair, small regular features, and nothing distinctive in my face. In all my photos, I'm smiling mindlessly, hiding behind an affable facade.

I hadn't much vocal volume due to a small mouth. But though I'd hated practising the piano, I never could spend enough time working on my voice. In school, I did reasonably well in elocution contests, and among the parts I played during my years at Glasgow University were Bella, the fluffy young cousin in *The Barretts of Wimpole Street*, the Grand Duchess in *Children in Uniform* and Ann Whitefield in George Bernard Shaw's *Man and Superman*. I suspect this play encouraged my latent feminism.

The Dramatic Club was dominated by a divinity student, John Stanley Pritchard, who put so much energy into it, it took him a long time to graduate. He managed, directed and, above all, performed. Small but dominating on stage, and passably handsome with slicked-down fair hair, a hawk-like nose, extremely false teeth and popping blue eyes, Stanley's disadvantage was a "Glesca eccent" of which apparently he was unaware. He was also a method actor long before that term was coined.

Years later, on a visit to Edinburgh, my mother called to me from her bedroom, where she had switched on her radio. Through a background of organ music came the announcement, "This is the Bee Bee Cee Hourrr of Prraya!"

"That's Stanley Pritchard!" I cried.

She nodded. "He's a pastor for Scottish broadcasting." Which has always struck me as a happy blending of talents with interests.

> "Through a background of organ music came the announcement, 'This is the Bee Bee Cee Hourrr of Prraya!' "

I won the part of Ann Whitefield in *Man and Superman* in an open audition and I felt I was pretty good in it too. Maybe I agreed with Ann's ideas about marriage. And on the opening night Mummy sent me a gorgeous apple-blossom bouquet, which was handed up to me on stage.

I don't think it's possible to fail in a Shaw part because there's only one way to speak the lines. During an all-star performance of *Man and Superman* in New York in the 1950s, with the great Maurice Evans as John Tanner, the actors put the same emphasis on every line that we students had done.

Shakespeare's plays, according to Emmett Robinson, who ran Charleston's Dock Street Theatre for many years, are production proof and actor proof. This, to my mind, also applies to Shaw, who went beyond Shakespeare in deciding every position on the stage which a director changes at his peril.

The 1930s was a golden age for drama in Scotland. The great James Bridie was writing for the Citizens Theatre and stars like Alastair Sim, Robert Donat, Edith Evans, Sophie Stewart, and Flora Robson appeared in Bridie plays like *The Anatomist* and *The Sleeping Clergyman* in Glasgow or Edinburgh before opening in London.

Contributing to Scots' sophistication as audiences was the Brandon-Thomas Repertory Company which before, during and after World War II staged plays ancient and modern, well-produced, well-acted and well-attended by season ticket holders. The repertoire wasn't controversial but its scope was wide. And if the box office was sluggish, Brandon-Thomas would put on a J.M. Barrie play and the house would be sold out.

While I was at the university, I wrote a one-act comedy called *A Matter of Opinion* about Lord Bacon writing a play which he shows to the actor-manager William Shakespeare who takes it over! Telling no-one, not even Mummy, I sent a copy of this curtain raiser to Jevan Brandon-Thomas. He responded at once, inviting me to come in and discuss it. I met him backstage and what a thrill that was! He was a big affable man who treated me like an equal, and his suggested revision taught me the essence of playwriting.

"Your idea's excellent," he told me, "but the way you've written it, you have Shakespeare going through the script and infuriating Bacon by his criticism to the point where he walks out. Now instead of Shakespeare being all prepared with his remarks it would be much more fun if he hadn't read the play at all, he'd been too busy dilly-dallying with the Dark Lady. So he's thumbing through it, spotting things as he goes, and maybe she's trying to prompt him behind Bacon's back."

I rewrote it this way, it came out well and Brandon-Thomas wanted to cast his leading actor, Wilson Barrett, as Shakespeare. But World War II intervened and when I returned to Glasgow in 1946-7, I had other things on my mind and never followed through with Mr. Barrett who by then had taken over the company.

In my final year at Glasgow University, Mummy and I went to a meeting where the guest of honour was Mrs. Alfred Hocking, the lively wife of a famous American academic. From her, I learned that Yale University had a pioneer course in playwriting. I got the address and with Mummy's approval, wrote to them and applied for admission, offering *A Matter of Opinion* as a sample of my ability together with a letter from dear Doctor Pryde. The Yale Drama School wrote back accepting me as a graduate student.

So my Alma Mater led me towards my future, though not by the most direct route.

By then, of course, the war clouds were gathering but as a history student, I didn't believe hostilities would really break out. Or, if they did, that they'd involve the British. A number of projected holidays in Europe had been threatened by international crises while I was growing up. I didn't approve of war anyway.

That summer, I went down to London to a summer session at the Central School of Speech Training run by the great Elsie Fogarty. She was a stout unadorned lady in sensible shoes and brown suits who called a spade a spade in a consistently resonant voice. We admired and liked her but we were also awed by her. Most of my fellow students were Americans, all anxious to learn something they described as "standard English." Miss Fogarty didn't approve of my going to Yale. "You'll just marry an American and then divorce him," she forecast.

But my motivation in going to the Drama School wasn't just to learn playwriting. It was to get far enough away from home so that I could learn how to live my own life, and make mistakes in peace. I had acquired enough self-confidence at Glasgow University to believe I could do this. I had met students less intelligent and far less cocooned in cash than I was, who had few misgivings about their future.

Perhaps this exposure to the real world and how other people went about making careers for themselves was the most important information I picked up at Glasgow University.

11

Why America?

At Glasgow University, I'd thought a lot about how one became a writer, a playwright in particular. The only one I'd met was the great James Bridie, whose real name was O.H. Mavor. He had a flourishing ear, nose and throat medical practice, and when I encountered him socially it would have been impossible for me to ask him how he'd become a dramatist.

My father knew the novelist Neil Munro but never brought him home. Apart from Mr. Davidson, the only journalist I met in my youth was W. Kersley Holmes, who contributed brief, witty items to the local press and visited us occasionally at Strathblane. The only remark he made that stayed in my mind was that he'd be writing poetry all the time if he could do it at the "Den" window. Mummy considered him a lightweight. "He's awfully clever, but is what he does worth doing?" she'd ask me. I often remembered that remark when rolling out the funny columns my editors most liked for the *Glasgow Herald*.

I've often felt I should apologise to the great Scottish writer Maurice Lindsay for secretly hating him when I was a child. We never met but our fathers used to lunch together regularly and Littie would come home and hold up to me the example of the young Lindsays who published what they wrote and won all kinds of literary prizes. I was of course left in the dark as to how they found these outlets for their creative endeavours. I knew that one of my favourite authors, John Buchan, and his sister who called herself O. Douglas had, as children, learned to write and earned pocket money through sending articles to newspapers, but apart from the Levana column in the *Queen*, I hadn't a clue as to how they'd gone about this. The few times when in deepest secrecy I sent a story to an editor, I got it back without encouraging comments.

Littie, as a banker, knew members of the Collins family, the publishers, and we visited them, occasionally, during my adolescence. When I told one of them I wanted to be a writer he said, "Don't write when you're young. You'll just copy other people."

> "In addition to my longing for independence was my need to get away from my father."

This doesn't agree with R.L. Stevenson's advice about "playing the sedulous ape" to learn style and in any case I couldn't stop myself scribbling away but I remained unguided on how to turn my facility with words into a career. Anthony Spalding, my literary lover, wasn't any help either because he wasn't selling so well himself in those days.

While I was a student, another "ship passing in the night" – for I never met her again – profoundly affected my view of the writing life. She was Florida Scott-Maxwell, an American psychologist who had married into a Scottish family Littie knew through the Royal Bank. Somehow, Mummy had made contact with her and was invited to lunch at her hideaway, the country cottage where she worked on her books and articles.

I went along and from that brief, wonderful visit, I carried away a picture of a happy, mature, handsome woman in attractive, offbeat, comfortable clothes, and wearing only one earring because she'd lost its mate. As she fixed a tasty snack she and Mummy discussed ideas. These were far beyond me but extremely stimulating.

So were her surroundings – her simple little house in the woods with books, papers, filing cabinets and a typewriter unabashedly part of the livingroom's decor; the tiny functional kitchen; the plain bedroom and bathroom in back. They suggested a way of life rich with work.

Florida Scott-Maxwell's life style wasn't like any I'd previously encountered. It was an example of Virginia Woolf's *Room of One's Own*, popular feminist reading in those days. It took me over thirty years to achieve almost similar surroundings – at Wavertree Hall, an artists' colony now known as the Virginia

Center for the Creative Arts and located near Sweetbriar College in America's South.

In addition to my longing for independence was my need to get away from my father. Always a difficult man, he developed symptoms of manic depression. He was never admitted to hospital and, unless Dr. Boyd was quietly keeping the disease under control with homœopathic remedies, he was on no medication. In those days, mental problems weren't as treatable with drugs as they are today.

Littie's problem grew less after he retired but the illness was at its height during my college years and it was terrible to live with. He would be in tearing high spirits during the upbeat phase, talking nonstop, telling us at every meal, even breakfast, how he was going to make a fortune on the stock market from tips passed on by one of his luncheon companions, a man who cost him a lot of money.

Mummy and I would just sit and eat in silence while he ranted, knowing that eventually the change would come. This would happen without warning. Something – the most innocuous remark from one of us – would set him off. He'd suddenly shut up, retreating into dour angry silence which would continue until, like the manic phase, it had run its course and he returned, more or less, to normal. I used to try to stay out of his way and discouraged my friends from visiting at these times, although he usually turned on charm for them "while you and your mother sat at the tea table and shot him down" Fay commented to me, years later.

Mummy and I discussed his illness – which we both recognised as such – and she read many books in hopes of finding how to handle him but nothing worked. So far as I know, she never looked for professional help. It "wasn't done" in those days. After the War, however, when she moved to Edinburgh, she became an active volunteer at the pioneer psychiatric Davidson Clinic, founded in 1939, and its director, Dr. Winifred Rushforth, greatly admired her.

I did try to help Littie, in my juvenile way. Once, when he was in a low mood, I took him in my arms and tried to cuddle him. Since one of his regular complaints about me was that I tried to evade the kissing rituals he felt daughters should engage in with their fathers, this physical approach was uncharacteristic. It was also unsuccessful and I didn't try it again.

The incident that most strongly influenced me during that time took place in the car, driving home from Glasgow. I sometimes met my father at his office at the end of his working day, always the dot of five o'clock. That afternoon he was all wound up and sounding off about his overwhelming responsibilities, what an important man he was and how neither I nor my mother could possibly appreciate what he did at the Royal Bank.

I just sat beside him, looking out of the car window, and we were passing the Bardowie Loch when his tirade suddenly focussed on me. I would never, he informed me, amount to anything without him. In fact, no one in Scotland would ever hire me unless he used his influence to get me a job.

I was so angry I couldn't speak. My silence, of course, prompted further denigration. When we reached Bluerisk, he went upstairs to his room to lie down for an hour before dinner. He did this every night – it was suppose to relax him but it never did. In those days, respectable middle class families didn't have cocktails before their evening meal. I've often wondered whether Littie might have been better off unwinding over a whisky, which he was allowed even though he had a duodenal ulcer. I don't think he and Mummy and I would have had a "happy hour" but a couple of drinks might have taken the edge off his tension more effectively that lying in a darkened room on his single bed brooding on the problems of the working day.

Intellectually, I knew that diatribe about my only finding employment through his influence was a symptom of his illness. I'm sure he never remembered that he'd made such a ridiculous forecast. But, turning twenty, full of powerful but unfocused ambition, and searching for an identity behind the facade I'd created to protect me from my strong-minded parents, never having had to look for a job, I had no frame of reference and what he said could well be true. If so, I had to get out of Scotland, out of Britain indeed, because even London was too close. He could take a train and invade my life within eight hours.

I had heard other earnest Scottish parents tell mine about

evaluating every career move their offspring made and always from the family's point of view, not that of the child. Next door to my aunties in Milngavie, the sibling of an invalid daughter fled to a Protestant convent and became a nun.

"If ever a girl was needed at home, she was!" said Auntie Jane.

Should anything happen to Mummy, with her bad heart, I would be expected by society to take over the management of Littie's household and spend the rest of my life walking around the Strathblane roads in sensible shoes and with only a dog for company.

I don't remember telling Mummy about that diatribe of Littie's but I suspect some of my real reasons for wanting to go to America had been in the back of her mind too. Certainly she did all she could to encourage me to leave home as she herself had never been able to do.

As long as my father was alive, I never looked for work in the United Kingdom, though at one time I considered the possibility of doing so. Only after his death did I start my long association with the George Outram Company, which at that time owned the *Glasgow Herald* and the defunct tabloid the *Bulletin*, where I first published articles about America. I progressed to becoming a regular columnist strictly on my own journalistic merits. Catherine Gavin gave me the initial lead to my first editor, the late Alison Downie, but I took it from there.

I suspect that by the time I quit in 1994, Helen Lillie's name was far better known throughout Scotland than her father's ever was. He would, of course, have been terribly proud. He'd have boasted and talked about me to his businessmen friends whose families would undoubtedly have disliked me as much as in my childhood I disliked the unknown young Lindsays.

Littie was greatly admired by his peers. And intellectually I have long since forgiven him for what he said, then and on a later occasion when his own anger and distress led to an outburst which hurt me greatly. But emotionally it's hard to forget accusations aimed at the core of a young person's identity. As the poet Jessamyn West put in, "A broken bone can heal, but the wound a word opens can fester forever."

12

The Land of the Free!

Was it a foretaste of the future that the New England hurricane of September, 1938, was blowing full blast when I landed in America? Mummy and I had crossed the Atlantic on the *Ile de France* and the massive ocean liner tossed around in New York's harbour like an 18-foot yacht in an open sea. Fortunately we were both past being seasick and didn't realise the storm's gravity until after we docked but it was a hairy introduction to an enormous unknown continent. Even so, I don't remember being scared. It was too exciting.

There was also a taxi strike in New York City. However a female connection-by-marriage met us, and, somehow, transported us to the Barbizon Hotel for Women on Lexington Avenue. Mummy had read about this place and thought it might be suitable for me to stay in if I visited New York alone. It was, but so reminiscent of a girls' dormitory I switched to the Roosevelt Hotel on my second solo trip.

The night we arrived, this same connection and her husband took us to dinner at a midtown restaurant. When I ran my eye down the list of desserts seeking something with no milk, they complimented me on being knowledgable enough about America to order apple pie!

Then they took us to Radio City. I'd never heard of it and was surprised when it turned out to be the biggest movie theatre I'd ever been in. We saw *You Can't Take It With You*, a superb film I remember to this day.

Next morning, Mummy and I travelled by train to New Haven, Connecticut, observing the hurricane's damage en route. My first impression of the America beyond New York City, was of impermanent wooden houses at the mercy of the elements. I thought if these weren't rebuilt as soon as they were blown down, the primeval wilderness would move back and snuff out all trace of human habitation.

In New Haven, we had rooms at the Young Womens' Christian Association. Alladean Bell, one of my Drama School pals who also stayed there, used to threaten to write a play called *Why the Y?* She never did but I wish she had, though as Ys went, ours was luxurious and had an excellent cafeteria in the basement much frequented by young men trying to pick up dates.

The Drama School in 1938-9 was headed by a Scotsman, Allardyce Nicoll, a notable scholar with a quietly pungent sense of humour and a slightly Glesca' accent. His wife was an extrovert European who had entertained us to tea a couple of months earlier in Malvern, where they had a summer home. With hindsight, I suppose I was being evaluated by the shrewd Mrs. Nicoll, who, I remember, impressed upon me that I'd be working so hard I wouldn't have any time for sightseeing while in the USA.

At the Drama School's reception for incoming students, Mummy met Mrs. Stanley McCandlass whose husband was the professor of stage lighting. The couple had just moved into a new house equipped with every available labour-saving device powered by electricity and consequently useless because of the hurricane. "Don't ever live in a house with only one source of light and heat," Mummy advised me. "Look what happened to these people when it failed!" I never forgot this, and always demand a gas stove wherever I live.

My first impression of my fellow students at Yale was that they ranged enormously in age. Some, to my 22-year old mind were downright elderly, in their forties at least. "And the place is overrun with homosexuals," an incoming costume designer told me. I was so shocked I kept this from Mummy. I did tell her, though that drama students frequently worked far into the night at the theatre rehearsing or on crews, so she'd better warn the Y. This establishment didn't like residents who came in late, for a staff member had to stay up at the front desk until everyone was accounted for each night. But I never had any problems when I came in at 2 am or later, indeed they often commiserated with me for having to work so hard!

Pretty soon I had a steady boyfriend, Francis Woodburn Leary, known in those days as Frank, a history student in the Graduate School and later my first husband. When he found that other young men were escorting me home after these late nights on crew, he took to working late at the library then picking me up himself.

Sometimes we'd stop off for a snack at a bar called George and Harry's. Frank told me that beer would relax my tensions and help me sleep. I still wasn't used to alcohol, and a non-Drama Schoolgirl who regularly rolled into the Y very late had been ordered to get out the morning after she showed up circa 3 am, greeting the sleepy lady on the desk with a boozy "Hiya, Toots!"

If I drank more than one glass of beer, Frank would say as he left me at the door, "Now go in and call the old lady Toots!" I never did, but in my second year I moved into an apartment where I could come and go as I pleased. In more comfort, too, with a carpet on the floor. I've always liked to go without shoes and found the linoleum in the Y bedrooms unsympathetic.

I loved Yale University. It suggested Oxford where Anthony, still a regular correspondent, had been a student. The undergraduates were all male in those days but there were a lot of wispy, unattractive females working on PhDs in the Graduate School. Frank often took me to dinner there and I heard the disparaging comments he and his friends made about academic women. I also learned that in America you were an old maid if you weren't married by the age of twenty-four which I was fast approaching.

In the Drama School, for the first time in my life, I was working alongside dedicated professionals who loved what they did and knew where they wanted to go. Like Glasgow, Yale offered little formal career counselling but students had a closer relationship with their instructors, even called them by their first names, which struck me as lacking in respect.

Everyone disliked Frank MacMullen, a youngish blond man with a perpetually raised eyebrow who had stepped into the professorship of Stage Direction on the sudden death of a brilliant and famous predecessor, Alexander Deane. Conscious that many of his students had already accomplished far more in the

American theatre than he ever would, MacMullen hid his insecurity behind sarcasm. He cast me as an amateurish rich girl and tried to weed me out until I set him straight. In my second year I insisted on my right as a playwriting student to a direction assignment and eventually got one. I staged the first act of James Barrie's *What Every Woman Knows* and my biggest problem was discouraging the cast from using what they believed to be Scots accents. Predictably MacMullen criticised me for letting them speak like Americans.

But I absorbed more about play construction in the Direction classes than in the famous Drama 47, the first college course created to teach stage writing. It started at Harvard under George Pierce Baker. Isabel Wilder, who died in 1995 at the age of 95, was in the class of 1928. Though she published three novels in her youth, Isabel, like Dorothy Wordsworth, is better remembered as the secretary, hostess and general amanuensis of a famous brother. Thornton Wilder's play *Our Town* is the greatest of American plays and I wonder how much it owed to Isabel's expertise? If she had been born fifty years later would she have surpassed him in what she created?

In 1938, our mentor was a former New York dramatic critic, Walter Pritchard Eaton, a taciturn New Englander, who read aloud our efforts in class in neutral tones. He would then light a pipe and invite our comments. These fell regularly into two categories. The earnest souls who believed the theatre should have social significance, judged every play from this angle and despised comedy. On the other side were those, like me, who believed that "We who live to please must please to live," so our primary job was to entertain.

Among the serious-minded was Rae Dalven, a Jewess of Greek extraction, erudite and earnest, with the kind of mind that couldn't see the wood for the trees. All year she struggled with a play about the romance of Pericles and Aspasia. Eventually she brought it to class and Eaton read it to us. She had included examples of behaviour from every rank of Ancient Greek society and the result was a lengthy hodgepodge. Knowing how much the play meant to her, we tried to be constructive but she argued vehemently against leaving anything out.

Five minutes before the end of the exhausting hour, our professor removed his pipe and spoke for the first time. "Rae," he asked her. "What's the subject of this play?"

"Why, Aspasia and Pericles!" she explained. "Their relationship . . ."

"Okay. Aspasia and Pericles. A love story. You're not writing about women's rights, Greek attitudes towards homosexuals, Athenian politics or anything else."

"Only to show how these things . . ."

"The structure of this play," he interupted her, "is very simple."

We gasped!

> "There were those, like me, who believed that 'We who live to please must please to live,' so our primary job was to entertain."

"Act One: Boy meets girl," pronounced Papa Eaton. "Act Two: Boy can't get girl. Act Three: Boy gets girl. That's your play."

He put his pipe back into his craggy face, the bell rang, and as we thankfully made ready to escape, a beautiful light of illumination broke over Rae's intense features.

"You're right!" she cried. "You're so right!" She was beaming. "Now I know how to revise it! Of course! Just Aspasia and Pericles!"

She did do some rewriting but at the end of the year, returned to academia. She published many books including translations and poetry collections, but her obit in the *New York Times* didn't mention anything about either Aspasia or Pericles.

I liked Rae though she could be tiresome. She too stayed at the Y, and used to pace up and down the corridors at night, deep in thought. Her intellectual respect for me was based on a misapprehension. Talking about how neither of us was working towards a degree, she once commented with pride, "We already have our Masters." I didn't enlighten her that Scottish universities awarded MAs only, and mine, without Honours, was more like an American BA.

Among my contemporaries were Fred Coe, later a distinguished director; Herbert Brodkin of television fame; Richard Fleisher who went into movies; and Otis L. Guernsey, a notable critic and editor. Many others made their name in the American theatre, like a wacky undergraduate, Burton G. Shevelov, whose efforts in Drama 47 we so despised we once reduced him to tears. He had the last laugh with many successful Broadway productions. Everett (Bud) Gammon wound up in advertising but I and others remember him for his evil, brilliant Richard III, handsome in spite of hunchbackly padding in his doublet and a limp added during the final rehearsals in an effort to make him look less sexy. The women students tended to go into acting or the ubiquitous teaching profession.

That I didn't keep up more closely with these people shows my inexperience. Perhaps if I'd made better use of my contacts, I wouldn't have wasted so many years doing silly office jobs but when I moved to New York City I needed regular pay cheques and I'd learned what a chancy employer the theatre was. Nor did I know enough to seek out freelance script assignments. "And you're not old and bald enough to be a drama critic," someone said to me kindly.

I did a lot of acting at Yale, including a repeat performance as Bella in *The Barretts of Wimpole Street*. In the most memorable production of 1939, Ben Jonson's *Silent Woman* directed by Wilson Lehr, later a professor of drama in Brooklyn, I was bolstered by petticoats, and played the stout, strident Mrs. Otter. My stage husband, played by David Langworthy, owned a bear garden. The set was a reconstruction of Shakespeare's Globe Theatre. We used this for many shows and it grew so rickety I screamed with real fear rushing across the upper level fleeing from an imaginary fire in that Elizabethan tear-jerker *The Changeling*.

I learned perfectionism at Yale. Mary Percy Schenk, a stout, motherly costume designer with a dry wit who later worked at the Metropolitan Opera, created spectacular eighteenth century clothes for *The Beaux' Stratagem*. I worked on the crew that made these, sewing long and hard through many a late night and at the last dress rehearsal, to which select members of the public were admitted, not even the cynical Direction students had any criticism of the costumes.

Except Mary who wasn't satisfied with one beautiful gown.

Everyone, even McMullen, told her it looked fine, but she went off muttering to herself. Next morning, her crew found her in the workroom stretched out on the floor fully dressed and dead to the world among pages of sketches, piles of discarded material and empty bottles of Coca Cola.

On the leading lady's dress form was a glorious, shimmering new dress with intricate underpinnings, and many lacy frills and furbelows. Mary had designed and made it from scratch, working alone all through the night.

I did notice that when I brought the Sunday *New York Times* into the Green Room, no-one borrowed anything except the theatre section. Shows went on, regardless of world crises, backaches, colds, or as once happened, a diagnosis of tuberculosis for the director who consulted a doctor in the midst of staging a bawdy restoration comedy called *The Squire of Alsacia*. I was cast as a "Mistress Margaret" and I was so busy on Mary's costume crew, it wasn't until the first run-through that I discovered I was playing a whore. This explained some curious business shortly after my entrance with another girl during a party scene. "Eat this, my dear!" suggested the country bumpkin, handing me a stick of celery.

"Why celery?" asked the stage manager, when told to supply some.

"It's an aphrodisiac," explained the student director. "Doesn't everyone know that? If not, then for goodness sake, spread the word so we'll get a laugh." The stage crew usually forgot to refrigerate the food and I had to wolf down some disgustingly soggy stalks. In that same scene I was also handed money which I stuffed into my cleavage. During one performance, as we were dancing and singing a bawdy song down by the footlights, I felt those big cold pennies working their way out below my formidable corsets. They landed with a clunk on the stage. Well, it was a comedy after all and we were hard put to for merriment, so I bent over, picked the coins up and stashed them away again!

Our director disappeared into a hospital immediately after the show closed. We never heard if he recovered from his TB but I hope he did. He was a nice guy and he'd had the imagination to cast everyone against their known nature i.e. a gay played the heterosexual lecher, and we two ladies of the town were the most inhibited of the female students. Years later, I remarked to that other actress, "We must have been the only virgins in the Drama School."

She snorted. "Speak for yourself, sweetie."

"But – you used to proclaim in a loud voice that you were!"

"Yeah but that was for protection. I'd had one affair and I wasn't about to have another before I found a husband." I'm glad to say she had a long and happy marriage but, like my Scottish classmates, she never fulfilled her original career ambition.

Student plays given major presentations attracted sponsors and talent scouts from New York. Faculty members usually staged these which made it difficult for the playwright to get across his or her own ideas. My friend Alladean Bell, brilliant but insecure, claimed her comedy *Jackrabbit Flats* missed out on a Broadway production because of wrong direction at Yale. Would protests from a male playwright had more effect than hers, I wonder?

This could well be true. Walter Pritchard Eaton regularly lectured Drama 47 on the advantages of staging one's own dramas, citing the case of one popular woman playwright. And down at New Haven's Schubert Theatre that season, there was the example of *The Time of Your Life* by William Saroyan. According to the rumours, it was so bad during the try-out the management was about to give up on it until the playwright convinced them to fire the director and let him stage it exactly as he'd written it. The result was a longrunning Broadway hit.

But, despite the undercover double standard, the Drama School was years ahead of its time in being integrated both by sex and by race, though in 1938, there were only a couple of Hispanics and a mere handful of African-American students. But the most admired and ultimately successful playwright of my generation there was Owen Dodson, a leader in the Harlem Renaissance of black drama and later associated with Washington's Howard University. At Yale he rewrote the Medea legend setting it in the antibellum South with Jason a white slaveowner. After that show closed the local beauty parlour made a small fortune washing inky dye out of our hair and skin since all the actors were white.

I wasn't creative during my two years at Yale. I was too busy absorbing new experiences. But I was learning to take a professional attitude towards whatever I did and to have respect for technique. I saw too many examples of plays written like novels and vice versa. And I've always found useful the old theatrical adage, "Don't tell 'em. Show 'em."

> "A good play, we'd been taught, should start with an explosion and end with an earthquake."

The producer Eddie Dowling, giving us a lecture while he was in New Haven with a try-out, told us that he read every script submitted to him until a character delivered "The Message". Then he'd reject it. If the "meaning and significance" didn't come across through the action there was something wrong. Another visitor, the European director Otto Preminger, challenged every high-falutin' statement we students made to him with "Vy?" spat out in his most Germanic accent. It became a legend around the School.

As a novelist, I have to guard against developing every situation through dialogue. I once picked up at the library a thriller written by a fellow-Drama 47 student. I enjoyed it, but I could feel him working up to his first act curtain, then the second, and finally building towards the climax. A good play, we'd been taught, should start with an explosion and end with an earthquake. This is a good format for a news story too. And just as a playwright has to keep audiences sufficiently intrigued to return to their seats after every intermission, so non-fiction writers and novelists must entice readers to move on from paragraph to paragraph and keep turning pages.

I have always agreed with W. Somerset Maugham who points out in *A Writer's Notebook*,

> "One fusses about style. One tries to write better. One takes pains to be simple, clear and succinct. One aims

at rhythm and balance. One reads a sentence aloud to
see that it sounds well. One sweats one's guts out. The
fact remains that the four greatest novelists the world
has ever known Balzac, Dickens, Tolstoi and
Dostoievsky, wrote their respective languages very
indifferently. It proves that if you can tell stories, create
character, devise incidents, and if you have sincerity
and passion, it doesn't matter a damn how you write.
All the same it's better to write well than ill."

This I learned at Yale, and also the need to stand up for myself
as I did with McMullen over the direction assignment.

My acting experience later became a useful job hunting tool.
Before setting out on any employment interview, I'd carefully
dress myself for the position I sought. If you look the part and
perform as though you're in control, people tend to believe in
you. It's a useful way to mask uncertainty and grief, too. During
some of the most unhappy periods of my life I'd remembered
Bud Gammon's voice as Richard III snarling,

> Why, I can smile and murder while I smile.
> And cry content to that which grieves my heart.
> And wet my cheeks with artificial tears
> And frame my face to all occasions.
> Can I do this and cannot get a crown?

13

The War that Would Never Come

Though I did work harder in the Yale Drama School than ever before in my life, I played too. I didn't socialise much with the male drama students because most of them were either gay, married or strapped for cash. My sexual innocence aroused match-making attitudes in the women, who took me in hand as soon as Mummy went back to Scotland. They included me in foursome blind dates and I met undergraduates and young men who were specialising in professional fields like law. On one of these occasions with Diane, a Southern divorcee studying directing, I met Frank Leary.

He was in his mid-twenties, solidly built and with arresting blue eyes at once sharp and dreamy, a long wandering nose, a well-formed mouth, and dark hair, already receding. He wasn't handsome but he was attractive. "You look like an Irish cop!" his mother once remarked apropos of a photo taken for a bookcover. To me he suggested an Irish intellectual with a touch of the poet. Dear Miss Christine Renton once asked me what his attraction was? "It was his wonderful mind and the way he could write," I told her with partial truth. "He was incapable of writing a bad sentence."

A sense of fun also made him good company, when he was in the mood, and he had an attractive resonant voice. He loved music and owned a victrola on which he played classical records while he studied. This was something I'd never done, but I soon found myself working on my reading assignments in the student rooming house at 54 Trumbull Street where Frank had a small, pleasant room with a studio couch, a desk and a typewriter. It was easier to concentrate there than at the Y, and more comfortable.

His landlady, Katharine, had been a concert violinist before her marriage. I never knew why she'd abandoned her profession because she was good. In the afternoons she often practised the Mendelssohn Violin Concerto – never anything else, and I often wondered why? But I'd been brought up to consider such a question as rude so never asked her. Later, I saw how women frequently had to discard vocations they'd worked hard on after they got married.

Frank came from Binghamton in upstate New York, the only child of an incompatable and now broken marriage. His father, a lawyer, was part Dutch. His mother, Eve Woodburn, was of Scottish descent. Eva, as her son called her, was a talented writer who published many short stories and after her divorce went to Manhattan and became a successful literary agent. One of her most grateful clients was Earle Stanley Gardner. While she was building this mystery writer's career, her young son was being raised by his adoring grandparents, Hiram and Della Woodburn. Hiram was a wonderful erudite self-educated man. He had been a conductor on the Delaware Lackawanna and Wabash (DL&W) Railroad and spent his time on the long train trips reading books about American history, an interest he passed on to his grandson. Later, he went into business and became Mayor of Binghamton.

If some men marry their mothers, Frank married his grandmother. At least 'Grammy' and I were so temperamentally alike we recognised each other the moment we met. "Helen, I just wanted you to know, whatever happens you'll always be my little granddaughter," she told me when she got the news of our divorce. Since my generic grandparents had died when I was too young to bond with them, Grammy filled that role in my life.

She was a nurturing woman, and Frank told me a revealing anecdote about how one hot summer afternoon she'd said to her husband, "Hirie, I'm going to scoot down to the store and get Little Lover Heart some ice cream." To which Mr. Woodburn growled, "For Gawd's sake, let him go get his own ice cream!" But she never did, and this was not good training for marriage. Nor did she teach him how to cook for himself or cope with such domestic chores as sewing on buttons, like my wonderful second mother-in-law. But there was a generational factor involved too.

My second husband is ten years younger than my first.

The Woodburns were ambitious for their appealing, attractive grandchild, who like me, had had health problems in his youth. Some affluent relative underwrote his going to a prestigious boarding school where he was among boys from families much richer than his. He followed them into Princeton University then to Yale where for a year he studied law. He realised, however, that this profession wasn't for him, so switched to the History Department. Shortly before we met he had had a nervous breakdown due to the tension of the uncongenial study and an abortive romance. From time to time throughout his life he suffered from bleak periods of depression, as impossible for me to cope with as Littie's manic moods.

I don't regret the ten years I was involved with Frank. Though he caused me much unhappiness, not all of it was his fault, and he did two wonderful things for me. He taught me how to work towards good writing and also how to enjoy the company of cats, animals I'd never been exposed to because Mummy didn't like them.

In his student days Frank was already gestating the Great American Novel. A few years later, when he had a job reading for a publisher, he handed me a manuscript with the comment, "An interesting example of Early Leary." After I'd read a few pages, I told him, "It's more like fourth rate Thomas Wolfe." "That," he answered, "is what I mean." He moved on from there to develop his own distinctive style and his literary achievements should be far better known than they are.

We listened to music together. We went to the theatre and to films. We saw the first showing of the movie *Gone With the Wind*. He came to all the Drama School shows, often said he should have studied there.

One of his Princeton friends, Bob Sincerbeaux, was studying law at Yale. At Frank's suggestion, I introduced "Sincy" to my best friend at the Y, a dedicated art student called Betty Morley. She had curly black hair and brilliant blue eyes set in a lively, intense little face. She got up at the crack of dawn every morning and worked at her sculpture. She'd grown up in a comfortable home in Short Hills, New Jersey, and her father worked on Wall

Street so we had similar backgrounds. After she met Bob she started to pay increasing attention to her appearance and he began to pay less attention to other girls he'd been dating, notably a lively young Italian who, according to Frank, would have been an unsuitable spouse for a Wall Street lawyer.

I went home after my first year at Yale, in the fateful summer of 1939. Although the Americans were much aware of the "gathering storm" in Europe, Betty and a girlfriend with the same first name, came to Britain on holiday and my parents planned to sail back with me to see some of the United States. To this end Littie had booked three passages on a ship leaving from Liverpool in early September.

My strongest recollection of that summer is how Ian Neilson reacted to my American clothes. He thought them too far out. He was also aware that I'd become interested in someone else and didn't empathize with my increasing determination to become a professional writer. For my part, I was thoroughly out of sympathy with all the war talk. From what I knew of European history and my pacifist convictions, I felt proper diplomacy to create a balance of power should be able to keep Hitler in line.

But by the time Bet Morley came north to visit me in Strathblane, the international situation had grown into a crisis and security was suddenly tight. She'd brought along one of her friend's suitcases which she planned to leave in the station in Glasgow. "You'll have to open it," Mummy warned her, when we met her off the London train.

"I don't have the key," said Bet. Unfazed, she hauled the bag to the Left Luggage where the dour Glasgow attendant asked suspiciously, "Whit's in there?"

She gave him her radiant smile. "A bomb!" she announced. He grinned and took it without more ado!

Mummy and Littie had by now decided to cancel their trip and, after some phone conversations with Bet's parents, who had also been holidaying in Europe, offered to turn over their sailing accommodations to her and the other Betty. But when we arrived in Liverpool, Cunard refused to change the names on the tickets in the midst of the international crisis. For once, Littie acted unemotionally and like a businessman. He simply held onto his two reservations until the shipping office was closing and at that point the company gave in.

So the two Bets and I sailed away from World War II which broke out when we were in mid-Atlantic. The *Athenia*, the ship that left after ours, was sunk by a German submarine. We, on the other hand, had a high old time with a group of Naval Reserve officers en route to the West Indies and, like us, anxious to eat, drink and be merry as long as possible.

But underneath the nonchalance, I was reminding myself every day, You're on your own now. You'll have a living allowance for a few more months but after the school year ends, the money'll be cut off and you'll have to support yourself.

But I'd be free to do whatever I wanted. In America, unlike Scotland, there was no social stigma attached to menial jobs which brought in cash. I'd seen how my fellow students coped and knew I could do equally well.

Moreover, I wasn't entirely alone. Frank, who had learned somehow which ship Bet was on, cabled her frantically, "Is Helen aboard?" Our first port of call was Boston, and there he was on the pier. So I disembarked and went down to New Haven with him where, instead of staying in the Y, I found a one-room apartment at 100 Howe Street and settled down to my second year at the Drama School.

That was the year of the "Phoney War" so I wasn't unduly worried. I visited Bet's family in New Jersey. She hadn't gone back to Yale, but was living at home and making sculptural models of the neighbours' dogs and horses. She was also wearing nifty clothes. Bob Sincerbeaux was working in a prestigious Manhattan law firm and taking her out a lot. By Spring they were engaged, then married. The other Betty and I were bridesmaids, in ethereal blue organdy creations trimmed with cerise ribbon.

The newly weds moved into a small house near the bride's family and as the academic year drew to a close I found a job through a Drama School acquaintance, Sally Stearns. Her mother owned the Peterborough Players in New Hampshire and needed someone to write publicity. There was no salary, but I was given room and board and tuition in acting and direction.

That was one glorious summer! We lived in a small farmhouse near the theatre and ate the most wonderfully fresh food. "I've always wondered why Thornton Wilder didn't mention corn on the cob in that last act of *Our Town,*" someone remarked, as we were gobbling up ears dumped straight into the pot from the garden. Like every other New England summer theatre that season, we put on *Our Town* and I wrote myself out in the local press proving that it had been inspired by Peterborough and not Keene or the other New Hampshire villages with rival stock companies. After all, Wilder wrote his masterpiece at Peterborough's MacDowell Colony, an artists' retreat which provided us with highly intelligent audiences.

Meanwhile, Frank had been in New York looking for a job, and when he found one, teaching at a private school in Westchester which provided an apartment and offered spouses work too, he asked me to marry him.

The War in Europe was then moving out of the phoney stage. I was still a pacifist and I might have had a hard time getting home even if I'd tried, though I could have been deported as an illegal alien since all I had was a student visa, viable only when I didn't work for money and stayed at Yale.

But, apart from practical considerations, I believed I was in love with Frank, though I knew he wouldn't be easy to live with. He was self-centered, possessive, jealous, and impervious to explanations of any conduct which diverged from his own ideas or didn't contribute directly to his comfort. However, I thought these grey areas in our relationship came from insecurity and would disappear once we'd made a commitment. I did not marry him to change him although of course I hoped to make a few improving modifications in his behaviour patterns. Didn't wives usually accomplish this?

"Your marriage didn't have a chance, with the war breaking out and the future so uncertain," Eba Haddow said to me later, but I am more inclined to agree with Louanna Wilcox, a perceptive and learned astrologer whom I met when the marriage was long past. I once mentioned casually to her that I'd been married and divorced before I met Charles, and she asked, "What was your first husband's date of birth?"

"January 29th," I recalled.

"Aquarius," she pronounced, "and you're a Virgo. You'd never have got along."

Among my marriage photos is one showing me, in Bet's white dress, surrounded by the male ushers, Frank's Princeton pals. It looks like every girl's dream situation – all those handsome affluent-looking men and a husband too. The naivete of couples contemplating marriage in the late 1930s is unbelievable nowadays. And I was not alone in my ignorance.

"A man, I have since discovered, exhibits the same characteristics in bed that he does elsewhere"

Frank and I didn't realise that we disagreed fundamentally about almost everything except writing and music, starting with money and sex. Throughout the two years we'd been at Yale we'd both been living on small fixed incomes supplied by our families and seldom discussed the pros and cons of finance. Before wartime regulations went into effect, Littie had transferred some money – a handsome amount by the standards of the time – into an American account for my use in an emergency. Although by then it was accepted that women controlled their own money, after we were married Frank felt I should draw on this whenever we were short of cash. I wouldn't do so because I'd been brought up to consider capital as untouchable save in a dire emergency.

As for sex, we had never, as they say, gone all the way or even engaged in more than rather heavy petting. My only instruction came from an embarrassed Bet, whose parents were hosting my wedding by way of thanking Littie for getting their daughter safely out of beleaguered Britain. I wore her gorgeous white gown and she was matron of honour in my blue organdy.

I stayed at the Morleys' the night before the ceremony, and appealed to my more experienced friend for some basic information about what happened next. She spelled out the logistics of intercourse, more or less, showed me how to insert some horrible jelly alleged to prevent conception, the pre-Pill form of birth control, then she said, "I guess that's about all I can tell you. Just remember it's fun."

It wasn't for me, on an unhappy honeymoon in Montauk on Long Island. A man, I have since discovered, exhibits the same characteristics in bed that he does elsewhere, and if he is primarily interested in his own sexual gratification, he isn't going to take the time and trouble to arouse and then guide an inexperienced woman towards a shared climax.

My ignorance was typical of the times as I discovered a couple of years later, when working in a small New York advertising agency. With their boyfriends being "caught in the Draft" my female co-workers were all getting engaged. One girl, whose sister was about to marry a young serviceman regularly took me aside and whispered, "Gloria wants to know. . ." One question was, "Does a woman have to Give Herself to her husband every night?" I burst out laughing. "Tell Gloria," I said, "that people do get tired!"

I had had another problem before my own hitching. My parents, of course, had been notified well ahead and had reacted in character. Mummy's letter was short and filled with an unusual outpouring of love and desire for my happiness, adding, to my surprise, that it broke her heart to miss my wedding. Littie wrote that the financial arrangements weren't satisfactory, then burbled on about the fine Woodburn family, saying he was "half in love with Eva already."

Neither parent bothered to tell me that they'd also sent an announcement of my engagement to the Scottish press. I had, of course, written a most carefully worded letter to Ian, mailed to his home since he was by now in the Army and "somewhere in England." But unluckily, he bought a paper to read in the train coming home on leave and there was the news that Helen Mary Lillie would become Mrs. Francis Woodburn Leary on September 20, 1940. All I remember of his heartbroken telegram was a plea to cable him immediately if my decision wasn't irrevocable. I still feel sorry that our romance ended that way and am thankful that, fifty years later, we're friends once more.

14

Thank Heaven for Little Boys

My career as a teacher was brief, in a job I hope no modern girl would ever consider, it commanded service under such sexist conditions. The experience illustrates just how women were exploited in 1940. My husband was paid a pittance and our employers got my MA and two years of graduate work, unpaid, in return for an apartment and some free meals of dubious nutritional value. And I wasn't the only unpaid wife there.

After our marriage, Frank and I were seeking both paid employment and a place to live. The offer from Scarsdale Country Day School, which came through friends, promised to meet both needs. The school enrolled boys only, and since that well-heeled suburb of New York offered excellent public education, our pupils tended to be children with problems, usually behavioural ones, which came from being brought up with an exaggerated sense of their own and their family's importance. Teachers, far from being authority figures, were thought of as servants and expected to tie shoelaces and perform similar chores on demand "or else my father will take me away from this stupid school".

However they were, by and large, a delightful group of lively youngsters, avid for entertainment, sometimes even instruction. Frank taught English and History and there were two other masters in addition to the head, 'Uncle Sherry', who had recruited his pupils largely by turning on charm while sharing drinks with their parents in fashionable local watering holes. When he was hungover, as often happened, he made Miss Lee seem in retrospect positively benign. Even one of the toughest boys, whose name was Du Pratt, would beg teachers not to punish him by sending him to Uncle Sherry "because he shouts so!"

I'd thought I was to teach Drama or at least stage some plays. Instead I found myself instructing the First Grade in my old Achilles heel, Arithmetic. However to my Scarsdale pupils I was "an ace" because I could total up long columns of figures, to the best of their knowledge, correctly.

I didn't have disciplinary problems either if Du Pratt was in my class. He was sharp, intelligent and he loved to be told stories. He also claimed, with truth, that he could "lick any guy in the school", and he was part of an afternoon group assigned to me entitled Crafts. This was a dumping ground for assorted pupils nobody knew what else to do with during that period. I had as little aptitude for making things as for mathematics, so I'd hand out paper, paints and plasticine and suggest that everyone draw or make something that especially interested them. In 1940, this meant war planes. The modellers would build them, then divebomb those the artists were drawing.

One afternoon, as all Hell was starting to break loose, I hollered through the noise, "Would anyone like me to tell a story?"

"Geez, Yes! Mrs L!" yelled back Du Pratt who shared my boredom with Crafts.

"Then be quiet and sit still! Du Pratt!" I looked him in the eye. "I'm putting you in charge. It's your responsibiility to keep order." I then launched into a tale aimed at holding his attention, and from then on at the slightest sound of unrest among his peers, he'd clench his small fist and snarl, "Shut up or she won't tell us what happens next." Even Uncle Sherry complimented me on what a quiet class that was!

We ate every meal except breakfast in school. The midday dinner was solid dull meat and potatoes with dessert to follow. Supper for the staff was skimpy leftovers. Uncle Sherrry usually had a few drinks from what he called "the Faculty bottle" but he never invited us to join him. We were so hungry we filled ourselves up on peanut butter, which I've never eaten since.

None of the teachers stayed long. In our first term, one enlisted in the Navy and shortly after, Frank tangled, legitimately, with Uncle Sherry. So, after three months and at short notice, we lost not only our jobs but also our living quarters.

15

"New York! New York! A Wonderful Town!"

When Frank and I moved into Manhattan, I became an instant New Yorker – a typical one since I wasn't a native but lived there from choice. And what followed for me – ambitious, clever and with special talents which didn't fit into the job market's requirements – was the typical fate of naive young married women fifty years ago.

The city gave me what I'd always wanted – a flexible lifestyle and anonymity to pursue my own interests, make mistakes without having to explain them and cultivate people I liked regardless of who their parents were or what they did. I wrote to Mummy and Littie every week, sometimes more often, but I usually edited what I told them about my circumstances and my friends.

Neither of my husbands have shared my love for the city which has never lost its fascination for me. I sincerely believe that,

> You may not see
> In Gay Paree,
> In London or in Cork,
> The things you'll meet
> On any street
> In Old Noo Yawk!

Dr. Samuel Johnson wrote that he who was tired of London was tired of life. I'd substitute Manhattan Island. It has the advantage of being so condensed you can, given time, walk on level streets to every theatre, museum, art gallery or store and, if not, get there by subway, bus or cab.

It's one of the few places in the world that isn't dependent on the automobile, and after growing up in the country, I appreciated that freedom. The climate is horribly cold in winter but the sky stays blue. And the summer isn't as humid as Washington's Southern climate.

When you're given an address in New York, you can figure out the location from the logical pattern of the streets and avenues. Of course, in Greenwich Village you also find West 12th Street crossing West 4th which in turn intersects itself in four directions on the next block but that's like life. Every street offers a cross-section of lifestyles too, with offices, luxury apartments and old rundown brownstones and tenements co-existing side by side. It's a dirty city but there are trees and many parks. Plants and flowering bushes abound on the avenues and are especially noticeable and precious among the skyscrapers. Above all, you're never far out of sight of two great waterways, the East and the Hudson Rivers, on which huge ships and every variety of smaller boats are constantly navigating.

I also enjoyed my fellow New Yorkers, who push and hassle and don't hesitate to speak their minds. As neighbours they're caring beneath the brashness and with no strings attached to their spontaneous kindness. They seldom interfere, respecting their neighbours' privacy. They're emotional, illogical and larger than life and congregate in ethnic neighbourhoods. When I went to San Juan in Puerto Rico, I could identify every little shop from having once lived near Eighth Avenue. And on my first trip to Italy with Mummy she was impressed by how confidently I read menus.

"I didn't realise you knew Italian," she commented.

"I don't," said I, "but I eat out in Greenwich Village."

If it weren't for the indecipherable script, I imagine I'd feel equally comfortable with menus in the Middle East, the Orient, or indeed anywhere in the world. Nowadays, of course, I'd find such restaurants everywhere, but not in the 1940s.

You never knew what might be happening in New York, either. One cold March day during my first year, I saw so many policemen lining upper Fifth Avenue, I went nervously up to one of them and asked him why?

"Sure and it's St. Paddy's Day, m'dear!" said New York's tall, handsome Finest. I never lived in any city that had so many

110

parades! They can be a nuisance, but they do add colour to the passing scene.

When we left Scarsdale for New York City, Frank and I rented a room in an East Seventies brownstone, long since demolished. Round the corner was the Madison Avenue Presbyterian Church which I later joined. While living in that first lodging I came down with German measles. We knew no doctor but a student psychologist in the bedsitter next to ours diagnosed my feverish rash and advised me to stay put quietly since I had a reportable illness. Unasked, he also lent me his radio for entertainment and talked the woman who cleaned the place into bringing me food. This was my first taste of Manhattan in-house friendliness.

We then moved into a cheap but spacious apartment in an ugly, dreary district of Queens where we were the only Gentiles in the building. Later, we had a beloved doctor and friend, a German refugee called Frederic J. Heilbroner, who described himself as "a good anti-Semite" despite his racial origin. He wouldn't have liked our Rego Park neighbours any more than we did.

We only stayed there a year, hating the subway commuting and the surroundings, then moved to a reasonably priced two-room apartment in New York's Tudor City. Eva, Frank's mother, lived two floors above us and after Mr. Woodburn died, Grammy joined her. Our seventh floor bedroom at The Manor on East 43rd Street, looked out over the East River at least until the United Nations bulding went up and cut off our view. However, that also meant the end of the insalubrious meat markets and abattoirs on First Avenue which we were unpleasantly aware of when the wind was blowing west.

Whenever we had some cash – and sometimes when we didn't – we took advantage of the city's entertainment. We saw the Metropolitan Opera "live" from good seats and like a true Drama School alumna, I criticised Tristan's dying with his feet to the audience though his faithful servitor, in his own final throes, did contrive to pull a blanket over them.

Ten years later, my cousin Nancy Donaldson made her first trip to New York one Easter time and wanted to see the Met, for

111

she'd listened to many of their Saturday afternoon opera broadcasts. The Sadlers Wells Ballet starring young Moira Shearer was playing. I went to the box office – and found the house sold out except for the topmost gallery – "the gods" – costing $1.95 a seat! It was a long climb and accommodation so hard and tight we had to walk miles to restore our circulation after a magnificent performance which I never heard or saw better! Thereafter I've always sat in the topmost back row for ballet, the better to enjoy both the choreography and the music.

Frank and I had always wanted to see Bruno Walther conduct so went one Sunday afternoon to hear the New York Philharmonic Orchestra at Carnegie Hall. But the maestro was indisposed and so, it was announced, the conductor would be his assistant from Tanglewood, Mr. Leonard Bernstein. We'd never heard of him and Frank was muttering about asking for his money back when a slim, youthful figure in a dark suit walked up to the podium. He bowed briefly then turned to the orchestra and proceeded to give the music all he'd got, which, as we now know, was plenty! After the overture, the audience applauded appreciatively and at the end, we all stood up and cheered!

In summer, we trekked out to the Lewisohn Sports Stadium for jazz concerts. One sultry evening the soloist playing Gershwin's Piano Concerto was Oscar Levant, notorious for his dislike of fresh air. The sky was darkening rapidly as he started the last movement and, with frequent glances at the clouds, Levant played faster and faster, the orchestra keeping up as best it could. The heavens opened just as he crashed out the final chords and rushed offstage, a quick hand wave acknowledging the tremendous applause from the rapidly soaking audience. Nor did he take any curtain calls!

Frank found an editorial job in a publishing house. I forget why he lost it, but by the time he did, companies were reluctant to hire young men likely to be called up by the Armed Services. So I was able to find work more easily than my husband.

I was less choosy about what I'd do to pay the rent and our living expenses. I didn't mind doing this for he was working hard on a promising novel, but his prickly male ego led him to make demands on me which were hard to handle.

In pre-World War II New York unless a girl could type and take some shorthand, the only entry position she qualified for was as a receptionist. Young men were hired as trainees but not women. So I started a crash course at a business school but dropped out when I found a job. By then I knew how to touch type but, like piano playing and probably for the same reason, i.e. lack of ability to relate to an inanimate object, it's a skill I never mastered. I've often had an urge to describe myself in a resumé as a "rapid and inaccurate typist." Chances are, no one would catch it.

At business school, I met an attractive girl who modelled on Seventh Avenue but wanted to move into something more sedentary. She gave me some introductions but I didn't know enough, then, to utilise my acting skills, to put myself across, and cover my inexperience so never became a model. When I applied at an employment agency for a job advertised as "research" I discovered this didn't involve pouring over library books, it meant handing out candy samples on the street and asking passers-by for their reaction. I thought it was fun but Mummy commented in one letter that she didn't think she'd tell any of our friends what I was doing!

After that project ended, I worked for a Scottish entrepreneur who told me he ran "a kinda racket" selling used cars and similar merchanise to foreigners. He was a nice old boy and I hope he didn't catch the German measles that made me so ill I fired myself after four days.

I'd landed that job by coming on strong at an agency which had advertised for "A Correspondent. Scotch (sic!). Attractive." That I got it gave me confidence, and after recovering from my unreported rubella, I set out one Friday dressed in a chic dark-yellow suit originally Mummy's, with a green blouse and a turban to match. In mid-afternoon, I swept into the Maud Lennox Employment Agency in Rockefeller Centre, a small office with half a dozen women busy on phones. The receptionist started to tell me they only took applications in the morning, then in mid-sentence, had second thoughts, handed me a card to fill out, disappeared into a backroom, and came back to say Miss Lennox herself would interview me.

Maud was an elegant, formidable blonde of uncertain years who put me through a tough interrogation. I had by then absorbed enough street smarts to question why the boss would bother with such an unimportant applicant, so when she asked me if I could work under pressure, I smiled and suggested that since the young lady on the front desk seemed very busy, perhaps I could prove my ability by helping her out for the rest of the afternoon?

"However did you guess?" cried Maudie throwing up her well-manicured hands. "She's just been promoted and we have to replace her by Monday. So take off that turban and go to work!"

"I can't!" I told her. "I washed and rolled up my hair before I came out. It's still damp."

"Then come in good and early on Monday morning and she'll show you what to do. You must be awfully nice to applicants even if they look hopeless. They fill out an application, you take it to the appropriate interviewer. In the afternoons, you file all the cards."

"No typing?" I queried. She shook her head. It seemed too good to be true.

On Monday, of course, the office was swarming with aggressive jobseekers but I survived. The half dozen interviewers, mostly female, who handled the placements were tolerant of my inexperience locating cards in the bulging files. But I had a gruelling job and the pressure never let up. We even worked half a day on Saturday.

However, it was fun and gave me invaluable insights into the hiring process. I learned, for example, how Jews were subtly weeded out if a prospective employer didn't want them. In those days African-Americans didn't look for office jobs in white corporations, but I'm sure the same system of making a small mark on the card signifying race is still used among personnel specialists. Discrimination may be against the law but human nature doesn't change and in a business underwritten by commissions, the client's privately expressed wishes come first.

"I was born in the same year as President Roosevelt," a well-qualified woman protested when turned down on grounds of age for a secretarial position, "and no-one says he's too old for his job." But companies wanted women who were beautiful, chic, not greedy about salary, and under twenty-five though with ten years' experience and a college degree.

Single, too, and without dependents. I'd remove my wedding ring on my way to work and didn't tell Maud I was married until I felt established. Then I brought Frank in to meet her, for by then we needed male applicants – older women, too! – for the War was escalating overseas, new jobs were opening up and we were scraping the bottom of our file drawers looking for bodies.

Within six months, I realised I was not just overworked, I was grossly underpaid. My salary, without deductions, was $16 a week, which went a lot further than it would today. I also got a Social Security number without anyone questioning my citizenship (I was by now an illegal alien). Soon I recognised my own assets as an applicant. I was good-looking and pleasant and wore nice clothes. Also I knew what employers needed, sometimes better than they did themselves.

There were other employment agencies in Rockefeller Centre and I registered with all of them in my lunch hours. They were delighted to poach from their competition, were discreet about contacting me, and willing to send me on interviews after five o'clock. We always closed on time since by then even Maud was worn out.

A small advertising agency called Bermingham, Castleman and Pierce (BC&P) needed a receptionist who could operate a plug telephone system. Maud's efficient operator had, like me, been recruited on a Friday afternoon and told me later she'd never handled a switchboard, but a sympathetic expert in her father's office had given gave her a crash course of instruction after she'd been hired.

At the advertising agency, a sweet-faced young blonde who introduced herself as Bobbeye Washburn, talked to me while I waited to see the vice-president, Mr. Stewart Wark. She was, she told me, quitting work because she and her husband no longer needed two salaries. "But I'll stay on to train whoever takes over," she reassured me.

BC&P's quarters were in an attractive brownstone at 38th

Street and Lexington Avenue. The janitor, a horrid black man called William who only Mr. Bermingham liked, lived in the basement. A client, an agent for Gilbey's Gin in the USA, rented space off the reception room. Mr. Bermingham, Mr. Wark, and Mr. Castleman's Radio Department were on the second floor (no TV in those days!), Production and Accounting occupied the third. "Up and down those stairs . . ." William would complain. He took a teatray around every afternoon until sugar rationing gave him an excuse to stop.

Later I learned how BC&P had inadvertently been involved in international affairs. They'd hired a talented artist to design a bottle for a cosmetic account. His name was Osmark and he was a European. He kept to himself socially and one day he just didn't come to work, then or ever again. The accountant, trying to forward his salary cheque, discovered that the Social Security number Osmark used was that of someone long dead. William claimed his spirit haunted the building.

By chance, I solved the mystery of Osmark many years later. I'd told the story to Elizabeth Byrd, the popular writer who used it in one of her books. She got a letter from Switzerland signed "Osmark." He had been, he said, a German spy observing the Brooklyn Navy Yard and left his art job because he'd been re-assigned by the Nazis.

But that happened before Mr. Castleman's pretty secretary gave me the once over as she escorted me up to Mr. Wark's big pleasant office. He became a respected father image in my life but when we met he just looked old to me, with hawk-like features and kind but gimlet eyes. In an extrovert profession, his technique was to listen. So I found myself conducting the interview, which I knew how to do. I didn't mention that I'd never touched a plugboard. Mr. Wark asked if I could start work in two weeks and I said I could.

Next day, I went into Maud's office and asked for promotion to interviewer, like my predecessor. Helen MacDonald, a hard drinking, heavy smoking, oversexed Scot who handled the best accounts, had told me she'd already recommended this. Maud, however, said the agency was no longer growing fast and didn't need another interviewer. In that case, I told her, I was leaving because I'd been offered a job elsewhere.

She was furious. She was losing a useful employee and the commission was going to a rival agency. "If you're determined to leave, Miss Lillie, we can find what you want," she said.

"I won't take less than thirty-five dollars a week," I shot back. That was a good salary in those days. BC&P had only offered me twenty-three.

"Why, of course, dear," said Maud, "you're worth it."

I didn't ask her why she didn't pay me that herself, but I agreed to sleep on my decision. When she went off to the hairdresser I talked to Helen, who promised to find me something else if BC&P didn't work out. I also discussed the situation with another interviewer, Mary-Madeleine Lamphier. MM, as we called her, was beautiful, charming, unconventional, newly-wed and coping with two teenagers from a previous marriage. She was in analysis and if people disagreed with her she'd remind them sweetly, "Of course, you're neurotic too!" Like me, she was looking for a more remunerative job.

"A small advertising agency's a wonderful springboard for a writer," she told me. "You could wind up in the copy department or on the creative side as an account executive. These people sound nice, so go ahead and take the job."

So I refused to recant my resignation, and the boss made my life hell for my remaining fortnight. With the moral support of MM and Helen, I kept my cool and departed fully reimbursed, and on civil terms with Maud.

Years later, this paid off. When I was with Media Representatives, in a job I didn't want to lose, I had to go to Scotland on short notice for an indefinite period. I phoned Maud, outlined the situation to her. She immediately promised to help, tripped out and told her staff, "This client once worked for us and you're to send her the best applicants you've got." They did, and came up with the right person.

During these years, Bet and I drifted apart. She had abandoned her sculpture to concentrate on her home and children. Although outwardly she seemed sympathetic to my having to take mundane jobs completely unrelated to my education, I think subconsciously she was a little jealous.

16

Politics, Sex and Divorce

Mr. Wark always hired attractive girls in their twenties who got along well. There were half a dozen of us, and twice that many men. In *Murder Must Advertise* Dorothy L. Sayers, once a copywriter, describes an agency similar to the one I'd just joined.

On my first day, I confessed my inexperience with switchboards to Bobbeye who willingly instructed me. Mechanically it was easy. She also briefed me on the art of handling callers, usually salesmen, on the phone or in person. And she filled me in capably on the office power structure. "Bobbeye's not simply a receptionist," someone said of her later, "she's a number one diplomat."

Like me she lived in Tudor City so we stayed in touch. Her husband, Whit, was an agreeable, pudgy sales type with a sharp mind. Frank liked him and we played bridge together. The men were good, Bobbeye and I were not.

Frank's other interest, apart from music, reading, and writing, was tennis, a game I'd always hated. He spent every weekend on the courts, leaving me alone, which I complained about. I was having to cope with domestic management, a field for which I'd had no training other than that summer in Switzerland. I hated cleaning but became a passable cook for I liked to eat. With hindsight I realise my husband had plenty of legitimate complaints about me as a wife, but his ego was under attack from the constant rejection he was getting from the publishing world, and I was part of his frustration.

We also disagreed about the War. After Glasgow and Strathblane were bombed, I put my pacifism on hold and started hating Hitler. Frank, however, didn't want the USA to get into the fight. He joined the America First group and brought home their literature. I threw it into the trash. Then, on Sunday afternoon

December 7, 1942, we were listening to a broadcast performance of the New York Philharmonic Orchestra, when, just ten minutes before the end, the programme was interupted with the news that the Japanese had bombed Pearl Harbour. Overnight American public opinion changed and so did Frank.

" 'You're very pretty, Helen,' he told me over coffee. 'It won't be hard for you to find another husband.' "

He enlisted in the US Navy and was sent to Northwestern University to be transformed into a "Ninety Day Wonder" i.e. an Ensign. That Christmas, in horrible weather and in transport already overloaded by troop movements, I went by train to Chicago to join him for the holidays. A Princeton friend in Evanston had introduced him to a predator called Sylvia. In my hurt and rage, I made stormy scenes.

At the end of the three months, he was sent to New Orleans where the ship he'd been assigned to was being outfitted, and wrote asking me to take my two weeks' vacation down there. The journey involved more long nights on crowded trains and I arrived exhausted though I immediately loved New Orleans.

Frank had rented a room in a stately Garden District home. After I'd had a bath and dressed myself up in a new outfit bought for the occasion, we went out to one of the city's most beautiful restaurants.

"You're very pretty, Helen," he told me over coffee. "It won't be hard for you to find another husband."

He then informed me he was being posted to Florida and would be there long enough to satisfy resident requirements for a divorce! Sylvia, he added, was joining him in Miami.

I was stunned, shattered, taken not completely by surprise but knocked sharply off base. I was also angry. Why had he not prepared me for this, given me a chance to think things over before investing so much money and energy on that long, horrible trip? This may sound superficial but in wartime everyone was living from day to day. Everyone was tired and working under

119

pressure. Everyone, "let's face it," as we said, "was scared shitless about the future".

I couldn't even cut short my trip, it had been too hard to arrange. And, in a fit of furious reaction to grief and the way I'd been used, I determined to see New Orleans even though my heart was broken. I forced myself to go on guided tours of the city. To keep my mind occupied when my feet gave out, I went to movies. That's when I saw *Casablanca* for the first time. It was just out. Frank wouldn't even let me tell him about it. "You always have to outline the whole plot," he shouted at me, "it's one of the things I can't stand about you."

On our last evening, when I had worked through my emotion enough to act calmly, he took me to another lovely restaurant where we ate outdoors in balmy weather and by candlelight. When I managed to appreciate the ambiance he told me he shared it, although of course he'd rather have been there "with Her" . . .

Travelling back north was even more traumatic than going south. I had to change trains in Washington DC, dragging a heavy suitcase, with little time to make connections and disoriented by the huge, busy station. But young, tragic-eyed, pretty women travelling alone arouse male protectiveness. Soldiers helped with my bag and pushed me through the crowds onto my train.

The second worst moment of that trip was opening the door into my empty apartment. Now I'd have to live with myself as a failed wife. It started when the nice people who worked in the building carried my bag to the elevator, and wanted to know how Mr. Leary was and if I'd had a good holiday?

"Yes. Oh yes. He's fine. So am I, but awfully tired from the journey. Goodnight. Thank you. I'll tell you about it in the morning."

I got through my first day back at work using that tack. I'm sure my co-workers knew something was far wrong but, being New Yorkers, they didn't ask. For the first week I couldn't bear to go home after work. I went to films, double-features if possible, at seedy late-night movie theatres on Times Square, taking the 42nd Street crosstown bus back to Tudor City long after midnight. I never worried about being mugged or raped or otherwise attacked. Maybe I didn't care.

Then sheer lack of sleep caught up and I did go straight home from work. Alone in bed, I fell back on my childhood trick of telling myself a story to induce relaxation. At work, I'd been promoted to be Mr. Wark's secretary. My prececessor, Leslie, was a smart salty character who did a lot of copywriting and had also found herself a husband. I told her frankly I was a lousy typist and had never learned proper shorthand.

"Don't worry," she said. "The company'll send you to a refresher course. Wark dictates so slowly you can take him down in longhand. He isn't under pressure, his job's management. What's important to him is that he likes the girl who works for him. He's used to you and you know the ropes around the agency.

"There's just one thing!" she added. "In Spring he goes off to his summer place in New Hampshire every Thursday night and you may think you'll be able to spend Friday filing and balancing his personal cheque book. Forget it. Keep the typewriter going at all times or you'll have everyone in the next office coming in with little jobs." Following this advice, I'd transcribe my own writing after I'd finished my weekly letter to Mummy.

I didn't include my father in my correspondence. In my first period of shock, I'd said nothing to my parents about my marital problems. Maybe I hoped Frank would have second thoughts. When the Navy moved him to Florida, he did bring Sylvia down from Chicago to join him but, as he once let slip, he'd never promised to marry her. Eventually she went back to Chicago and was last heard of going for long walks with her dog.

When I got legal notice that my marriage was no more, Bobbeye was sharing the apartment with me for Whit, also a "Ninety Day Wonder", was en route to North Africa. In those days, mail arrived first thing in the morning and I received the Florida lawyer's letter before we left for work.

This unplugged a backlog of tearful confession. Dear, reliable Bobbeye, who'd get all upset about trivialities, always came through in emergencies. She held me in her arms, phoned her own employer to say she'd be late, then called Mr. Wark, who immediately came over to the apartment. When I'd calmed down enough to be coherent, he rang the BC&P lawyer. Before he handed me the phone, he'd said, "I want you to do your best for Mrs. Leary. She's my secretary and I'm very fond of her."

An undemonstrative New Englander, Mr.Wark's only sign of affection was to pat a shoulder occasionally. He didn't kiss the girls in the agency even at the Christmas parties.

The New York lawyer sent a letter which protected my right to the apartment and tidied up some loose ends. Now all I had to do was tell my parents. I appealed to them, in my letter, to hold their comments and please! please! to bear in mind that I was in a fragile emotional state and trying hard not to fall apart.

Mummy immediately sent me a loving, supportive note. But Littie mailed a reply typed by a public steno, because, he told me, he didn't want to embarrass his "Wee Darling" disclosing her troubles to his private secretary. My reaction to this was that maybe he didn't trust her to keep my news to herself in the bank, and he would be embarrassed. Divorce was anathema to Littie's Victorian values, and probably equally unacceptable in Glasgow business circles.

His letter, which I tore up, was an emotional polemic against Americans and me for living among them. As soon as I could, i.e. when the War permitted, he ordered me to come home "and as Miss Lillie." I could feel that dark woolly twinset scratching my skin under a raincoat and knew I'd have no more relationships with men.

Littie of course was deeply distressed, but although I've long since forgiven him, I still think it incomprehensible that as a father he was so insensitive. I also find it strange that a successful businessman could be so unimaginative. He was negating several years of my life and major accomplishments in my own development just to put back the clock – the last approach likely to entice me back home. One result was that, although I disliked its Irish connotation, I continued to call myself "Mrs. Helen Lillie Leary" until in 1956, long after Littie was dead, I became Mrs. Charles Marwick, a name I'm proud of and like for its sound, too.

This communication threw me into more storms of tears, again coped with by dear Bobbeye, who had just enough problems with her dour New England parents to understand how I felt.

If I wrote a reply, I never sent it. I ignored the letter, just stopped including Littie in the notes I sent Mummy. Formerly, I'd written to my parents jointly, unless I had something for her ears alone.

After six months, he sent me an apology, saying he "accepted the silent rebuke." I responded with a polite letter and resumed occasional communications. But I never felt close to him again. Years later, I accompanied a newly widowed friend to a psychic in Washington and during the session, she claimed Littie sent me a message from the Hereafter saying he considered his treatment of me "rightfully wrong".

The experienced Mary-Madeleine informed me that "the best cure for a man is a lot of other men." She invited me to parties at her Village apartment, where I met her old beaux. Her then husband worked in defence and had a widowed friend called Bill. Apparently I was the spittin' image, physically, of his late wife who'd died of polio leaving him with two small children and a house in New Jersey. Within forty-eight hours of our first meeting he not only got me into bed, he proposed to me.

I'd noticed that after a divorce people either married disastrously on the rebound or took a long time to form a better relationship. I was still too numb to cope with emotional involvement, and knew Bill and I were not as compatible intellectually as physically. Nor did I see myself as a suburban housewife with a husband off visiting his children on weekends. So this relationship was brief.

I didn't miss sex, for in marriage it had given me little pleasure. This changed when I met a handsome Naval officer, a lieutenant commander who answered a classified advertisement I ran in the *New York Times* grandiosely offering "editing and part-time work of a literary nature by an experienced writer." This man, a lawyer in peacetime, was having such interesting experiences at sea he wanted to record them, and whenever he sailed into New York, which happened regularly, he'd take me out to dinner.

"Four Daiquiris," he'd tell the waiter. "Two for the lady and two for me, and get lost until I signal you that we want our food." We'd then go over his manuscript which, in the form of a short story, we did sell to a major magazine. It was never published but we got a cheque, which we split. I blew my half on a rabbitty topper from a bargain basement and wrote with relish to my co-author, by then overseas, telling him he'd just bought me a fur coat! He'd been so contemptuous of men who "had to buy women expensive clothes to get them into bed."

It hadn't taken long to do that with me, and he introduced me to rewarding intercourse. He had a wife in a New York suburb, but didn't seem much interested in visiting her when ashore. I've often wondered if the marriage lasted. After the War he tried to get in touch with me again but it was during a reconciliation with Frank so I didn't respond.

My friend Viola, whose sister Gloria I had instructed on the facts of married life, had moved to Washington but came back to New York frequently. One Sunday afternoon, she phoned and suggested we meet at the Roosevelt Hotel for supper. The bar was busy and the waiter disinterested in two lone women to the point where I had to call the manager to get service. We were finishing up our snacks when a nice male voice said, "Excuse me!" and, looking up, we found two Naval officers whose brand new uniforms identified them as "Ninety Day Wonders".

"I wouldn't say this if it didn't happen to be true," the first one said. "We really did just come into town and we really don't know anyone. And we'd be awfully pleased if you two ladies would join us for a drink."

Viola and I had scarcely time to make eye contact before our waiter materialised. "You can't pick up men here!" he told me.

I glared. "Bring us our check. Right now." He did so. I threw down some cash and turned to the Naval officers who were looking horribly embarrassed. "We'll be delighted to have a drink with you," said I. "But not here. Settle your bill and meet us at the door."

Laughing, and properly introduced, we wound up at the Biltmore Hotel next door. "You know, it was because you two girls were so obviously *not* trying to pick men up that we were attracted to you," said Carol who was a farmer from Kansas. "We're on an eight weeks' course at Fort Schuyler and we want to see the New York sights, and go dancing."

Viola went back to Washington but Carol came over to my apartment every weekend as long as he was in town and took out either Bobbeye or me. He also fixed our radio, the vacuum cleaner, and other household gadgets for he was awfully handy. "I'm married with two kids," he told us. "And I miss my home. I'm not used to being around men all the time. Do you mind if I phone you girls now and again in the evenings, just to talk?" We didn't.

He left New York for a port below the Mason Dixon Line but a few months later, on a brief excursion through New York, he told us, "You two spoilt me. Those darn little Southern belles were just husband hunting. They'd drop me as soon as I told them I had a wife and kids. Finally, I informed one chick – she was a pretty good dancer – 'Look you're supposed to be here to entertain us officers not to promote your own ends.' So she stayed with me for the rest of the evening. Then I escorted her home and when she asked, 'Will I see y'all again?' I said, 'No, Ma'am. You don't go out with married men – remember?' And I saluted and left her on the doorstep of her stately home."

Another Naval officer, a friend of Whit's, liked Broadway shows. Through a servicemen's canteen he got standing room for the sold-out musical *Oklahoma!* I wasn't even tired by the end of that show, even though I was wearing four inch heels and knew I'd have a struggle getting rid of my date at the end of the evening. He couldn't understand why I didn't want "to fuck", a word I heard for the first time on his lips.

Gradually, I was starting to enjoy single life again. Several of the men at BC&P were enlisting and we had a farewell party for them at the office one Friday night to which Bobbeye was invited. An account man called Charlie took her on to dinner and they both had far too much to drink. Next morning she wasn't just hungover, she was upset at how far they'd gone and also by what he'd told her. "He's a creep," she confided in me, "and awfully ambitious. He says he's going to be vice-president when he gets rid of Mr. Wark."

On Monday afternoon, my boss remarked out of a clear sky, "You know Charlie keeps hinting around. He wants to know if

I'd heard anything from you about his date with Bobbeye. I told him you were much too discreet to discuss your room-mate with me."

I laughed it off. I did not want to compromise her but I wish I'd told him what Charlie had said because, soon after, he started easing me out of the agency. He complained to Mr. Bermingham that I didn't pull my weight helping out the other departments when the vice-president was in the country. My boss of course didn't want to let me go and suggested I return to my old job on the switchboard. I knew that wouldn't solve the problem but couldn't bring myself to tell him why. Besides, I was ready to go on to a war job.

About a year later, Mr. Wark opened his own agency in Vermont. We kept in touch but we never discussed why he left BC&P. I've no idea what happened to Charlie. I hope he got his comeuppance from some predator smarter than himself.

I was sorry to leave BC&P but for some time I'd wanted more active involvement in the War effort and a British friend, Diana Martin Lowery whose aunts, the Miss Kers, lived in Strathblane, had given me an introduction to Philip Hewitt-Myring, head of the News Room at the British Information Service. He told me frankly I hadn't enough journalistic experience for his department but said there was an opening in the Information Division, where his American wife Eleanor worked. They needed someone for the front desk, which, I later discovered, was the first line of defence against the public! My suitability, quite apart from being young and good-looking, was that I could understand the Americans, which wasn't always true of the academic experts imported to enlighten Britain's most important ally, the USA.

I applied for the job and was hired without much background investigation.

17

'Giving Americans the Facts'

The British Information Service was located on the fifty-sixth floor of Rockefeller Centre's RCA Building, where we had an uncensored view of troop and supply ships on the Hudson River.

The Information Division was supposed to have an answer for any and every question curious members of the American public could think up. And it must be correct since we were spokespersons for His Majesty's Government and "there was a war on." This called for a savvy staff with an ability to cope, and it was assembled, apparently, without prejudice as to sex, age or even origin.

Our head librarian was a German refugee, Dr. Maria Lowe. One day a British army officer came in looking for material on some esoteric military device. I summoned Maria who listened attentively, then stated, "Ve have zat information. You vill vait, jah?" As she stomped off in her sensible shoes, he turned to me and echoed incredulously, "'You vill vait, jah?'"

One noon she came to the front desk and said, "Helen, zis new female arriving from England . . . Vill you please tell her I'll be back from lunch soon?"

Gawd, thought I, another one who'll start criticising the Americans . . .

But, duly alerted, when I spotted an unknown and pleasant-looking young woman wandering around as if searching for something, I went up and asked if I could help? "Yes!" she said, smiling. "Please tell me where to find . . ." she paused then enunciated slowly, "the water cooler."

"It's right behind you," said I. "Are you the new recruit from London?"

"I am. And in all the mystery novels I've been reading to learn about New York, every office has a water cooler."

"You actually want to 'learn' about this city?" I exclaimed.

"I do. American whodunits kept me sane during the worst of the Blitz. I'm Dorothy Harmshaw. Do tell me your name."

I gave it and added that I too liked whodunits. She became one of my best friends, and never lost her open-mindedness. When the War ended, Dorothy wanted to stay on in America. Before she found a niche at the British Travel Authority, she supported herself with odd jobs like baby sitting, starting with a family on Riverside Drive who left her in charge of a little monster. As soon as his parents were out of earshot he informed her, "You speak funny. Why d'you speak so funny?"

"I speak this way because I'm British," Dorothy explained.

"Geez" he said. "You're British. I'm American. I'm free."

She told me it was one of the few times in her life when she couldn't think of any comeback!

The most effective people in the Information Division weren't the academics but those who answered questions quickly. My predecessor on the front desk, an efficient lady called Betty Baird-Murray used to say she'd gone to a ladies' school and had had no education. "But I do beautiful embroidery," she'd add.

Our most common query was how to send packages to Britain for which we had a comprehensive handout. One Oxford-educated lady, hired as a backstop in case our nice young British lawyer was caught in the American Draft, just couldn't grasp dealing with the public. Incoming queries were rotated and while she was saying into her phone, "Parcels to Britain? Oh I don't believe we'd have anything on that . . ." the elegant blonde sitting next to her, who'd never gone to college, would yank the receiver from her and provide the information.

Second only to parcels for Britain came requests for exact quotations from Winston Churchill. Once at a party I met a woman who worked in a *New York Times* information office and she said they got similar requests involving Hitler's speeches.

"How do you go about checking these quotes?" she asked me. In my best Temporary Civil Servant style I said we usually began by asking around the department. "Yeah, it's the same with us," said the American. "You put your hand over the phone and holler, 'Hey! When did Churchill make that speech about

The author's parents, Helen Barbara Lillie and Thomas Lillie, at the time of their marriage in 1912. This picture "says it all" about their relationship

The last joint public appearance of the author's mother and her two brothers
(l to r) (a neighbour), Helen Barbara Lillie, Sheriff John A Lillie QC LLD, and Dr Robert A Lillie MBE. Taken with some of Robert A Lillie's picture collection at a reception honouring him in Edinburgh in 1970

Breaking the mould – the author on the desk at the
British Library of Information in New York, circa 1942,
talking to the director G D'Arcy Edmundstone.
Situated on the 56th floor of 50 Rockerfeller Plaza in
New York, this was the first defence of Britain against
the great American public

The author's two husbands Francis Woodburn Leary (l) and Charles Robert Scott Marwick, pictured in their apartment at 224 West 11th Street, New York shortly after her marriage to Charles

Just married!
Helen Lillie and Charles Marwick on 26 September 1956 with New York's Stuyvesant Town in the background

Albert C Capotosto – known as 'Cappy' – long-standing favourite boss (1947)

Independent and with style!
Helen Lillie – the last Easter in New York City (1965)

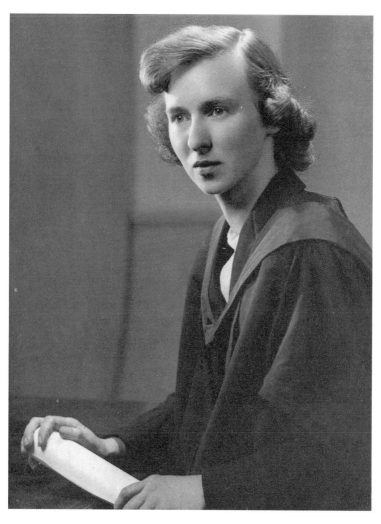

The author's second cousin, Dr Morag L Insley on her graduation from Edinburgh University's medical school – their first 'specialist' in geriatrics (1940s)

Helen Lillie in contemplative pose (1959)

Forty years on . . .
Charles and Helen Lillie Marwick outside their
Washington home on return from celebrating 42 years
of marriage (1998)

fighting on the beaches?'"

Our public relations officer was a charming retired military doctor called Major Cummings, who always wore impeccable British tailoring, carried a cane and, I seem to remember, used a monocle. Some of his success was attributed to his fulfilling the American concept of an English gentleman, although from his name he was more likely a Scot.

Eleanor Hewitt-Myring, short, blonde, intense, heavy smoking, and full of wit and fun, was a graduate of the Columbia School of Journalism and answered queries on education. One day a young woman came in looking for her. After they'd greeted each other warmly at the front desk, an envelope with a big bound manuscript changed hands.

"The most effective people in the British Information Service (Information Division) weren't the academics but those who answered questions quickly."

When the girl left, Eleanor remarked to me, "There goes my PhD. on the British school system. She got the degree but I did all the research and documentation. Well, she did offer to buy my lunch . . ."

Eleanor's brilliant and diplomatically experienced husband, Philip Hewitt-Myring, as head of the News Room also acted as public relations officer for the Duke of Windsor when that dubious Royal and his Duchess visited New York City. One day Philip phoned his wife who rushed out at lunchtime and came back wearing her best suit. When we asked her where she thought she was going, she snorted, "To the Waldorf to have cocktails with the Windsors. And Philip wants me to curtsey to Wallis which I won't do, because she's just another American!"

Next morning, we all rushed in to work eager to hear what had happened. Problems of protocol had been evaded. The Duchess, convalescent from an operation, was elegantly stretched out on a couch, her guests gathered around her, and there were no formal presentations. We got a rundown on everything she wore except her earrings, which Eleanor hadn't noticed.

Philip had, though. "Aquamarine clips," he said promptly, when she phoned him in the News Room.

The Duchess was scared of flying and later that week, Eleanor had to accompany her to the ship which took the couple to the Bahamas, where the exiled former King Edward VIII had been stationed as Governor-General. The couple's two Cairn terriers were in the car and one of them snagged Eleanor's last remaining pair of nylon stockings, which didn't improve her feelings towards her fellow-countrywoman.

Two savvy ladies of uncertain years handled questions on India. The department head, Miss Herrington, had never been there but she'd been so good at her job HMG wanted to send her on a trip after peace was restored. By then her health was bad, and I don't know if she ever went. Her associate was a former schoolteacher of the hockey-playing type, "all girls together" as someone put it, and how she became so knowledgeable about India I know not.

A formidable British spinster, Miss Wilson, one of several volunteers in the department, clipped newspapers, always wearing a hat. She'd grown up in a Foreign Service family and was rumoured to have been offered the Order of Chastity Second Class, which she had turned down. The First Class, apparently, is only awarded to royalty. She lived in a hotel and got little pots of jam with her breakfast. These she'd bring to the office and distribute among carefully chosen recipients.

On Saturday mornings, before the hoards of school children rushed in to sweep all the handouts off the front desk with "Miss, I-gotta-have-some-pamphlets-for-my-school. . ." we'd sit around and chat, and all too often the topic under discussion was how to rid our apartments of cockroaches. One morning, Miss Ledbetter, who handled the Government documents, said, "I bet HMG has something on that!" Sure enough, there was a pertinent pamphlet.

The Sales Department for these publications was run by a salty old musical hall artiste called Bessie Slaughter and an extremely public school type with the delightful name of Timothy MacOstritch. It was claimed that an Old Etonian from the Information Division encountered this gentleman socially, couldn't remember the name but knew it was some kind of big bird, so throughout the party addressed him as Mr. MacAlbatross.

When I needed a pamphlet from backroom files, I'd seek out Phyllis Lintott who'd always drop whatever else she was doing and help me. Attractive and thirty-fivish, she'd been an Arthur Murray dance instructor and lived with an overpowering elderly mother, the widow of an artist.

Katie Lintott had been a pioneer woman journalist in England and in youth conned a British publisher into letting her cover the Spanish-American War of 1898 from New York, where unexpurgated dispatches arrived by telegraph and were recycled by local press representatives. As soon as news came in, Katie wrote it up and relayed it to London, innocently scooping all the other foreign correspondents who had a gentleman's agreement about the time they'd file their daily stories. When their editors began complaining that a rival publication was ahead with the news every day, they went to the cable office and learned that, "a pretty young lady with long blonde hair files her copy a couple of hours before anyone else."

Next day they lay in wait for her. "Good heavens!" Katie said. "Why didn't anyone tell me?" And from then on, she was a team player. So much for female aggression in the early days of careers for women.

Not content with working hard five and a half days a week, Phyllis dabbled in real estate, painting and maintaining her properties herself. She had a nice weekend cottage in Connecticut, and how she did it all, with her heavy job, coping with old Katie and leading an active social life, no one knew.

Being chic and single Phyllis was often called upon for public relations chores after hours. One afternoon Ruth Isaacs, the assistant to our boss Dr. Bennett, told her to leave promptly and drop by the New York Yacht Club. "BIS is invited to a publication party for the British writer, Alec Waugh," Ruth explained. Phyllis, hectically busy as usual, just said okay, she'd go.

When she showed up at the Yacht Club around 6 o'clock the party was in full swing. She completed her mission of letting both Mr. Waugh and his publishers know BIS had been there, but she couldn't learn anything about the book. All the free copies were gone and there was no one to ask about it except the author, who was too busy shaking hands. When she eventually achieved a sherry, Phyllis thought it odd that the bar was serving tea as well as cocktails. She didn't stay around long because she had to cook her mother's dinner.

"What's Mr. Waugh's book about?" asked the nice but steely-eyed Ruth next morning.

A good information officer never admits to lack of knowledge. "Oh . . . you know . . ." said Phyllis, thinking fast. "Affairs . . . Foreign affairs."

Ruth gave her an odd look but left it at that for her co-worker had uncomplainingly carried the flag after a long tiring day.

All became clear to Phyllis next noon when she went out to lunch. She passed a book store with a window dislay of Alec Waugh's latest publication. It was a biography of Sir Thomas Lipton, the famous yachtsman who made his fortune in tea.

Phyllis stayed on at BIS until the late 1960s when her health broke down so severely she had to be fed through a tube in her side. Diabetes was a complicating factor. By then, Katie was dead so her faithful daughter had some leisure. Only the unmarriagable of her innumerable boyfriends were still available, but she had many friends, and was nominated for a well deserved MBE.

This was presented at the British Embassy and a retired personnel officer from BIS, a sweet lady called Elsie Marshall, accompanied Phyllis to Washington where HMG put her up at an elegant hotel. Elsie stayed with me in my Georgetown home.

Although she was in fragile health, Phyllis on that memorable afternoon looked like her old self in a beautiful maroon silk ensemble with a small hat to match. The BIS had been on the phone to the Residence stating in no uncertain terms that she was to be given VIP treatment, including use of the Ambassador's private lift to reach the second floor drawing room.

There Elsie and I, in white gloves and our best hats, sat nervously among the guests. Phyllis, seated up front with the other honorees, among them Henry Brandon of *The Times*, just smiled as she always did.

In the area organised for the presentations stood a small group of impressive Brits, among them a Brigadier with an formidable array of campaign ribbons and decorations. While we were waiting for Ambassador John Freeman to made his entrance, this platform party was joined by Bluffie, a homely alley cat with a sawed-off tail, well-known in Washington as the Embassy's First Feline.

Bluffie settled himself in front of the lectern and gave the assembled guests an experienced appraisal. The Brigadier, probably a dog owner, stepped forward and went "Shoo!" with one hand.

The cat just looked at him, his dignified body language deploring that someone would try to order him around in his own home. For probably the first time in his life, the Brigadier beat a retreat, and a ripple of laughter went around the room.

Then Mrs. Freeman with her children came in and sat down to one side. Sizing up the situation, she beckoned to Bluffie, who got up, walked over and jumped onto her lap, leaving the platform clear for the Ambassador.

At the reception afterwards, Phyllis was made much of and her strength held up so well we had difficulty dissuading her from joining a group going on to a restaurant dinner she couldn't have eaten. "But I do want to keep in touch with that man who invited me," she remarked to me next morning as she and Elsie boarded their train to New York.

Six months later, dear indomitable Phyllis went into a coma at her Connecticut home and by the time someone found her, she was dead.

Val Merivale was another favourite of mine at BIS. Brilliant but unassuming she handled people at the desk when I was busy. Her father was Philip Merivale, the handsome actor, and her features resembled his, though her face was marred by several long scars. One morning, when a group of inquirers left, Val lingered by my desk as though seeking comfort. Finally she said, "That man who just left asked me if my face had been injured in the Blitz. I just said no . . ." I gasped. Our eyes locked for a few minutes then she went back to her desk and we returned to fighting the War.

BIS taught me that the English when you were working with them, weren't obnoxious like so many pre-war visitors to

Scotland from south of the Border. Besides some of them were Scots.

During my first week on the job, someone said, "You've got to meet Dr. Daiches. He's from Edinburgh," and led me to a quiet, tweedy, wee man who sat in the backroom smoking a pipe and writing readable pamphlets in a formula which called for a fact in every line. His greatest achievement was a Complete History of Scotland which kept readers turning every one of its six pages.

"So you went to St. Trinnean's," said David to me. "I'd an aunt who taught Latin there. Rose Phillips."

He was such a good writer, he was transferred to the Embassy in Washington, and before he left, he wrote a poetic farewell to the Information Division which had an extensive undercover circulation. Here is an excerpt:

> Some things I shall rejoice to have remote.
> No more rewriting what rewriters wrote.
> To have one's re-rewriting done again
> By secret forces in some hidden den.
> Henceforth when facts elude me I will let 'em.
> Or call the BIS, by God! And get 'em!

18

Illegal Alien

Even with such congenial co-workers, I hated that job so much it literally made me sick. My stomach would fill out with painful gas which nothing would release. The pressure of trying to be helpfully polite to endless relays of demanding and often stupid people, and constantly checking out at least two or three unrelated inquiries concurrently became too much for me. I often felt I was in one of the War's front lines, as in a way I was.

Also, I had a chip on my shoulder. I'd applied for a writing job and instead I'd been hired as a receptionist which, to me, was going back to Square One professionally. Moreover, although it was an unusually democratic office, there were a few experts from London who treated me like hired help, expecting me, at my busiest, to phone the drugstore for snacks, which most people did for themselves. "This is the eatingest office. We're always nibbling," someone once pointed out, a sign of anxiety according to psychiatrists.

Every few months I went down to Personnel and asked for a change of job. Instead, I got several raises and once an upgraded status, which as a Temporary Civil Servant was supposed to improve my morale. But it didn't relieve the constant pressure of being on my feet from 9 until after 6 coping with the great American public.

And, at the end of the day I went home to . . . Francis Leary! He had dropped out of the Navy, and although we were by now legally parted, he'd staged a reconciliation and moved back into the Tudor City apartment with me. I'd said so little about the divorce it wasn't hard for him to slip back into my life. And around that time I began calling him Francis instead of Frank.

So, like many another ill-matched couple, we made a second try at marriage but it proved as unsatisfactory as it did the first time. I, at least had changed. Wartime living was hard in New York City, with rationing, food shortages and overcrowded public transport, to say nothing of the constant underlying fear of bad news. But, like other young women, I'd had fun too, and also learned that I was a survivor who could cope with many things.

I never told Mummy in so many words that Francis and I were living together again. I'm quite sure she figured it out but she was much too clever to ask me point blank. As for Littie, I don't think he would have been able to face the thought that his daughter – His Daughter! – was "living in sin" so he didn't think about it. But I had to be careful. I let nothing slip writing to British friends, another pressure on me.

During the winter of 1944, I came down with a bad cold and stayed home for a week, typing up a four-page single-space memorandum to BIS Personnel which boiled down to the two words, "I quit!"

This produced immediate action. Elsie Marshall phoned me the day I returned to work and asked, "Helen, do you have your identification card on you?" I had. "Good. You're going to get a call from a Mr. Hill. He has just the kind of job you want but I can't tell you anything about it. I'm simply letting you know, we recommended you."

As soon as I hung up, the phone rang again. "Mrs. Leary? My name is Tom Hill. Do you have an identification card with a photo? If so, bring it with you to Room 3606 in the International Building and say I'm expecting you."

I proceeded without delay. The weather was nasty so I was wearing an old blue tweed suit, not what I'd have picked to impress a prospective employer but it didn't matter. A wee Scot called MacLeod barred the entrance to Room 3606. I produced my card and stated my business, which he confirmed by telephone. Someone came and escorted me through an area filled with office workers, mostly female, who pointedly didn't look up as I passed.

Around this space, were small private offices with outside windows, one of them Mr. Hill's. He was a short, blue-eyed, balding, unthreatening man with an endearing habit of constantly raising and lowering his eyebrows. He put me through a sophisticated quizzing on my background and experience, but said he couldn't tell me anything about the work involved before I had a security clearance. However, I could rest assured it involved writing. With a guard between me and the Great American public, I wanted it anyway!

Soon after I was recalled to Room 3606 to see a Personnel officer, identified as from British Passport Control. I filled out an interminable questionnaire, covering where my family lived and what they did, going back for at least two generations. I had to supply information, with dates, on my education, not just what I'd studied but the political groups I'd belonged to at Glasgow University, my reason for living in America, everything I'd done there and, of course, my marital status. I didn't mention my reunion with my ex-husband. After all, I didn't know how long it might last.

The Personnel man, after running his eye over all this, asked what kind of visa I had and there followed a variation of an old music hall routine – "I don't have a visa." "You must have a visa." "I don't have a visa!" "You MUST have a visa!" I DON'T have a visa! I entered the country as a student then I married an American and I've never had the time or the money to legalise my status."

To do that, I'd have had to leave the USA and re-enter the country with proper documentation, which could be a long and expensive procedure. The war had cut off funding from home. When I married Francis Leary, I'd notified the authorities, which got my married name onto the records of the U.S. Immigration and Naturalisation Service. Periodically they'd sent me complicated form letters asking what steps I was taking to legalise my status? I'd point out that "unnecessary journeys" were unpatriotic in wartime and if I quit my job I might become a public charge. "Just keep the letters going back and forth," Bob Sincerbeaux had advised me before he joined the Navy, and using the street smarts I'd learned in New York City, I answered the next inquiry on a grubby sheet of paper. "dear sir, don't know what this is all about yours truly mrs. leary."

This halted correspondence for nearly a year and after I joined BIS I felt safer, although several co-workers had had such hairy experiences our lawyer, who'd had one of them, claimed, "Every horror story you ever heard about US Immigration is true!"

In capsule form I told this to the Personnel officer. He then asked about my passport and we went back to the old routine. "I don't have a passport." "You MUST have a passport." "I did but it expired!" "Then go right down to the 35th floor – there's an interoffice stair – and they'll give you one." I got it as soon as my mugshot was developed. In it I looked dazed but relieved.

Eventually, after an outside investigation which I heard about from Mr. Wark and other friends, I found myself a member of British Security Coordination (BSC), a department of MI6.

I was working for the British Secret Service!

19

The Perils of Propaganda

H. Montgomery Hyde, who worked there, wrote several excellent books about British Security Coordination (BSC). The first and best, published in 1962, is *The Quiet Canadian*, a biography of Sir William Stephenson who created the organisation with the cooperation of Churchill and Lord Beaverbrook.

Before the United States came into the war, BSC operated with uneasy and questionable legality on American soil, keeping an eye on foreign embassies and groups potentially hostile to Britain. Sir William's friendship with the maverick American general, "Wild Bill" Donovan, led to the evolution of the Office of Strategic Services (OSS) and later the Central Intelligence Agency (CIA).

British Passport Control was our cover agency and the OSS had offices near our one in Rockefeller Centre. Sir William's personality dominated our lives. Though we seldom saw him, he seemed to know about everything that went on, even in the mailroom. Years later, the writer William Stevenson who wrote an excellent book about his near namesake entitled *A Man Called Intrepid* told me that even in the 1980s, he had trouble persuading former members of BSC to talk about their wartime activities. Sir William by then had retired to Bermuda, but they were still scared of him.

My boss, Tom Hill, an experienced Canadian reporter, managed Section One – Communication – and I was his Research Assistant. Officially, I "wrote reports" on foreign groups within the USA. I also rehashed a pamphlet of Eleanor Hewitt-Myring's on "British Women at War" which a sympathetic Congressman had reprinted in the Congressional Record. This earned me an extra five dollars a week, real money in those days and untaxed to boot. I don't remember my exact salary, but it was around fifty bucks, paid weekly and in cash, for security reasons.

I also recycled outdated espionage reports as offbeat news stories, fed by contacts to influential columnists in hopes of keeping them sympathetic to Britain. Our most influential ally in the American press was the legendary Walter Winchell, then in his prime. Over two thousand daily newspapers syndicated him and an estimated 50 million adults out of a US population, numbered in those days at 75 million, read his columns.

So, as a gossip writer, I started at the top. It was also a thrill to tune in on Winchell's Sunday night radio programme and hear him lead with one of my juicy snippets of international dirt. And I had to think up excuses to listen to these because I couldn't tell Francis what I was doing in the job which paid our rent.

One morning Tom called me in to say that "Our Friend," as we called Winchell's legman, wanted a whole column on an Italian writer the Allies had just arrested. As seemed traditional, this "Senor X" had been captured while in bed with his mistress and was now loudly protesting he'd never been a Fascist. "Find something juicy on him and write it up by tomorrow noon!" Tom ordered.

Our files had nothing nor did the individuals I queried discreetly within BSC. When I reported this to Tom, he just said, "Oh come now." And repeated, "We need the story tomorrow noon."

Around 2am after a fruitless day, I got an idea. En route to work next morning, I stopped off at the BIS library, and in a back issue of the magazine *Current Biography*, found a long piece about my subject, who, as I'd hoped, had visited America in the 1930s.

I scribbled notes, rushed through Rockefeller Centre to BSC, ran the material through my typewriter imitating Winchell's style as best I could, and met my deadline with time to spare. "Our Friend's" legman, a large nameless trench-coated individual, picked it up pronto and Tom and I celebrated over our afternoon cuppa tea.

Next morning, I shared the elevator to work with one of Sir William's senior secretaries who remarked, "Winchell has a long piece in today's column about That Man You Were Asking About." "Has he?" said I deadpan. "Thanks for telling me." And rushed to Section One where Tom was gloating over the newspaper. Not a comma had been changed! Our euphoria was brief. For the first and only time, Winchell had a question. How did we know that "Senor X" had dedicated his first book to Mussolini?

"We can't tell the most powerful journalist in America that we found his 'inside scoop' in an old magazine!" Tom groaned. "We'd never get another item in his column! And he's Britain's best propagandist!"

> "Sir William's personality dominated our lives. Though we seldom saw him, he seemed to know about everything that went on, even in the mailroom."

"Don't worry," I soothed. "*Current Biography* lists sources and I have 'em in my notes."

"Then look them up pronto! I gotta call Our Friend back before lunch."

I rushed down to the Library on 42nd Street which we Brits called "The New York Public". Their newspaper back issues were on microfilm which took time to call up. None of the stories on Senor X mentioned his books, much less to whom they were dedicated. Back at the office, I phoned the US Information Service, claiming I was with a British news service. A helpful female voice directed me to "Winchell's column in yesterday's *Mirror*."

"Helen!" Tom ordered. "Find a source! Anywhere! Now!"

I started dialling Italian publications listed in the classified section of the telephone directory. Editors were no more anxious to be identified with Fascism that Senor X. But eventually someone answered whose English was limited to "Yeah? Yeah? Senor X?. . . Yeah?. . . Yeah? What about him?"

"Did he," I asked rapidly, "dedicate a book to Mussolini?"

"Mussolini? Yeah . . . yeah . . ."

"Thank you." I hung up, typed up the name of the newsheet, dumped it on Tom's desk and went out for a drink. I only hope that the FBI's director, J. Edgar Hoover, didn't subsequently investigate that little Italian paper. Hoover incidentally was another of "Our Friends" and to keep him happy I wrote a most laudatory article about him but never knew if anyone used it.

On May 8, 1945, VE Day, hostilities ended in Europe, but Sir William vetoed celebrations. His staff must stay on the job, otherwise our neighbours in the OSS would think Britain wasn't interested in the Pacific War.

None of us felt like working not even Tom who said our allies across the hall were all out getting drunk. Besides we couldn't concentrate with noisy outdoor celebrations in Rockefeller Centre. The Free French had taken over the bandstand and every European musical star in New York was belting out *La Marseillaise*, led by the coloratura Lily Pons from the Metropolitan Opera.

Tom was working on a special report, so kept his door locked, phoning for his staff when he wanted them. Now he called us all in. "Damn it, Section One's going to celebrate VE Day!" said he. "But it's got to be a top secret operation. What's the drill on the afternoon tea?"

Marion, his secretary, reported that she brewed it up in the office kitchen, brought the pot to her desk, and took a cupful into Tom's office. Her assistant, Barbara and I then poured our own, and were responsible for cleaning up.

"Today, Marion," said our boss, "you fill that teapot with ice, and bring it straight in here. Then I'll buzz for Helen and Barbara and – who else do we want to invite?"

"How about Ginny?" I asked. She was secretary to another executive and shared my office.

"Can she be trusted to observe security?" Tom asked. I nodded. "Okay then. Anyone else?" We suggested a couple of other girls. "Okay. Be sure everyone brings a teacup. I'm going out now, back shortly." He picked up his hat and a leather holder. "Remember! This party's Top Secret! If Sir Willie ever finds out about it, all Hell'll break loose."

Tom returned with a bulging briefcase, locked himself into his office then buzzed Marion. She sauntered down the hall and came back carrying a teapot, following her daily routine. The rest of us in turn knocked on Tom's door and were admitted upon identification.

We had a jolly party, telling bad jokes and getting drunk on a horrible gin concoction, allegedly a dry martini mix served over ice. Every time the phone rang, we froze for fear it was "the Most High" or one of his staff summoning Tom to a conference.

BSC wasn't usually such a matey office, we were so brainwashed about never discussing what we did. Ninety percent of the female help was Canadian and strictly on the secretarial or file clerk level. Many of them came from the prairies and were away from home for the first time. The executives were mostly male, usually imported from London. And there was a handful, like me, who were "neither fish nor fowl", who were seldom invited to fraternise with either group. I kept to myself anyway on account of my dubious domestic situation. No-one was supposed to share an apartment with an American, though rumour had it one man had done so with Lauren Bacall before she went to Hollywood. We compensated for our security consciousness by being the gossipiest office I ever worked in!

Around 5pm on VE Day, Tom announced that we were now winding down our secret operation and it was vital to cover our tracks by following routine. So, one by one, the guests returned to their desks and I headed for the pantry with the teapot. En route I met a very senior Britisher, a stuffed shirt Tom and I didn't like, and for once he recognised my existence.

"Aw . . . Mrs. . . Er . . ." He stopped me in my tracks. "How . . . ah . . . is Mr. Hill doing on that report?"

I stepped back to avoid breathing gin all over him. "The report's going well but Mr. Hill hasn't completed it yet." How could he, drinking martinis all afternoon? "Sir William will have it very soon." I lied, and sashayed off towards the pantry, my heart pounding with fear that our cover was blown.

Tom raised both eyebrows, when I reported this incident on my return. He then solemnly kissed us all, stuffed the empty bottle into his briefcase, and, as he departed, reminded us to lock everything up as usual before we left. We thought we did, but next morning he found at least two file cabinets open and kidded us we'd make lousy agents in the field.

Shortly after, he offered to recommend me for a job opening up in Washington, but while I was considering it Truman dropped the Atom Bomb and clearly the War was nearly over.

Besides, my work in New York had become fascinating. Section One was writing BSC's official history, and I was reading through all the files, looking for incidents worth recording. One I didn't use was an exchange of TKs (telegrams) at the height of the Blitz between our office and London. The first read, "(So and So), important American journalist sympathetic to us, en route to London. Suggest he be LIONIZED REPEAT LIONIZED upon arrival."

Back came the terse reply, "Ref your TK Number (whatever). Subject being lionized." Under this, Ginny's boss had scrawled, "Where is this bloke now? Is he still being 'lionized' somewhere?" And below this query some unknown wound up the operation with, "Subject back in USA. No further action."

After the democratic BIS, I found BSC a throw-back as far as the acceptance of qualified women was concerned. Maybe this came from the agency's predominantly Canadian make-up. I lunched mostly with my old pals on the other side of Rockefeller Centre and made no lasting friendships with my later co-workers.

In another respect, however, BSC was ahead of the times. It offered us free medical care and a capable staff nurse encouraged us to have our physical problems taken care of at the expense of HMG. I never availed myself of this service but several of the other women did.

20

To Canada with Roald Dahl

Shortly after VE Day, Tom called a group of us 'girls' into his office and asked us how we'd like to spend the summer at Camp X in Canada, a BSC training ground for agents? It would be cool, we could swim every day, we'd have no living expenses and we could save on summer clothes. Economy-minded bureaucrats in Britain's incoming Labour Government were concerned about the high cost of office space in Rockefeller Centre and Sir William worried about security for the project we were working on.

"So," Tom explained, "it's been suggested that Section One move up to Ontario where we'd be undisturbed. We'd be there at the most three months, working and eating at the camp. Where," he added, looking at the young Canadians who'd had so few dates in New York, "there are also lots of men!"

Could he miss?

Tom's team consisted of his wife, five office workers and three writers – myself, Grace Garner, who'd been head of Sir William's secretariat, and a mysterious tall, dark, personable RAF Wing Commander named Roald Dahl. He was "Our Man in Washington" and today would be called a lobbyist. His particular assignment was to keep the influential columnist Drew Pearson on the British side, as we did with Walter Winchell.

Roald had injured his back in a plane crash in North Africa, and had an odd, stooped walk. He was tall and slender, with straight, thinning, black hair, quizzical blue eyes and a fair skin inherited from British-Scandinavian parents. By his own account, he really got around socially in wartime Washington, and was making a name for himself as a writer, having sold short stories to literary magazines.

Later, Roald became famous for his juvenile and horror fiction. My favourite concerned a wife who killed her husband by clunking him with a leg of lamb, then putting it in the oven and serving it cooked to the cops while they were searching vainly for a murder weapon.

Roald informed Tom he planned to drive north in his own car and could transport two girls. When Tom asked which ones he wanted, he said, "Grace Garner and Helen Leary." Grace was also a writer.

So early on June 20, 1945, having kissed my ex-husband au revoir, I turned up, lugging a suitcase, at a midtown hotel, phoned the Wing Commander's room from the lobby, and a cheery male voice told me "Roald's in the shower. This is Flash Gordon. Just relax downstairs like a good girl."

I did, after phoning Grace and telling her not to rush. "Thanks for letting me know," said she. "Isn't he a bum!"

Eventually Roald loped out of the elevator carrying a crated picture. "It's my Picasso," he explained. To this day I don't know if it was real or a copy. It could well have been either. We picked up Grace then took off so fast, we were barely out of New York City when a traffic cop stopped us for speeding. Peering suspiciously into the car, he saw an RAF officer and two young women in summery dresses obviously going some place although every billboard asked if this trip was necessary?

Roald, with Anglified good manners, produced identification and explained we worked for the British Government and were en route to Canada on official business.

"Well," said the policeman, stymied and not believing a word, "just don't drive so fast. There's signs everywhere. The President puts them up."

"I don't see any, officer," said Wing Commander Dahl, looking around.

"Well – they're there. The President puts them up," he repeated, and perforce, let us continue on our way.

We didn't bother with lunch but pushed on to Elmira for an early dinner. Roald pointed out it was on HMG so we had a drink and a good meal and discussed stopping for the night there or pushing on towards Toronto. Roald went off to make inquiries and came back looking puzzled. "There's a place we can stay in Dansville," he told us," but something's odd about it. All this hotel will say is that the beds are good. However, they did phone and made us reservations, and I warned that we'd be pretty late in arriving."

So off we drove towards Dansville. The sun went down and so did the petrol gauge, with no filling stations in sight. Twice we passed a sailor trying to hitch a lift at an intersection so concluded we were lost. Grace who was thirtyish, an intelligent but highly strung type, asked nervously what we should do?

"Open the glove compartment," said Roald. In it lay a quart of Scotch whisky. "We're a little tired and we need a drink."

"But Roald!" she fluttered. "We've no ice . . . no glasses . . ."

"Grace," ordered the Wing Commander. "Open that bottle and take a good slug. Then give it to Helen who'll do the same and pass it along to me."

She unearthed a dainty white handkerchief, cleaned the bottle's neck and raised it to her lips. Then she wiped it off and passed it along. We did this twice and eventually, ominously low on fuel, we found Dansville, where the only light on its long main street came from a pub, obviously popular.

"Girls," said Roald, "lock all the car doors while I go in and get directions." As soon as he left us, a couple of drunks hove in sight and made obscene solicitations through the car windows.

"We're nearly there," he told us on his return. "Which is lucky because the gas station's closed and our petrol's nearly gone. And I got this funny reaction again about where we're staying."

He turned up an incline at the next intersection and our headlights picked out a neon sign over a huge gate reading:
PHYSICAL CULTURE HOTEL.
Bernard L. McFadden, Proprietor.

Roald braked. We sat there and laughed from relief! McFadden was a famous health food guru of the era.

The building was huge, white and silent. An old, old man rocked in a cane chair in the cavernous lobby. The thin, disapproving clerk, who'd had to wait up for us, eyed us as suspiciously as the New York policeman. However, he couldn't deny that we had reservations, so took down three large keys.

"You, Sir," he said pointedly, "are on the second floor. The . . . er . . . ladies are on Three and next door to one another." None of us dared catch each other's eye as we got into the rickety lift. Grace's and my rooms were close to the staircase and Roald loped up it as the clerk was unlocking our doors. "I have to inspect your quarters," said the Wing Commander formally.

Suddenly the silent corridor filled with eldritch screaming. A door flew open and out catapulted a ruffled soldier hotly pursued by a young woman in red pants. She was yelling imprecations along the lines of what kind of girl did he think she was? Chinks opened in adjacent doors and old ladies with bathrobes and curlers peeked out.

Grace and I, exhausted but fascinated, just stood there. Roald went over to the soldier and asked him what the trouble was? "Geez,sir, I picked her up in town and she asked me to come back here for a drink so I thought . . . but then she started screaming at me."

The girl rushed back into her room. Roald said something quietly to the GI who squared his shoulders, followed her, and slammed the door shut. Silence returned.

"She's sent here to dry out. She's very rich," an elderly female voice informed us. "They should give her something to calm her down."

"I think the soldier's doing that quite effectively," said Roald, deadpan. The old lady reared back in alarm, stared at the three of us, and defensively pulled her robe up around her neck as she retreated into her room and turned the key.

"Sleep well, girls," said Roald, heading for the stair. "See you tomorrow."

The beds were indeed comfortable or maybe we were so tired we'd have slept anywhere. Next morning, while Roald paid our bill, I cased the diningroom. Every table held packets of evil-looking branflakes and dietary supplements.

"We'll have breakfast downtown," said the Wing Commander when I reported this. After he'd replenished the gas tank, we had a marvellously high cholesterol meal of bacon, eggs, doughnuts and coffee. This sustained us as far as Buffalo where we had a bibulous lunch, relaxed and comfortable with each other.

"Grace," said Roald, sipping his third Bloody Mary. "We should send Sir Willie a progress report." She nodded. Our telegram read more or less as follows:

"Personal attention Sir William Stephenson. Progress Report Number One enroute Toronto. Spent night Physical Culture Hotel, Dansville, New York. More physical than cultural. Grace said it's lovely here. Helen said it's lovely anywhere. Hope to make Niagara Falls today. Regards Harry Hillward."

The famous Falls were anticlimactic after Dansville and since we'd detoured to see them, we arrived very late at Toronto's King Edward Hotel, a more comfortable and traditional hostelry than Bernard McFadden's.

From the lobby, Roald telephoned Tom, who hollered, "What-in-hell have you characters been up to? Sir Willie's been on the phone! He read your telegram to me. No one's left in the New York office he could share it with."

"Details upon arrival tomorrow afternoon," Roald replied. "We're tired and we're going to bed."

In the car, he'd told us massage helped his bad back and I'd offered to give him a rub. After we'd checked in at the King Edward, I unpacked some hand lotion and went to his room where by arrangement he'd left the door open for me.

He was lying face down on the bed, fully dressed and to my surprise, acted downright coy when I suggested he take off his shirt. But he did so, uncovering a long, terrible scar.

As impersonal as I knew how, I gave him a careful back rub which he obviously enjoyed, and we talked of this and that. But our relationship had lost the cameraderie of the past two days. He was defensive, although I'd never made any sexual overtures for he didn't attract me.

As I was leaving, I asked if I should close his door? "No," said he, "women are supposed to lock their bedroom doors but men leave them open. See you in the morning."

Not even Roald Dahl, talking with the author David Stafford, who wrote a book about Camp X, could describe the mess and confusion we found in Oshawa, Ontario. No one had unpacked our many fileboxes or cleaned our working quarters. We girls spent a couple of horrible days grubbing around, literally scrubbing floors and furniture surfaces. By the time we were able to start unpacking our materials, the sophisticated elegant Grace, in shabby dungarees, was muttering darkly about what she'd like to do to "that bloody Stephenson." Our morale was not improved by a visit from some military big shots who stood around in their smart uniforms while we crawled around the dirty floors. Needless to say Roald didn't help us either.

Tom and his wife were housed in Oshawa's one hotel. So were Grace and Roald. I was among five incompatible females living in an apartment with a single kitchen and bathroom.

Army lorries transported us to and from the Camp but I don't remember any transportation problems for the War was winding down and the drivers weren't busy. We'd start work early, take a long midday break and go down to the shore of Lake Ontario where we'd swim and work on suntans. Then we'd return to our desks and keep on working far into the evening, usually over weekends too.

Why not? There wasn't anything to do in Oshawa, a small town which offered for recreation two Chinese restaurants, the Globe and the Grand, and a movie house that changed its programme once a week. The military didn't fraternise with us. The women resented that we girls could keep cool in shorts and flimsy tops while they had to wear hot khaki uniforms and stockings. The men were mostly married or otherwise involved.

But I had one date with a soldier. Bert was an old Englishman who had lost his whole family in the London Blitz and re-enlisted for work in Canada after he was demobbed. Before the War, he'd been a pierrot playing seaside resorts. I think as a little girl I'd once seen him on the stage. He was pathetic, although he was always clowning and telling mildly dirty jokes.

When a good movie came to town, Bert invited me to see it and have dinner at one of the two Chinese restaurants. My roommates remarked snootily that he wasn't the class of person one normally dated but if I didn't mind his Cockney accent etc. etc... I didn't. Next morning I told them, "I had a lovely evening. We enjoyed a good show then had a nice meal and conversation that was aimed to entertain me. I was picked up and taken home and always treated like a lady, didn't have to fend off unacceptable passes and fumblings. Who cares about speech patterns? Bert is much more of a gentleman than some of those uppercrust characters we've met in Oshawa."

For I'd had plenty of dates. Roald, early on, had joined the country club and, telling Tom that "these girls need men," he'd taken us up there with him.

"Don't say one word about where you work or what you're doing!" the boss cautioned us.

We were greeted with, "So you're the new girls at Camp X . . ."

And we met the promised men, who all had hollow legs. Their second idea was that since we could buy unrationed booze, we should drive to the town's liquor store and buy our dates a bottle for joint consumption while copulating in unheated, uncomfortable cars.

I preferred to spend the evenings at the apartment with the other girls. I remember no radio or television, certainly no piano, no place to read except in bed and no continuing supply of books. So we drank. I discovered boilermakers, a shot of whisky washed down by strong Canadian beer. After a couple, I'd have to lie down so I'd head for my room where the end of my bed would rise up and swing me round in circles before I either passed out or vomited into the wastebasket.

It was not a stimulating summer for any of us, even Roald, though he found himself a well-connected local blonde to date.

Periodically visitors from Ottawa or New York would show up, talk with Tom in secret, and I'd find out via Marion the secretary that the approach of our report had been so drastically changed he was redictating my copy with many changes. When I confronted him with this and suggested that I could write it any way he wanted, he waffled. A nice, competent man, he was disoriented by conflicting directives from superiors and demoralised by the grumblings of his staff.

On VJ Day, the country club tried to close its bar at 11 as usual and Roald blew his stack. "The War's over!" he roared. "We're celebrating all night!" And we did.

But morale kept plummeting and by September, it was obvious that the project might linger on into the grim Canadian winter. On Labour Day, I quit and so, independently, did Roald. Tom acted resigned. He assured me I'd get my War bonus and he had already expedited the legalising of my dubious immigration situation. I re-entered the USA in style with a diplomatic visa, which put me at the head of a long queue seeking permanent residency in America.

The night I left Oshawa, after my co-workers had had their usual rounds of drinks, someone cried out, "Leave us organise!" They then composed a long cable listing their grievances and resigning en masse. This they sent to Sir William and it led to the operation being wound down fast. Its final days and how Tom and his wife had to cope with the actual printing as well as the final rewrite is described in *Camp X; Canada's School for Secret Agents 1941-45* written by David Stafford. It's a fascinating book, even if doesn't give Grace or me any credit for working on that famous report. Well, some of my stories are quoted verbatim by H. Montgomery Hyde in his history of BSC.

A more recent publication, entitled *Wild Bill and Intrepid* by Thomas F. Troy, a former CIA executive, doesn't give me or Grace any credit either, although he took me to lunch and interrogated me during the writing. The Secret Services were still a man's world during World War II, even though they made full use of women as agents and office workers. I was happy to notice, however, that in the James Bond movies, Judi Dench was now playing M, the head of the British outfit that superspy worked for.

Back in the New York office, the Personnel Officer handed me my severance pay then sat back in his chair and asked, all buddybuddy,

"What's really going on up in Oshawa?"

I had just signed an Official Secrets document promising not to disclose anything about BSC or my activities there for twenty years. His question was probably a straight plea for information, but it could also have been a test and I was taking no chances. Roald had followed me down to New York and was, at that very moment, in Sir William's office. Let Roald do the telling.

I replied simply, "I'd rather not say."

As I left, several women in the office who'd never bothered to socialise with me before suggested I join them for lunch. I just smiled, said I had another engagement and for the last time took the elevator down to the concourse of the International Building.

21

Peace – more or less

World War II was over. I had money in my purse. I was, as in one of my favourite Fred Astaire songs "Fancy free and free for anything! Fancy free!"

But first I had to work out of my involvement with Francis Leary. He never abused me physically but constant emotional put-downs can be just as eroding to female self esteem and when I read about women who stay with husbands who beat them, like Nicole Simpson, I remember how long it took me to learn behaviour patterns don't change and the only thing any woman can do is get out of such a relationship.

The problem was that Francis and I did share many interests and still do. He developed my abilities when we read manuscripts for a literary agent. I got a part-time job with my old pal Mary-Madeleine in a public relations agency with an account called The Cleanliness Bureau. We turned out educational material on the use of soap for health, education and possibly even welfare.

When I struggled over the recycling of press releases into entertaining newspaper fillers, MM told me to "put a piece of paper in the typewriter and just start typing." I also parked my tongue in my cheek. Even Francis admired the results, chuckling over copy I brought home. "I couldn't roll out this funny stuff!" he exclaimed. Thus it was I discovered that I had, in Noel Coward's words, "a talent to amuse."

By the Spring of 1946 I'd also found that, although it was easy to board a ship heading for Britain, it was well-nigh impossible to book a return berth to the USA. So, with my War service bonus, I bought a round trip plane ticket to London. Mummy, always eager to travel, came down there to meet me.

I'd never flown before but, on boarding, passengers saw a

sign announcing this was the three-thousandth-or-so trip of American Airlines across the Atlantic, a reassuring thought. I sat next to an elderly Scottish lady also on her maiden flight. When the stewardess asked if we wanted a beverage, I ordered sherry, not knowing how my airborne system would react to anything stronger. My seatmate, however, stated she'd like a Manhattan, and when the attendant moved on, turned to me and exclaimed, "Mercy! What kinda cocktail is that?"

"A real strong one," I warned her.

"But it's free, isn't it?" said she, and subsequently downed two without visible ill effects.

Mummy and I hadn't seen each other for over five years. When I knocked on her hotel bedroom door, a little stooped old woman opened it and for a split second I didn't recognise her. But then what a happy reunion we had! We stayed in London several days, and saw the effects of the Blitz. Our hotel on Park Lane had gaping holes on its outer walls, and the hall porter climbed long stairs to let us into our rooms. American troops had taken all the keys home for souvenirs and every night I braced myself for the arrival of some large inebriated Yankee in the wee sma' hours.

We found nothing in the shops, but we saw old friends like the Twins, and the theatres were better than ever. Women in the audience wore vintage barebacked evening dresses while I huddled in a topcoat, determined not to admit how cold I felt! Later I learned it was one of London's chilliest summers.

In Strathblane, the balance of relations at Bluerisk had changed and my parents were better friends. War had given Mummy the career she'd always longed for as head of a widespread female network in the West Stirlingshire division of the Womens' Voluntary Services (WVS). They coped with any and every emergency like caring for Glasgow refugee families left homeless by German air attacks on Clydeside heavy industry.

Strathblane had been bombed too. A direct hit from a Nazi plane demolished the valley's worst slum, built the same year as London's Crystal Palace and so known as "The Paelas." Another bomb, designed to cripple Glasgow's water supply, landed in the Punchbowl Loch, miraculously missing a rock formation. The blast blew out a lot of windows and cracked a front wall of Bluerisk. "I was in bed fighting off flu," Mummy told me. "I just pulled the blankets up over my head and shut my eyes.

"My worst moment of the War was when a man came up from London to brief the WVS on what to do if the Germans invaded Britain, which seemed likely. Someone asked where they'd land and he put his finger smack down in the middle of my territory!"

The experience had transformed Mummy from a reserved person into an outgoing one. Everywhere we went, she'd stop off for me to meet "one of my people in the WVS." The welcome she got from these women warmed my heart. They saw her as I'd always done and appreciated her for her ability and her great, imaginative heart. She never lost the confidence this gave her.

My father had retired from the Royal Bank. He wasn't a reader and, like me, had no mechanical ability, so he had nothing to do except balance the books of the Parish Church and exercise Sandy, a Cairn terrier who'd replaced the original wonderful canine character. Littie had also learned to change the sheets on his bed and, on occasions, to wash dishes. Sometimes he went into Glasgow and lunched with other retired businessmen whose conversation, Mummy told me with relish, turned on their wartime domestic duties. A wealthy stockbroker one-upped them all by saying he dusted the drawing room.

Annie, now married, and the cook who'd gone into the Army, had been replaced by a slovenly Irish biddy called Isa. "Why do you keep her?" I asked Mummy. "You always said you couldn't stand dispeace in the kitchen but you won't go in there, she's so full of complaints. And she can't even boil potatoes properly."

"But I might never find anyone else!" sighed my mother, who, although she was in such good mental health, was physically exhausted and suffering from arthritis in her hands. (Doctor Boyd treated it with homœopathic remedies and in later life she could again play Bach and Mozart on the piano.)

"The Lord," I told her, "will provide. Meanwhile, I'm here and I'm a better cook than she is. And I'll gladly fire her for you. It won't upset me if she makes a scene."

Accepting me as a grown-up, Mummy asked, "Would you really get rid of her?" I nodded.

Isa took time off in the middle of the day and went out. Next afternoon Mummy left Isa's ration card and a carefully worded letter of dismissal on Isa's bed, got in the car and drove away. Littie retreated upstairs to lie down.

I hung around and at 4 o'clock went into the kitchen to put the kettle on for tea. Isa came out of her room wearing her coat.

"I'm catchin' the next bus into Glasgow," she informed me tonelessly.

"You'd better be going then, Isa," said I. "It's due in a few minutes."

At that moment, the door from the hall to the kitchen began to open and Littie hissed, "Is she gone?"

I signalled him to get lost and escorted Isa to the back door. She'd been fired so many times, she had her departure technique down pat. Mummy's car backed into the garage before I had warmed the teapot.

The Lord provided an efficient and refreshingly pleasant Highland girl called Chrissie who worked at Bluerisk until my parents left there. Mummy and I had resumed our discussions about Littie. His manic depression was in abeyance but she worried about his having so little to do. "He's in such low gear," was how she put it.

"And what about You nowadays?" I asked. "What would You like to do?"

Without hesitation she said, "I'd like to sell Bluerisk and move to a small house in Edinburgh. But he'd never do it," she added. "He loves this place and I can't bring myself to raise the subject."

"Go to bed early tonight," I told her. "I'll see if I can sound him out. He must be thinking about the future, too."

He was. "Helen," said he, almost as soon as she'd gone upstairs. "I'd like to ask your advice." (That for sure was a change!) "I'm worried about your mother. She worked so hard all through the War, she's exhausted. This house is far too much for her but she's so fond of it, she'd never give it up."

"She might," I said. "What would you like to do?"

He answered in almost the same words as hers. "I'd like to

sell Bluerisk and move to Edinburgh. Living here," he stated, "is interfering with My Career."

I was speechless.

"My Career," he explained, "in the Church of Scotland."

"You always did say you wished you'd been a minister . . ."

He chuckled. "If I had been, I'd be a fair hypocrite by now! But I've become very interested in ecclesiastical finance. Since I retired, I've been on several central Church committees in Edinburgh. If I lived there, I could be on at least two more."

> "I asked sternly, 'What kind of wife are you to stand in the way of her husband's career?' "

But like Mummy he didn't want to bring the matter up, in fact, he asked me to do this for him. So when we went upstairs to bed and I saw a chink of light under Mummy's door, I walked in on her.

"Well?" said she.

I asked sternly, "What kind of wife are you to stand in the way of her husband's career?"

She dumped down her book and asked, "WHAT career? The man's over seventy."

"His career," said I, "in the Church."

Fortunately Littie took his hearing aid out at night. He mightn't have appreciated our ribald laughter.

However, with communication opened, they started debating the most strategic and profitable way to sell Bluerisk. For years people had been asking Littie to promise he'd let them know first if it was for sale. "Don't do that," Mummy warned him. "It'd just cause bad feeling among our friends. If we give it to an agent the matter will be out of our hands."

He agreed.

"And it's likely to be snapped up fast," I added. "So don't put it on the market until you've found what you want in Edinburgh."

I also assured both of them that I'd help with the "flitting" which would involve clearing out the home where they'd lived for thirty odd years, the kind of hard physical labour neither of them could handle.

Somehow we got Littie to keep quiet about the projected move during that extremely sociable summer. No fatted calves were available to welcome this returned Prodigal Daughter, but whenever anyone found a chicken, we were invited to dinner. I couldn't bear to tell these hospitable old friends that in New York I'd queued for hours every Saturday morning throughout the War just to get a bird, the only unrationed meat in the USA and sometimes I felt I never wanted to see another one again.

I gave some talks to women's groups and was amazed at how little the British knew about wartime shortages in the USA. They didn't even realise Americans had had the same food rationing because all the beef and canned products like Spam went to the troops. Nor was there control over the allocation of hard-to-find items, so unless you were a regular customer at your local grocery store, you missed out on goodies like bacon and sugar.

During that halcyon summer in Strathblane, I had marvellous reunions with old friends and there was a historic family gathering at Bluerisk which Uncle Jimmy, a talented photographer, captured on some prewar photo film.

I flew back to America in a warm glow and, shortly after, Mummy wrote that she'd found just the place she wanted in Edinburgh. Its curious address was 2B Church Hill and it had been the garage of a large mansion now divided in half like many Morningside houses.

Her next door neighbour, Mummy added, was a Mrs. Melville, the widow of my grandparents' family doctor. This, though I didn't then know it, was to have a momentous consequence for me.

22

Scotland Postwar

1947 was one of the most important years of my life. In January I packed my clothes and most valued books and sailed to Southampton on the old *Queen Elizabeth*, hedging my bets on whether or not I'd come back to New York and Francis Leary after moving my parents to Edinburgh as I'd promised.

The North Atlantic in winter is pretty rough even in a big liner. Fortunately, when war broke out an enterprising Cunard executive had taken all the booze off the ship and stored it in a safe place for the duration. Now it was back aboard and on sale at prewar prices.

I had an innocuous shipboard romance with an Englishman who'd taken a job in California but became so sick upon arrival he'd had to turn around and go home. Neither of us drew many sober breaths during the week's voyage and one night we were the only couple dancing a slithering foxtrot across a wildly tipping floor as the band played on. When we docked a day late, at Southampton, all our luggage was tossed higgledy-piggledy off the ship then taken by boat train to London, where it had to be sorted out.

The press ran stories about the mess, so Mummy, who'd again come down to London to meet me, wasn't surprised when I fell into bed and slept most of the following day. The voyage had been, after all, a kind of last fling.

In Strathblane, we were then snowed in, and no one interested in buying Bluerisk could drive out from Glasgow to see it. "But when the roads clear," said Mummy, "the house'll be warm, with roaring fires in every room and one in the hall fireplace too!"

Every morning I'd turn out cupboards and Mummy would sort through what I unearthed. The wonderful Chrissie would make a hot midday meal then my parents would go to their beds armed with hot water bottles and I walked Sandy up and down outdoors in the sunshine until it got too cold for us. Then I'd make tea and Chrissie, having prepared but not cooked our supper, would depart for Glasgow where she shared an apartment with another girl. Mummy had been dubious about this arrangement but I'd convinced her it was the wave of the future. Now a few months later, my mother so enjoyed having no servants around in the evenings, she said she wouldn't have anyone live in again and she never did.

When it was too cold to go out, I'd sort through piles of old photographs and stick them in an album, but alas, I didn't write down the subjects' identities though I got the generations sorted out with my parents' help. But who, for example, was the sanctimoniously smiling black-bonneted lady Mummy described as "the old de'il who brought the neurosis into the family"? I wish I'd asked her name!

Bluerisk sold quickly and for a good price. Meanwhile, in Edinburgh, Uncle Ned's old chauffeur Mackenzie was supervising structural changes at 2B Church Hill. Periodically Mummy and I would go through to see how these were going and he'd meet us at the train, very dignified in a black suit and a bowler hat.

The renovations, of course, took far longer than anticipated, and I was shocked by the bureaucratic grip on every facet of British daily life. I also learned the Scottish male's attitude towards aggressive women. My cousin George had recommended a hot-shot architect to advise on 2B. When I went to see him, he brushed aside my queries, giving me instead a diatribe about how the garage had been turned into a dwelling by an entrepreneur who hadn't bothered to hire an expert like himself. "If I'd been consulted your mother would never have bought that place," he wound up.

I said coolly, "That house is ideal for my parents. It's in the right neighbourhood and it's the right size. I think it came straight from Heaven."

George reported that his friend thought I didn't understand how things were done in Scotland.

Soon Spring was in the air. The young couple who'd bought Bluerisk wanted to move in. Mummy and I went back to Edinburgh and found that all 2B now needed was some indoor painting. But even this called for inspection and evaluation from local authorities and an unknown waiting period for workers.

> "I was shocked by the bureaucratic grip on every facet of British daily life. I also learned the Scottish male's attitude towards aggressive women."

"But . . . er . . . Mrs. Lillie," said Mackenzie, coughing discreetly, "I could get it done for you right away if . . . you'd trust me with some cash. I know a couple of good painters who have time at the weekend."

"How much?" I asked. He named what sounded to me like a horrendous sum but my parents could afford it. "When could these men be relied upon to complete the job?"

"Oh, by this time next week at the verra latest," said Mackenzie. "They're first class fellows. They just keep at it until they're done, for they're no' working' union hours, ye understand. But they like to be paid in cash, so if ye could make a cheque out to me, Mrs. Lillie . . ."

"But, is it all right?" asked Mummy. She meant was it legal?

"Oh . . . aye . . . aye. It's maybe a wee bit irregular but it's the only way ye'll get the job done quick. It's what everyone's doing, these days."

I looked Mummy squarely in the eye. She wrote the cheque, handed it to Mackenzie, and asked him to phone her when the house was ready for occupancy. Throughout the train trip back to Glasgow she agonised and wrestled with her conscience. "It's a black market deal," she told me. "I wouldn't have gone along with it but I think Mackenzie had already hired those painters."

"And everyone's doing it," said I. "In America no-one would think twice about it."

We moved within seven days.

The flitting was traumatic. There were complicated logistics, packing and sending furniture to different destinations like 2B

Church Hill in Edinburgh and a sales room in Glasgow, to say nothing of dispatching individual items, in particular the grand piano which went to George's son in Eaglesham.

Mummy masterminded everything with my assistance and we had neither the time nor the strength for regrets about leaving our lovely home. We'd deal with those later.

Littie however had no need to curb his emotion. He'd asked me, at one point, what he could do to help? I told him he mightn't like it but the best thing would be to go to his club in Glasgow. The movers would most likely ask him for specific instructions rather than Mummy and this could lead to crossed signals, he was so deaf. He was furious and stayed under foot throughout the flitting, demanding, during one crisis, "Time to Ourselves, in Our Own House."

Finally Mummy and he drove off to Edinburgh, the car filled with stuff. Chrissie and I stayed until the van with all the furnishings left.

I then found her on her knees scrubbing the kitchen floor. "I always leave a house clean!" she protested. I pointed out that the incoming movers would dirty it up regardless, so she reluctantly headed for her bus after a fond farewell.

I went next door to the Kirsops' who poured me strong drinks and fed me a delicious meal before I tumbled into their spare bed. Next morning Jack drove me into Glasgow to the Edinburgh train.

That was the last night I spent in my beloved Strathblane, although I've revisited the Blane Valley many times and have both old and new friends there. But that Spring of 1947 ended a stage in my life.

23

You Can't Go Home Again

My parents adjusted quickly to their new lifestyle. Littie plunged into church finance, made friends with many eminent divines, and rebuilt his self esteem basking in their admiration for his business know-how. He was making a real contribution to the Scottish Kirk and knew it. He'd even stay downtown for lunch on occasions.

Mummy, who loved to decorate, was in her element and I helped out with the physical work. The front bedroom at 2B looked out over a little courtyard and beyond it, on the street, was a tram stop where some of the double deckers paused when they were ahead of schedule. The passengers had nothing to do but look out of the windows and this annoyed Mummy while we were hanging drapes in ours. She wasn't used to city living like me.

"I'll fix 'em," I told her. I focused Littie's old binoculars on the tram and the snoops, embarrassed, went back to reading their newspapers.

Soon after we moved, Freda Kennedy, the Strathblane minister's wife, phoned. Her eldest daughter Kirsteen had just been sent to boarding school in Edinburgh. Could she spend her first free Saturday afternoon with us? Her mother was too pregnant to make the trip.

I collected the teenager at the Eskdale School (originally the Ministers' Daughters' College) and found her a delightful companion. We went over to Princes Street, sampled McVitie's snack counter then did some sightseeing. On our way to Church Hill for tea, I showed her where to sit on the Morningside tram so that she'd reach her stop and get off before the conductor came around.

"You mean to say you showed a minister's daughter how to

163

gyp the public transport!" Mummy exclaimed.

"I gave her the benefit of my experience," said I. And to the best of my knowledge, it did her character no harm. Sometimes, though, I wonder what kind of mother I'd have made.

Whether or not I'd return to the States remained an open question, though the answer was growing increasingly clear to me. I still had a few congenial friends in Scotland like Jean Morrison, but the War had put a wide gap between me and some of the others. An undercurrent of anti-Americanism showed me how much I had come to identify with the country where I'd spent six formative years.

Moving a household in a bureaucratic Welfare State had also been depressing. There seemed no place left for initiative, except in evading the regulations. People were crochetty, tired, and burnt out. Unemployment was rampant, and I suspected the attitude towards women was worse than in the USA. Equal opportunity backed by legislation was still a long way off.

Moreover, in Scotland I didn't know how to find potential employers. I had no information network and wouldn't use Littie's contacts. Mummy had a subtle way of down-putting organisations she didn't approve of and if I approached any of these for work, the dinner table conversation would be sticky.

The logistics of a job-finding campaign, typing resumés, sending out mailings and getting phone mesages would also be difficult in my parents' house. Nor did I want them following my every actions, offering advice or consolation.

Without a salary, I couldn't move out. I'd left my little bit of capital in the USA and was strapped for ready cash since it never occurred to my parents that I needed any.

My experience in New York wouldn't count for much in Scotland or London and job openings in advertising or journalism would more likely go to returning servicemen than to a female outsider.

Mummy's friend Bella Walker did offer me a position teaching drama at her girls'club in Aberdeen but Yale had destroyed my attitude towards amateurs in the theatre. And if the job didn't work out, my boss's closeness to my mother could present problems.

Another powerful incentive to return to America was the realisation that I was subtly reverting into an only daughter again. Those brown twin-sets and the walking stick were almost upon me. I didn't have one *bona fide* date with an unattached male during my six or seven months in Scotland. The "nice boys" I'd known in college, starting with Ian, had married during the War. Maybe because I was a divorcee, no one introduced me to single men and I'd no chance to pick them up. They didn't go to church, at least in Morningside, and I had no business outlets offering the chance to meet people in a context beyond my family.

I was now in my early thirties and the biological clock was starting to tick more loudly.

Once Mummy took me to a tea at the English Speaking Union "to meet some young people." A few were male and one followed us home. Mummy sat in the living room making social conversation throughout his visit, meaning well, I'm sure. But she also subtly contrived to let me know she found him wanting. So when he asked me if I'd like to go out to a movie I declined. He was pleasant but not worth the effort of getting it across to her that I couldn't commit myself to saying whether or not I'd be home for supper or how late I'd be staying out. He didn't call again and the incident taught me something I'd already suspected. If someone "wasn't good enough" for their daughter, my parents didn't want me socialising with him. They didn't appreciate that only through dating whoever was available did one meet better prospects.

Uncle Jack was now the only bachelor left among his contemporaries at the Parliament House and his favourite golfing partner, with whom he always went on holiday, had just become the second husband of another advocate's widow. On one of his visits I asked my sharp-tongued relative how his old pal liked married life and he answered, "He likes his creature comforts, so it suits him very well."

He escorted me to a party given by the newly weds and the middle-aged bride and I immediately took to each other. "How would you have liked having your uncle along on your honeymoon?" she asked me.

"I can't imagine it!"

"Well, I did! Getting hitched couldn't possibly cut into the annual two weeks of golf at Saint Andrews."

It was a cheery gathering with a lot of drink taken, though not by Uncle Jack who also wanted us to leave at a decent hour. The hostess vetoed my going. "We'll take Helen home," she said. After he left I got pleasantly high and, when I eventually made it back to Church Hill, stumbled up to my room without going in to see Mummy, whose light was still on.

Next day she wanted to know who'd been at the party and gave me a rundown on the past of every one of them. Since they were Uncle Jack's friends rather than hers, she wouldn't let me reciprocate hospitality and invite the newly weds back, so that social avenue was closed to me.

If I went to Glasgow I'd have pleasantly flirtatious lunches with my cousin George Laird. Years later, he confided in me that he'd "always been awful' sexually attracted" but he was a husband and father and I didn't expect anything more than company. All his friends were married too but even if he'd introduced me to anyone, he'd have talked about him in front of my parents and I'd have had no chance to develop a relationship – or not! – in my own way.

I caught a bad cold which left me with a deaf ear and had an unsatisfactory consultation with a general practitioner whom I didn't like any better than I'd done when I was going to St. Trinnean's. So, although I was worried, I refused to see him again.

"Why don't you consult Kenmure Melville next door?" said Mummy. "He's almost a doctor. He's sitting his final exams next month."

So I phoned him. He enthusiastically hunted out a case of his father's instruments, gave my ear a much better examination than the GP and agreed that my problem was more than the residue of sniffles. He told me, correctly, I needed a specialist.

Then he poured us both gins and tonics, the only medical man I ever consulted to do so, and proceeded to unburden his problems about living at home, which were similar to mine. His mother wanted to know all about every date. "I can't even have a night out with the boys and get a little drunk!" he sighed.

"Kenmure," said I. "Get married. Your wife will take care of

Mama." What a pity he was too young for me, probably ten years my junior. As a sonsy widow, who'd once worked for us at Strathblane used to say, "Them that's desirable's not obtainable and them that's obtainable's not desirable."

Before we'd moved, I'd remarked to Mummy that if I found a job in Edinburgh I didn't think I should live at home. She agreed and told me she knew a woman who rented rooms to working girls. "And she takes such an interest in them," Mummy added. That, of course, was what I didn't want.

"Another reason 'you can't go home again' is that adult children reactivate old family behaviour patterns."

Another reason "you can't go home again" is that adult children reactivate old family behaviour patterns. Once I went to Glasgow for the day and didn't say why because I was looking into sailings. On my return home, Mummy's face had the white drawn look I associated with a domestic squall. Littie was unusually silent and went off to bed, right after supper.

"What's gotten into him?" I asked her.

She sighed, "He wanted to know what you were up to in Glasgow. I said I hadn't asked. He accused me of never telling him anything, the old story about how you confided in me but never in him."

So I was still a bone of contention between my parents. The only difference was that Littie remembered how I'd cut off communications after his emotional outburst over my divorce and now didn't dare confront me directly.

All I said about my trip to Glasgow was that I'd had lunch with George. I waited until my departure arrangements were completed before telling my parents about them. I let Mummy know first, and I remember I cried, I was so afraid of hurting her. But she understood. Littie said very little.

I didn't have to worry about the physical work of running 2B Church Hill. Mummy, with her usual foresightedness, had bought a small flat a few blocks away and then advertised for a housekeeper to clean and do some cooking in return for accommodation and a stipend. She was swamped with replies although, at the time, domestic help was almost impossible to find.

The job went to Helen Sanderson, a widow who'd been working in a doctor's home where she claimed she had "a position of trust." Her references bore this out. Mrs. Sanderson stayed on until both my parents died. She was an excellent shiner of brass door knockers but a terrible cook and she wouldn't take any culinary hints because, said she, she was "self-taught in the British Army during the War and produced great meals according to the soldiers."

She grew deaf and wouldn't wear a hearing aid. She was neurotic and crotchety. But she was also faithful, devoted and dependable. After Littie's death, she and Mummy developed into a domestic couple who accepted each other's weaknesses and put up with them. Mummy could be difficult when so inclined, as well I knew. So, although Mrs. Sanderson often infuriated me, I appreciated all she put up with. Her intentions were good, she was unimaginative, but she did the job she was hired to do, hanging in there, maybe because her home depended on it but also because she took genuine pride in her position.

Throughout my stay in Edinburgh, Francis had been writing to me. We missed each other. So I planned to go back to the apartment and assumed we'd get married again. To re-enter the USA, I had to be vaccinated against smallpox and before leaving Edinburgh, I knew I was getting an unusually bad reaction to the injection. However, I didn't want to worry my parents so said nothing. But as soon as I boarded the *Mauritania* in Liverpool, I summoned the ship's doctor who prescribed two aspirins every four hours throughout the interminable six days of the voyage. I spent nearly all the time in bed in a cabin I shared with a loud chattering woman and a cute young GI bride.

Since then, I always fly on trips to Britain.

I wired Francis from sea and phoned him from the ship when we docked. He was all set to come down and help me. "No," I told him. "Let Cunard put me into a taxi. Just meet me downstairs at the apartment. And call Dr. Heilbroner!"

My wonderful physician was there almost as soon as I arrived. He studied my swollen leg with professional fascination, and wanted to put me in hospital.

"No!" I protested. "It's so airy and peaceful here after that cabin!"

"I'll take care of her," said Francis.

"But she needs penicillin around the clock. And she can't get up and cook meals," said our medical adviser.

"I'll see to everything," announced my ex-husband, and he did. He set the alarm clock for whenever I had to take a pill, and in an era before home-delivered carryouts, he brought in delicious nourishing meals. He was wonderful and within ten days he was taking me out to enjoy the sunshine and to movies, steadying me on his arm.

24

We Made No Money
but We Sure had Fun!

Tuesday November 11, 1947 was when my life turned around for the better.

I was deeply depressed. After our happy reunion in summer, Francis and I had slipped back into our old ways. He showed no signs of marrying me and I was beginning to think this mightn't be a good idea anyway. He was working on a novel so had given up job-hunting.

Meanwhile we had to eat and pay rent. In the employment market I was in competition with returning service men. I wanted a writing job, not a secretarial one, but when asked for samples of my work had to explain I'd signed an Official Secrets document so couldn't claim any published stories for twenty years.

That November weekend, I'd studied the Help Wanted section of the Sunday *New York Times* and found only one possibility – a trade magazine looking for a copywriter. It was a long shot but I was desperate and it would give me a chance to try a new job-finding strategy. On Monday morning I dialed the telephone number listed in the ad, and when the operator answered with the name of the publication (something like Tots and Teens) I simply asked, "Where are you located?"

"475 Fifth Avenue," said she. "It's opposite the Public Library." I thanked her and hung up.

On Tuesday, I collected every scrap of copy I'd written for the Cleanliness Bureau then dressed myself like a successful fashion writer. Mummy had given me a beautiful dark green topcoat made from an unrationed rug so it had a red plaid lining. With it I wore a becoming little matching hat. This was on the eve of the New Look, and smart women looked smart.

I went over to 475 Fifth Avenue and took the elevator to the floor listed for the magazine office. I found a row of doors, most of them closed including the one I wanted. Too late I remembered it was Veterans' Day and a public holiday.

Few job-hunting situations are as frustrating as psyching yourself up for a big sales pitch and then finding you can't deliver it. Almost in tears, I paced along the narrow corridor and came upon a small, wide-open office where a well-dressed, dark-haired man was thumbing through a pile of newspapers.

What did I have to lose? I swept in there, inquiring confidently, "Is this where you're looking for a writer?"

It's true that you sell yourself in the first thirty seconds of an interview. He turned, looked me up and down, then said, "The job advertised is across the hall. But . . . I need someone too. So come back here after you've talked to them."

"I'll talk to you now," said I. He was extremely handsome and not much older than myself.

"They'd probably pay you more money."

"But they're closed for Veterans' Day."

He looked down at his fingers. "Just let me rinse off this newsprint. Have a seat. And would you like a cigarette?"

I shook my head, sat down by the desk, and while he was washing his hands at a small corner wash basin (it was that kind of office), I picked up one of the newspapers which identified itself in bold type as the *Manila Times*.

Where-in-hell was Manila? And what nationality was he? Spanish?

"I am," he informed me, also sitting down, "starting up as a publisher's representative for a bunch of Far Eastern newspapers. The one you're looking at is the biggest."

I'd no idea what a publisher's representative did but it sounded promising so I smiled knowledgeably and he continued, "I'm moving out of this bucketshop into beautiful new premises in the old Marguery Hotel building on Park Avenue. It's been converted into offices. What kind of work are you looking for? And have you a resumé?"

I produced one. "I'm a writer. I was employed by the British government here in New York. After VJ Day, I went home to

171

Scotland to see my family and just got back." That would explain the lengthy time I'd been unemployed.

"I see you used to be in advertising. Do you have any samples of your work?"

That fatal question. "Only those clips from the Cleanliness Bureau," I said explaining the story about classified information and the Official Secrets thing.

He just nodded. "I'm not long out of the Army myself. I was a public relations officer in the Philippines. Tell me your job description and I can probably read between the lines."

"Officially I was 'Writing Reports'."

Our eyes met. "I've a pretty fair idea of what you were doing," said he. "Would you like to come to work for me, running my office?"

"I'm not a secretary. I type but I haven't taken shorthand in years."

"I want more than a secretary. I need someone who can handle office work of course. But she's got to be the kind of person who's presentable, knows how to meet people, whom I could send down to Washington if need be. And take responsibility, minding the store when I'm away."

"Well . . . I'm not sure that's what I'm looking for but . . . I'm free at the moment"

"Then maybe we could help each other out for a few weeks?"

"Maybe. I once worked for a personnel agency so I could help you find someone."

He took a gold fountain pen out of his pocket. He had nice expensive accessories, a good watch and a little pin shaped like a trumpet anchored the tips of his shirt collar behind his beautiful tie. On a *Manila Times* letterhead he printed in bold capital letters: ALBERT C. CAPOTOSTO.

"You're Italian!" I exclaimed off the top of my head.

"Born in Philadelphia. I don't speak a word of the language." We smiled at each other. "Look, I'll give you the phone number here so you can let me know if you find anything. And I'll be in touch as soon as I know when I'm moving to East 47th Street. If that's all right with you."

It was indeed. He folded up my resumé, put it in his pocket, and I floated euphorically home to Tudor City.

Next day I came down with flu and felt terrible. But towards the end of the week, as I was starting to recover, the phone rang.

"Mrs. Leary? Capotosto. I'm moving into my new office on Monday. Do you think you could meet me at 475 Fifth and give me a hand taking some stuff over there? It'd give you a chance to look the place over and we can talk some more. I'll pay you for your time."

"I'd be delighted to help you, Mr. Capotosto."

"Cappy. That's what everyone calls me."

So, on that memorable Monday morning, we walked together through the labyrinths of the Grand Central Station and into the beautiful old Marguery Hotel building at 270 Park Avenue. It has since been replaced by a glass monstrosity. Cappy carried a portable typewriter. I had an armful of files. The total furnishings in the new premises were two desks, a borrowed chair and a bar cabinet.

"If you can stay here for a while . . . er. . ."

"Helen."

"Helen. I'll go out and look for some more office equipment."

I was willing. The room was so spacious, after the apartment, and the atmosphere so peaceful.

By the end of the week, we had a file cabinet, two desk chairs, and a padded arm one. Two surly labourers moved these in, complaining about the trouble they'd had locating the service entrance. When they presented a bill, Cappy counted out the exact amount in cash, saying very quietly, "If you'd been a little more gentlemanly, I'd have given you a tip."

He had also stocked the bar with Scotch, soda and a bowl for ice and hung an interesting picture by a Filipino artist over the fireplace. We'd inherited light-coloured wall-to-wall carpeting and a charming mirrored entrance hall which we shared with two other small businesses.

We were subletting from three brothers named Zaro, Russian entrepreneurs who employed an attractive fortyish secretary called Peggy and, from time to time, odd bods, like an old European Colonel who was constantly on the phone yelling, "Allo! Allo! Peetsburgh?" We had to pass his desk en route to the unisex bathroom for this was, after all, a converted apartment.

Next door to us was a theatrical agency called Schaefer-Waible, referred to by Peggy as "Schaefer Wobbly" due to their precarious finances. Schaefer was a quiet type, Freddy Waible a sweetie-pie who used so many four letter words after a while we only noticed them when strangers were present and raised their eyebrows.

In the beginning Media Representatives didn't even have a telephone. Every day when I went out for lunch, I'd complain to the phone company from a booth in the Marguery's lobby demanding to know why-in-hell they didn't install one, with an extension. As a foreign newspaper office we had a priority rating etc. etc. Eventually I reached an executive-sounding female who listened sympathetically then said, "I'll look into it. Give me your number and I'll call you right back."

"You can't!" I fairly shouted. "We don't have any telephone!"

"You Don't Have Any Telephone?" she echoed, shocked.

We got our phones and a properly listed number the next day!

I stayed in that job for seven years, until Cappy moved to Manila and closed the office. By then he had accomplished what he'd set out to do which was to introduce the Far Eastern market to American exporters. Though I'd had no previous experience of publisher's representatives, from manning that switchboard at BC&P I knew what space salesmen did. They sold advertising. In addition to the *Manila Times* we peddled a string of Filipino magazines, a business publication called the *Manila Bulletin*, a Chinese daily with the unfortunate name of the *Fukien Times*, as well as the *Bangkok Post* in Thailand and a Hong Kong newsletter run by a salty Irish woman called Elma Kelly. We also had a tie-in with Philippine Broadcasting. Our financial arrangements with these companies were vague and we didn't do much business for the ones outside Manila.

When friends asked me what I did, I'd tell them to name it. I'd type Cappy's letters or compose my own, signing his name. I shampooed the carpet and shined two handsome brass pots on the mantlepiece. I gave out market information over the phone and sold one lucrative schedule myself when no-one else was around to do so. I entertained VIPs from the Philippines as well as clients from Madison Avenue in the small world of international advertising.

And I did once go to Washington – to interview the wife of an American Ambassador to the Philippines. The story ran on the frontpage of the *Manila Times* and that lovely lady told the managing editor, David Boguslav (of whom more anon), that I was a most intelligent journalist for never once did I ask her, "Who's your favourite movie star?"

Our constant refrain was, "We don't make any money but we do have fun." When our landlords the Zaros went bankrupt, I staved off our eviction as subtenants until Cappy came back from a trip to Manila and we took over the whole of the apartment in partnership with Edwin Seymour, an elder statesman in our business who represented publications in Bermuda and South America. This was an ideal arrangement. We weren't competitive because we were selling different markets, but we had the same clients and – God knows! – the same business problems.

"Schaefer-Wobbly" were replaced by a small international advertising agency run by a Viennese called Rose Lowe who shared the office with her husband, Fred. A delightful burly European with a thick accent, he had his own business and often worked over weekends and would phone me at home to read me the telegrams that invariably arrived after I left on Fridays.

The couple had season tickets to the Metropolitan Opera and late one afternoon Rose came in and said, "Honey! (She pronouned it Hawnee!) My ol' man's so tired. Could you go with me to the opera tonight?"

I knew her well enough to say, "Rose, I've had a rough day too. Is it Wagner? Because, if so, I couldn't take it either."

"If it was Wagner, my ol' man would go. It's *Lucia Di Lammermoor*."

'*Chacun a son gout*' and what a memorable evening! Lili Pons sang the title role and during the famous Mad Scene, as she started down the long staircase on centre stage, she caught one foot in the folds of her voluminous white draperies. For an interminable moment, she teetered and swayed forward. The whole chorus stretched up their hands as if to catch her, although from their stage positions this would have been futile.

Besides, the diva didn't need them! Through sheer will power she righted herself, kicked her toes clear, and kept on in her descent. She didn't miss a beat or even go flat as she often did! The audience couldn't wait for the end of the aria before bursting into applause.

Once Rose and I were going to an international advertising Christmas party and I went home with her after work to look over what she'd wear. We picked a black dress which needed some dramatic jewellery. Fred pulled open a drawer and offered his wife a collection of military medals.

"I can't wear those!" she protested. But of course she did. "And if anyone asks what they are I'll say my ol' man won them in the Second World War and I won them in the War of the Sexes," she explained to me.

Media Reps, in short, gave me far more than just a job. We were a family.

Working for Cappy restored the self-esteem which living with the unhappy, frustrated Francis had eroded in me. From the start, my boss treated me as his business partner. During our first few weeks together, we went through the motions of trying to hire a replacement for me. I phoned a couple of employment agencies, not Maud's, and they sent some applicants around but none seemed quite right. Then one Monday morning I came in early and found a handwritten message on my typewriter.

"Helen," it read. "Why don't you decide to stay on here? Maybe for a little more money? Anyway, on a permanent basis? Bestest, Cappy."

I stuck my reply into his machine. "I'll stay with anyone who writes me notes like this! Bestest Helen."

I didn't ask for more money because I knew he didn't have it. He had started the company on the basis of two major accounts – the independent *Manila Times* and a string of vernacular weeklies also owned by the Roces family, the major publishers in the Philippines and among the richest in the world. Like most Filipinos, they were canny and suspicious when doing business with Americanos. Moreover Cappy had taken over the projected opening in the States from an entrepreneur who'd been untrustworthy. So no contracts had been signed and only the *Manila Times* sent us a regular monthly cheque.

"I understand how they do business out there," Cappy told me. "They're waiting for me to prove myself. They'll come through eventually."

They did, but in the meantime we were operating on half our estimated budget, which covered the rent but so little else we had to decide which bills to pay each month. Mail from the Far East was also unreliable. One Friday, after a cliff-hanging week, I said to Cappy, "Look, if you want to hold off giving me my pay cheque until Monday, it's all right."

He shook his head. "No, sweetie. I don't pay you much but I'm damn well paying you on time."

Shortly after, he went out, came back and paid me in cash, then called his girlfriend and made a dinner date. Later that afternoon, he shot back the cuff that normally concealed his watch, then asked me what time it was? He wasn't wearing his gold trumpet pin either and borrowed my pen to sign some letters.

On Monday, when the cheque from Manila arrived, he went out to the bank to deposit it and came back sporting all his usual accessories. I said nothing but to have someone pawn treasured possessions to help me out was a new experience and a thoughtful gesture I never forgot.

Before the War he'd married an attractive socialite but they were now amicably divorced, and he was dating a beautiful actress called Virginia Copeland, at that time a star model for the dress designer Hattie Carnegie.

Virginia and I didn't trust each other although we were always polite when she swept into the office after work and found Cappy and me discussing the day's crises over a therapeutic Scotch and soda.

Francis didn't like this after-hours libating either. My job was changing our relationship and threatening his lifestyle. When I'd rush in, long after 5.30, loaded down with groceries but smelling faintly of whisky, he'd complain that the evening was his best writing time and he wanted his dinner by 6.00. I still wasn't much of a cook but in an age when carry-out meals were the exception rather than standard, I'd become an expert on fast food preparation.

My ex-husband externalised his insecurities by picking on me for innumerable small things, like crookedly sticking on the stamps I bought for his letters. My boss, by contrast, faced his problems by talking them out. Cappy would march into the office in the morning and say, "Keep out of my way today. I'm in a bad mood. If I snap at you it's nothing personal."

Pacing the floor he'd continue, "I'm worried because it's been two weeks since I wrote to Manila and I've had no reply. I know they work on the 'manãna system' but I'm afraid something's gone wrong." He would then spell out what that might be and he was invariably correct.

These sessions didn't exhaust me emotionally like Francis's nit-picking. Besides, after Cappy had talked the problem out of his system, he'd revert to his usual optimism, and we'd get a lot of work done. Our co-tenant Ed Seymour and our mutual clients from the advertising agencies often joined us in our after hours drink before catching their commuter trains. They preferred these relaxed visits to having their afternoon's work sabotaged by a boozy business lunch. So we did a lot of business around five o'clock.

Cappy, having been a general's public relations man during the War, was an expert on entertaining. "Good staff work makes a good party," he told me. "You must have plenty of booze, decent food properly served and also some good-looking dollies. Invite some of your girlfriends, sweetie."

And I did. A favourite was Louise Giraldi who was handsome, well-dressed and socially savvy. She'd worked with Francis in one of his brief office jobs and become my closest friend. Her stately widowed French-Canadian mother, a little like Mummy, lived in Brooklyn with her four children and Louise's sister Aline, a successful businesswoman, sometimes came to our office parties too. I spent many Thanksgivings and Christmases with this family who put on my wedding reception when I married Charles Marwick.

As devout Catholics, the Giraldis didn't care for my on-again-off-again relationship with Francis but to their credit, they didn't let it get in the way of their acceptance of me.

Acceptance, indeed, was what turned my life around. Cappy

had taken at face value the poised efficiency I'd presented to him when we met. I'd had to live up to this facade and eventually it became closer to the genuine article.

I was still an inaccurate typist and couldn't take dictation and the errors I made balancing two business cheque books and Cappy's personal account were the despair of Leo Seidelman, a personable, cigar smoking, laconic accountant who came in each month and brought order to our chaotic financial affairs. Leo got on Cappy's and my nerves but we trusted him.

He'd been recruited through Carl Messinger, an old school friend of my boss's who'd also been his sergeant in the Army and was now using our office as a mailing address while he set himself up in public relations. Carl was a Pennsylvania German with short straight hair and steel-rimmed spectacles. He was also a gourmet and, like Cappy, showed genuine appreciation for whatever I did for him. On his visits to the office, after he'd opened his mail and thumbed through the phone messages I'd taken for him, he'd give a dry chuckle and say, "Helen, let's go to lunch." So I got to know some of the nicest new restaurants in midtown Manhattan.

While stationed in Manila, the hard-headed Carl had taken the only illogical action of his life – he had fallen in love with a well-connected dark-skinned Filipino girl with an American child. When peace came, Carl and Conchita parted, but didn't forget each other, and my boss on a trip to Manila reopened communications between them.

"The fair Senorita," as Cappy called her, took her time before she accepted Carl's offer of marriage. She had Hispanic good looks but worried how her dusky complexion would go over in America. Moreover, she'd have to leave her little son behind.

I'd been one of Carl's few confidantes throughout this wooing so felt like the mother of the bride when she arrived. The Jewish Leo and his wife were best man and matron of honour at a Protestant church wedding staged for the benefit of Carl's mama who was more upset by his marrying a Roman Catholic than by her being a Filipino. The bride insisted on a civil ceremony the next day and that was the anniversary they'd later celebrate!

Conchita, who, like me, had never learned to prepare meals

at home, became almost overnight an artist at the kitchen stove. "If you can read, you can cook!" she'd say. But the recipes Carl cut out of the *New York Times* were often extremely complicated. I admired her tremendously and enjoyed her lively company.

Carl once told me, "I wanted a wife but with any of the women I met after the War, it'd have been like another public relations project. Conchita doesn't give a damn about business. All she cares about is living."

Sometimes, after a gourmet meal she'd cooked, he'd start pontificating about the philanthropical benefits of public relations until Conchita would interupt with, "Aw Carl! You just want to make more money out of these people!"

He'd come off his high horse, and chuckle, "You're right!"

25

Happy Days in 50s Manhattan

Our office sold a lot of advertising and after six months of limping along on half-pay Cappy decided to make a trip back to Manila to collect his commissions. Philippines Airlines was inaugurating flights to and from New York and in return for the promise of publicity in the Far Eastern press, he got free transport.

The week before he left, I started to panic and finally asked him if he wasn't worried about leaving me alone and in charge?

"Helen," said my boss, "as you know, I'm very concerned about this trip but the one thing I'm not worried about is how you'll keep the business going. You'll make mistakes because we all do but they'll be honest ones."

If he hadn't so hated women in tears, I'd have cried.

I had company in the office from an unemployed foreign correspondent called Norman Paige. He had some vague arrangement with Philippine Broadcasting which brought in no money. He didn't do much work either, he was too busy decompressing from glamorous War assignments. He wore a trenchcoat and, after hours, a khaki shirt with his name embroidered on it. He lunched every day – or at least held up the bar – at Twentyone, the "in" watering hole for his kind. There he hobnobbed with greats in the media and met predatory blondes, one of them a former Miss Germany and a darling girl. Norman was darkly handsome although neither I nor Cappy's ex-wife Jane, whom he dated, thought he had much sex appeal.

His only regular occupation was completing the *New York Times* crossword which he did early every afternoon. One day I was frantically busy getting out a mailing. The copy had been delivered late from the printers and there were many envelopes to stuff and stamp. It was exasperating to see an able-bodied male sitting there staring out of the window. Didn't he, I asked, have anything to do? He showed me his Byronic profile and asked, "What *can* I do?"

"You could help me get this release out on time," said I.

He grinned like a happy little boy, peeled off his sports jacket, sat down on the floor, and started collating pages. We worked out an assembly line and at some point poured a drink from the office bar. Everything went to the post office before 5.30 and both Norm and I were relaxed and happy! It was that kind of office.

Cappy was in touch from time to time on the trip, enough to let me know things were going well. On the day he was due back, I had flowers everywhere and was wearing one of my nicest outfits. But of course, when he actually walked into the office, I was busy on the phone giving out rate information! He stood by my desk then starting pulling dollar bills out of his pocket and strewing them around. He had also brought me jade earrings. When, eventually I lost one, I had the other made into a ring. All the money the magazines owed to us had been deposited into a Manila account but now our commissions and retainers would be sent to New York. From that time on, we were financially in the clear.

But Cappy had married Virginia and he was going to be spending more time in the Far East. Eventually, he told me we'd hire another salesman but until then I'd be in charge.

Relations between Francis and me had continued to deteriorate and I only stayed with him because affordable living space was almost impossible to find in New York. The night Cappy and Virginia left for Manila, we had a farewell party at the office with all our "usual suspects" and I cornered my boss in the hall. What, I asked,was happening to his bride's apartment in Greenwich Village?

"She's offered it to Norm," said he. "But if he doesn't take it, don't worry. The building's been sold and the tenants may be evicted."

I could take care of Norm. "If he doesn't want it, can I move in?" I asked. Our eyes met. "I'm leaving Francis."

You never had to explain things to Cappy. He just gave me a hug and said, "Gay Street's all yours."

Virginia wrote me a long friendly letter explaining that eviction was likely because some entrepreneur had bought the old brownstone and planned to remodel it into a townhouse for himself. She put me in touch with the basement tenant, the writer Elizabeth Byrd who had just changed husbands and moved uptown. Betty became one of my most treasured friends. Her previous spouse still lived there with Jack Morris, an alcoholic literary agent. Immediately above Virginia's apartment was an ancient naval officer's widow and over her, two pleasant lesbians and their Siamese cat, the first of this breed I ever met.

So I went home and gave Francis notice. He didn't argue, even helped me move my books and clothing down to the Village and some months later, he sailed for France and never came back to America.

I don't remember the exact months in 1948 when all these things happened. What I do remember is wandering out into the tiny garden behind the Gay Street house one autumn weekend, basking in sunshine and counting my many blessings. The apartment was furnished and only $45 a month. It needed redecorating but it had charm. There was also a ghost though I didn't find this out until Betty Byrd wrote a piece about it. I just thought the old lady upstairs moved around at odd hours.

Jack Morris downstairs could be delightful company. One Saturday he took me out to dinner then phoned Sunday morning contrite about standing me up! "Honey! I'm terribly, terribly sorry! I was so Goddamn' drunk I forgot!"

"You didn't," I said. "We went to Chumley's." That was a legendary restaurant off Morton Street frequented by aspiring writers which provided good cheap food and probably credit. Its peeling wallpaper was held together by bookcovers from the works of customers who'd achieved publication.

"Jesus! How did I behave?"

"Like a gentleman. We had a good meal and a lot of laughs, then you walked me home, kissed me chastely and left me at my door."

"Thank God" he said.

He wasn't someone I'd have introduced to Mummy but he gave me all kinds of insights into New York's literary establishment and introduced me to Jane McGill, a talent scout for mystery novels also, alas, an alcoholic. When her husband, an English professor, got a Fulbright Fellowship to Finland for a year, she steered her reading assignments my way, telling the publishers who employed her that my judgment was as good as hers on readable whodunits.

So, a year after leaving Scotland, I had an offbeat, fascinating job with a supportive boss, my own apartment in historic Greenwich Village, and emotionally I was a free woman.

Life hadn't been all bad with Francis. During our last years together, he had done most of the writing on a collection of political reminiscences, *Presidential Sweepstakes*, by an old time journalist Henry Luther Stoddart who regularly bought him lunch at the Union League Club. He had also published a well-accepted first novel entitled *This Dark Monarchy*. The story was based on the Constant Kent case, and I learned a lot about fiction writing, reading through it for him chapter by chapter, and sitting in on his discussions about it with his old Princeton friend, William Keinbush who was also dabbling in writing although he later became an admired painter of Maine seascapes.

"Frank, you've got to guard against the club sandwich technique," Bill would say. "You can't have a layer of description, then a slab of action, then another layer of description, like corned beef on rye. You've got to blend things together so it flows."

Excellent advice which stayed with me, as I gestated a novel of my own.

And once, when I was home sick with flu, Francis had gone out and on his return he'd rung the apartment's bell for me to open the door, which had annoyed me because I'd had to drag myself out of bed to do this. But his hands were full. He was clutching a caterwauling dirty little brown kitten.

"Dear. Don't get mad at me. He's a stray. He followed me down 33rd Street when I left and he was still there, as if he was waiting for me, just now. I thought maybe we could give him some food, let him stay here tonight then try to find a home for him."

"I don't like cats," said I. "And you told me you were allergic to them when you were a kid."

But of course I let him bring the little animal in and I served it some canned tuna fish which was promptly regurgitated on the living room carpet. The kitten then relieved himself fastidiously in the bathtub. We never did get kitty litter for him. Because, of course, he stayed on.

We called him Dennis O'Leary. He grew so fast that on the Fourth of July holiday, when I was taking him for rides up and down on the elevator, a ploy he loved, another passenger got on and exclaimed, "That's the biggest cat I ever saw!"

No wonder, the way he ate. He could also one-up my ex-husband. Francis wrote his books in longhand, and every morning would settle down in his comfortable armchair, having first sharpened several pencils and lined them up on a side table. When Dennis had slept off his breakfast, he'd try to get attention by carefully nudging these pencils one by one onto the floor. Francis, deep in creation, would pick them up and reposition them. Dennis would knock them off again. If that still didn't produce the proper reaction, he would then scamper around the apartment and wind up clawing at the back of Francis's chair.

That always did it. Francis would throw down his manuscript, and get the cat food out of the refrigerator! When I came back from work, I had to rinse off fishy little dishes left in the sink before starting to make the evening meal.

After we'd eaten and I'd collapsed onto the sofa in hopes of reading a book, Dennis would jump up and sit on my stomach, purring and demanding attention. In the beginning, I'd push him off me, until Francis, who had more understanding of cats than of working women, explained, "He feels that you haven't had the benefit of his company during the day. If you talk to him for a few minutes, he'll go off to bed."

Dennis did this at the same time – 10.15 – every night even when we had company, which he enjoyed. Sometimes he'd put on a sketch we called "playing Boris Karloff." He'd look very fierce, push his ears back, and rear up on his hindlegs.

When I moved out, Francis advertised for a male roommate and, after a few abortive interviews, a suitable prospect turned up. Unfortunately by the time he'd inspected the apartment's two rooms Dennis had figured out why he was there and didn't like the idea. So, when the prospect sat down to talk terms, the huge cat positioned himself on the floor and stared at him. Then, having disconcerted his victim, he rose up in his Karloff routine, gesturing with long claws towards the door.

"I'll call you, Mr. Leary," said the young man, as he left rapidly, never to be heard from again. Francis abandoned the idea of a co-tenant.

My ex-husband and I saw each other from time to time but couldn't work out a non-emotional relationship. When he decided to move to France, he asked me if I'd like to take Dennis?

"Have you had him altered?" I asked. I'd learned about male cats and their smell.

"No. I don't want to spoil his personality," said Francis.

"Sorry," said I. But then I slept on it and realised that we could make a trip to the vet after my ex-husband had sailed. So I phoned back and said I'd had second thoughts.

Francis laughed. "We don't need to worry about Dennis. Rich Uncle Luckie just died."

Uncle Luckie was a spoilt feline owned by Francis' mother. Since he'd have no heirs, we'd tell Dennis he might some day inherit all his canned shrimp, lobster and crabmeat. Luckie liked to sit at open windows but as his corpulence increased so did his danger of falling off the sill on the ninth floor. This was what killed him.

Comforting his distraught mother, Francis put Dennis in her arms and this heir apparent outlived her for several years enjoying luxury in a fancy cattery she'd provided for in her will. When Bob Sincerbeaux, her lawyer, complained to me about this, I told him Dennis was an unusual cat who expected and was entitled to enjoy the best of all possible feline worlds.

Years later, when John Hinckley shot the President, the Dean of Clinical Affairs at the George Washington University Hospital where prompt surgery saved Ronald Reagan's life was a Dr. Dennis O'Leary.

26

A Lady Doesn't Kiss and Tell

I'd found some truth in Mary-Madeleine's comment that "the best cure for a man is a lot of other men." Or, as a date who'd acquired two ex-wives before he was thirty, phrased it, "You've got to have your sex."

In the 1950s AIDS was unknown and six years of war had programmed single women to take their pleasure as men did. A popular song from that period, sung to music from an opera, was *There's no tomorrow, There's just tonight.*

Once, in our cups, I and a co-worker who'd grown up in the American West counted up the men we'd been sexually involved with and we were both mildly shocked, because we considered ourselves "nice girls" and not promiscuous, to find the total was a round dozen apiece.

One of the few things I've learned in life, one of "Lillie's Laws" in fact, is that a man is the same in bed as he is out of it, i.e. if he is intelligent and considerate or unimaginative and selfish, that's how he'll be between the sheets. I learned this the hard way and in this memoir will not identify the men I did or didn't sleep with. They were in the minority of those I dated. I had to know and like someone before I'd copulate and I never used my body for business purposes. I'm sure a lot of advertising people thought Cappy and I slept together but we never did. We were both much too smart. As a result, he still, fifty years on, sends me Valentines and Easter cards from his retirement home in Honolulu.

A charming Frenchman from Montreal called Pierre, who periodically came to town on newsprint business, always took me out to dinner and once, at short notice, suggested I find a date for his partner, Mac, who was with him. None of my friends were available but I got a name from Bill Farrell, a recently married Englishman who often stopped by my office. The girl his bride suggested turned out to be pretty and nicely dressed but dreadfully dull. The four of us went dancing at a Fifth Avenue hotel, and pretty soon, after clearing it with me, Mac said to her, "I've a long day tomorrow. Would you mind if I took you home early?" She nodded and they duly departed.

Next morning Pierre phoned me at work. "Helen, join me for a quickie drink before I leave town! I've much to tell you!" When I met him at a midtown bar, he asked, "Guess what time Mac got back to our hotel last night." I shook my head. "Six o'clock this morning. Seems she invited him to come up to her place for coffee and he went. She disappeared, he thought to the kitchen, but she came back in a sheer negligee and nothing more!"

"Well," said I, "I'm glad he got something out of the evening."

"Yeah," commented Pierre, "but you've still got to have some conversation."

This sums it up, to my mind.

In the six months following Francis's departure for Paris, I'd lost my lean and hungry look because Conchita had introduced me to a widower, a decent but dull telegraphic expert she'd met in Manila. In return for enjoying his excellent home cooking I introduced him to movies, theatres, dancing and socialising. When his married daughter came home for Christmas she was quite disturbed to find her father dating a Greenwich Village divorcee, although by then I'd moved uptown to an apartment on York Avenue.

After six months or so in Gay Street, I'd been evicted with the other tenants. However, we had presented our case so successfully to the City's rental agency, the entrepreneur who wanted the house had had to find us all "comparable space" and pay to move us out. I wound up in a horrible third floor single room apartment at 6 Jones Street in the Village. I had a memorable New Year's Eve party there to which I invited every unattached male I knew. A young man I'd met in a public relations course at the New School sent me three dozen pink carnations which do a lot for any surroundings so my friends couldn't understand why I despised the place.

Phyllis Lintott brought another Greenwich Villager whom she was frankly trying to unload on me. He was a small, dark

Irishman called Michael Joseph O'Brien, whose sister Kate was a famous writer. Mike claimed he'd been sent to America by the Irish Republican Army to influence public opinion but instead of following his youthful desire "to be out there with a gun" he'd wound up a vice-president in a New York bank. His extremely conventional associates reminded me of the prewar Glasgow business community.

Mike proved a good friend although he was difficult to handle. In his forties, he'd become unreasonably jealous around younger men after a few drinks. He was stubborn and set in his ways. He'd take me out to dinner on Fridays and Saturdays because they were the only two nights he could stay up late. He would also drag out the evenings until I was so tired I'd discourteously order him to go home before he lit yet another cigarette to pollute the air in my small living space. Launched on a bender, he'd stay up indefinitely.

One winter I had such bad flu it kept me off work for many days. Mike phoned and said, "Darlin', as a hard-headed banker, I know you must be getting short of cash. Can I bring you some, this evening?" I told him I could give him a cheque on his own bank, and added that Aline Giraldi would be there to make my dinner. So he brought some whisky too, and she invited him to stay and share the chicken she'd cooked. Later he took her all the way home to Brooklyn in a taxi.

A few years later Mike proposed marriage but I turned him down, pointing out that going out to dinner or to parties wasn't adequate preparation for combining life styles. After that, I didn't hear from him for some time – until he phoned to say he was in hospital. I gathered up a stack of paperbacks and dashed down to his bedside to find him very ill indeed. A sour old nurse told me bluntly he was an alcoholic and a heavy smoker so no wonder he had ulcers.

He went on a cruise to recuperate from the illness which also forced him onto the water wagon. We kept in touch but he was always going out of town to upstate New York. Finally he invited me to dinner, saying he had something to tell me. "You're getting married and your bride lives in Elmira," said I.

I talked to this lady once on the telephone and found her a

formidable retired schoolma'am. They had an apartment close to his office until they moved to Connecticut. When I read Mike's obituary, I phoned one of his banking friends who said he'd had cancer of the throat.

"I think he died of commuting," said I. "He so hated getting up, he told me once he'd tune his radio on high because the early morning talk shows exasperated him and made him hurry through dressing and eating breakfast just to get away from them. If he had to entertain a customer to dinner during the week, he'd ask me to phone him next morning when I got up and to keep talking until I was sure he was awake. I can't imagine Mike catching a train at some ungodly hour like 7.03 every day." His old colleague agreed with me!

God rest his soul, he was a kind, often entertaining man. My mother met him when she visited me in New York and they charmed each other. But on her return to Edinburgh she wrote me the news that a contemporary of mine who'd married a Roman Catholic just had her sixth child, then continued without even a fresh paragraph, "Kate O'Brien just published a life of Saint Teresa. Are the O'Briens Catholics?"

"Darlin'," said Mike when I read this to him. "I'm sending a telegram to your sainted mother saying, 'Am Catholic but believe in birth control'." I was afraid he might, after a few drinks!

One evening my home telephone rang around 6.30 and a distinctive and beautiful male voice asked if I was the Helen Lillie Leary who'd gone to Glasgow University? I said I was and who was calling?

"Jere Faison. Doctor Jere Faison. You and your husband spent a weekend with my then wife and I in New Jersey back around 1940."

I'd first seen him at his wedding to an attractive daughter of the General Manager of the Royal Bank. He was American and stunning, tall and dark-haired with acquiline features and hands with long sensitive fingers. He was taking a medical degree specialising in obstetrics at Glasgow University and came with his fiancée to my twenty-first birthday party, a dance at the Royal Automobile Club.

When they moved to America, his wife got in touch with me

in New York and Francis and I visited them. They had two small children and Jere was studying for an examination which would license him to practise in the USA. This was required by medical practitioners with degrees from foreign universities and was especially annoying to him because although he came from a fine old Southern family, it grouped him with the European refugees then flocking into New York.

My chief recollection of that weekend is that he and I had a lot of fun telling hoary old college jokes in the vernacular which our spouses didn't understand or appreciate! Later, during the War, I'd lost all contact with the Faisons but I heard that the marriage had broken up.

Jere practised obstetrics in Manhattan and had a patient called Mrs. Leary. He'd been looking up her number in the telephone book when his eye fell on mine. Since the pregnant lady didn't need him, he took me out to the first of many dinners.

I was now living uptown. Jere had a tiny apartment in the Village and at that time wasn't about to get married again. He'd given his wife control of his finances when he'd joined the Army and been sent to the Far East. By the time he returned, she'd found another man with better financial prospects and departed, taking his two children with her. He always spoke about her with restraint but he did resent that she'd tried to undermine his relationship with his young son and daughter.

Jere and I grew fond of each other but some vital element was missing in our relationship. I was never totally at ease with him although, like Mike, he was a dependable friend and there was a lot more physical attraction than with the Irishman. Jere and I also grew close during the creation of a Glasgow University Club of America in 1955, the brainchild of another graduate, a plastic surgeon called Leopold Glushak.

Dr. Glushak was an Estonian Jew who had grown up in Scotland, married a Glaswegian, then moved to New York City. He started rounding up fellow graduates to celebrate his Alma Mater's five hundredth anniversary and a visit to the USA of Principal Sir Hector Hetherington. Around fifty people attended that first dinner of the Glasgow University Club of America at New York's Plaza Hotel in December 1955.

191

As Vice President, Jere followed Glushak as President and I stepped into the second spot and became the first woman President. This resulted in our being dropped from the invitation list of the Saint Andrew's Society which is all male in membership. The Glasgow University Club of America has had its ups and downs and owes its survival as an entity separate from a fundraising group, the Friends of Glasgow University, to the persistence of Dr. Margaret Wallace Ferguson, a psychiatrist whom I first met when we were performing drama back in 1936. Neither of us had known the other was in New York until the formation of the Club!

"Helen's got it made," Carl Messinger would chuckle. "She's dating a banker and an obstetrician!"

I was dating a lot of others too, the most emotionally involving being a charming and incredibly rich South American from a publishing family. His first name was spelt in Spanish, Jaime, pronounced Hymie in New York. "Please call me Jamie, my darrrling," he told me. Although he rolled his rrrrrs his English vocabulary was almost as extensive as mine.

Jamie was a poor little rich boy. He once told me the only thing his parents hadn't bought him was his own airplane. He was also brilliantly clever and with no other outlet for his energies had had some kind of nervous breakdown which had led to his being sent up to New York to do some special job for a newspaper Ed Seymour represented.

So this small, blond, handsome Latin went past my office door every day and we started smiling at each other. I had had an extra telephone installed for some friend of Cappy's who wanted a listing in New York. He seldom got messages and I was surprised when it rang one afternoon. Jamie was at the other end of the line. "I came in and copied the number last night before I went home," he explained. "I like to come in late and work till seven or so. There's so much activity in this office during the day, I can't concentrate. Helenita, would you like to have dinner with me tonight? I could pick you up at your apartment with my car."

Why not?

One thing led to another, notably a second bottle of

champagne then back to his bachelor pad on Park Avenue. We were wonderfully compatible both in bed and as companions. We were also careful not to let anyone at 270 Park know about our relationship although I'm sure some of Seymour's staff had their suspicions.

In December of that year, (I think it was 1951) Jamie asked me what I was doing for Christmas? "I'm sharing it with my friend Grace," I told him. "We're both tired of being the odd female at family gatherings and she suggested that this year we cook our own meal and have our own celebration."

He looked wistful, then asked, "Could I join you? I've had invitations too but that sounds so nice. I'll bring champagne!"

I checked it out with Grace who said, "He can come if he does some of the cooking."

"I'll make South American rice," said Jamie, and did so. This seemed to take more effort that the rest of the meal but we all had fun. He'd collected Grace and her contribution to the feast and transported her in his Cadillac to my apartment. I'd bought a little Christmas tree and invited some neighbours, also business girls, to help trim it. For our feast, we stuffed ourselves with capon, fixings, and plum pudding, then Jamie and I drove Grace home and went down to St. Patrick's Cathedral where there was a midnight mass. We couldn't get in but we listened to the music from the steps outside.

Suddenly Jamie said, "Helenita, do you think I should get married?"

"Have you anyone in mind?" I asked. He had, I knew, many girlfriends.

He laughed, then said, "Several . . ."

"You'd better decide which one you really want," said I. I knew it wasn't me. He'd never let me think that our affair was more than a transitory one. Apart from other considerations, I was a divorcee and he was a devout though non-practising Roman Catholic. But I think we were both far more emotionally involved than we'd ever anticipated.

Once, when I'd gone out of town for a fortnight, he told me he'd been "very taste" in my absence.

"You mean 'chaste'?" I asked.

"Yes,'CCHHaste'! I've been faithful to you for six months, Helenita! That's a record, for me."

But, in his bedroom was a studio portrait of a youthful blonde inscribed in Spanish "I love you." Their families, he told me, had arranged they'd marry when she was old enough.

Jamie's brother Gabriel stayed with him in New York for several months to undergo some special surgery, and must have observed how close we were growing. Soon after this young man went back home, Jamie's intended arrived in town with her parents. She was eighteen and very pretty. He accompanied the family back to South America, got married immediately, and nine months later had a daughter christened Gloria Elena. From comments made by Seymour's staff, I gathered he'd settled down.

I really missed Jamie. I'd enjoyed his expensive lifestyle. One New Year's Eve he entertained elegantly at his apartment, the men in black ties, and with dancing. Mike O'Brien had invited me to join him at a celebration with some literary friends of his sister Kate, but he agreed to stop off at the Park Avenue party first and he was greatly impressed by Jamie whom I'd identified as a business acquaintance. Fortunately Mike was in a mellow mood, because when midnight struck and everyone kissed, I was yanked out of his arms by the host into a passionate Latin embrace!

Alhough I'd always known the affair with Jamie had no future, I suffered from the lack of his entertaining company and the most stimulating sex I'd ever known. I'd also enjoyed his friends. Once a group of us went downtown to a Spanish restaurant in the Village and in the wee sma' hours of a summer night and after much vino we piled into Jamie's Cadillac convertible and started driving rapidly up dark, deserted Fifth Avenue. I was jammed into the middle of the front seat next to the driver, and in the mirror we were observing the amorous exploits of the couple in the back seat when the young man on my other side remarked, "Jaime, I think that last traffic light was a little bit red."

No sooner noted than a policeman materialised out of nowhere and flagged us down. Eyeing us suspiciously, he asked Jamie for his driver's licence, then after this was most courteously produced, further identification, like proof of ownership for the Cadillac. This wasn't in the car. There was a cliff-hanging moment when we thought we'd all be taken off to a lockup, until the South American at my side produced, unasked, a business card which he handed to the cop. "Perhaps," said he languidly, "this will take care of the situation."

The policeman looked at it, then asked respectfully, "You, sir?" The young man nodded. "Okay," sighed New York's Finest, "Drive on."

"I work in my country's consulate," our saviour explained to me. "I've diplomatic immunity. I speed all the time, and the cops stop me. But they can't do anything about it."

Once when we were having dinner at Twentyone, I went to the ladies' room and there was Ethel Merman, the great musical comedy star whom I'd just seen in *Call Me Madame*. I observed how, after she'd washed her hands and fixed her face, she straightened up, took a breath and, as it were, drew herself into the character of a Broadway personality. Then she swept back into the restaurant and all eyes followed her as she joined her party.

A few drinks later, I went to the Ladies' again, and just for the hell of it, psyched myself into a celebrity before I started on my return trip to our table. Sure enough, the heads rose and people looked at me just as they'd done for Merman. I could almost hear them asking, "Who-in-hell is *she*?"

27

Enter – Finally – Our Hero!

In September, 1950, I was in the office at 270 Park when a young man erupted out of the elevator and approached my desk. He had a shock of reddish gold wavy hair, and the plaid jacket he wore with his grey flannel slacks was too wide in the shoulders and made him look even shorter than he was.

"*Manila Times?* Helen Leary?" He asked and when I nodded he continued, his words running together without pause, "My name is Charles Marwick. My family live across the street from yours in Edinburgh. Kenmure Melville told me to look you up in New York. I'm here to study at the Columbia School of Journalism."

Whew! Straight off the boat, thought I, and probably hungry. So, after learning that he was staying at the International YMCA, I invited him to supper at my apartment the following evening. By then I'd moved to York Avenue.

With a confident, attractive smile, he assured me he'd find his way there all right!

When he left, I phoned Conchita. "I seem to remember Carl's out of town. Can you come to my place tomorrow after work and chaperone me? I've invited a visiting Scotsman to dinner and don't want him to get the wrong ideas."

She came, and so did Charles, although he was late because he'd taken the wrong crosstown bus. He wasn't much of a drinker but he appreciated his food. I don't remember what I cooked but it was probably a chicken casserole, the fashionable fare in those days. We had a lively evening.

He was, I gathered, a good eight years younger than me and had been drafted into the Army straight out of Gordonstoun School, where one of his fellow pupils had been Prince Philip. Wounded in the knee during the Italian invasion, Charles had spent the remainder of the War running an army sick bay in the Orkneys, where the Marwick family had originated. His grandfather, father and an elder stepbrother had all been architects in Edinburgh and he had started out as a surveyor before realising he prefered a journalistic career and had applied to Columbia. Like me, he wanted to leave home. His mother had once lived in New York, so he knew a little about the city.

Our respective families on Church Hill hadn't got around to meeting but of course knew all about each other. One of his sisters had had friends at St.Trinnean's, so we had growing up in Morningside in common. Charlie had been studying in Paris when I was in Edinburgh in 1947.

It was a good thing that we met in America rather than in Scotland. We brought no family-engendered opinions to our friendship.

He'd arrived in New York too late to join the group just starting at the Columbia School of Journalism. So he'd applied for the Class of '52 and now planned to go up to Boston and try for a job on the *Christian Science Monitor*. He had sold freelance articles to that prestigious newspaper, but when he'd written and asked for regular employment, the reply had been that "without a personal interview," they couldn't promise anything.

"Anyway, I want to see some of the country," said Charlie.

A few days later, he phoned to tell me that the *Monitor*, possibly in mild shock similar to mine, had hired him as an apprentice reporter. "But I'll be back in New York this time next year," he added, "and I'll be in touch."

I wished him well, and he did call me when he eventually returned to town. He was pretty busy studying and didn't have much money but we saw each other now and again.

My greatest love became a part of my life so gradually I couldn't pinpoint when he became important to me. He was so much younger than I was, I considered him a nice friend rather than a marital prospect. Though I was now well over thirty I wasn't in any hurry to acquire another husband for I'd seen what becoming a suburban housewife did to my peers. I didn't want to abandon my career and carefree domestic living and I didn't care whether or not I remained childless.

There had been other major changes in my life. With the Korean War in the background, Cappy had moved back from Manila to New York for several months, bringing with him his three most valued possessions, his wife Virginia, Dandy their French poodle, and a prewar Mercedes Benz. This car had been stashed away in the Philippines by some prudent German. I had to cope with its return there after Cappy left.

Cappy, and I too, wanted to hire a US manager for Media Representatives and we had our eye on an outwardly able and amiable advertising man called Bill. He bore an uncanny physical resemblance to the successful presidential nominee 'Ike' Eisenhower. Bill worked for a large mercantile distributor, and had often been a useful source of helpful market information.

When my boss was in town, I tended to put my own life on hold and always got to work early. In those good old days, my mail would be delivered before I left home, so one morning I brought an unopened letter from Mummy to the office and read it after Cappy went off on a call. The news from home was that Littie had been having pains in his chest, and Dr. Boyd had checked him into the Glasgow Homœopathic Hospital for tests.

Mummy didn't sound worried and I don't usually get presentiments, but I picked up the phone and made my first transatlantic call. She wasn't at the hotel so I told the local operator to ring Dr. Boyd at his office on Sandyford Place.

"Hello, Helen!" said he, as calmly as though he talked across the Atlantic every day. Maybe he did. After all, he was on call for the Royal Family.

"Please give it to me straight," I said. "What's wrong? And should I come home?"

He was silent for a long moment then said, "You should definitely come home and before the end of the month. Your father has lung cancer. Treatment will just make things worse for him at the end. So I've advised your mother to take him home, make him comfortable there, and line up a local doctor to give him painkillers if necessary."

Would that all medical men gave such clear directives!

Cappy came back several hours later. I thought I'd calmed

down but he took one look at me and wanted to know what was wrong?

I told him. "And I don't know what to do. You need me here right now, while you're in town."

"Look, Helen," said he. "There's no question about what you have to do. You go to Scotland and if you haven't enough cash on hand for the air fare, you draw some out of the office account. I do need you here but we'll manage somehow."

I phoned Maud Lennox Personnel, and asked to speak personally to the boss. She remembered me at once, and came through with the perfect stand-in, a girl called Gert, who was attractive, capable, awfully nice and flexible enough so she didn't mind taking on a job of uncertain duration.

I left for Scotland the end of that week, having parked Topsy, a friend's cat I'd been boarding, with my old Gay Street neighbour, Jack Morris. While I was gone she presented him and his then wife with several kittens for which they found good homes. That was typical of New York.

Cappy and Ed Seymour saw me off on Scandinavian Airlines, pinning corsages onto my suit. I landed at Prestwick after a long night flight, took the airport bus to Glasgow and was dumped off outside a pub inhospitably labelled Closed. It was the Sabbath and no-one was around. I've often wondered what happened to the other jet-lagged, hungry passengers from America.

I'd left New York so quickly I hadn't had time to find out if anyone was meeting me in Glasgow, but on a hunch, I took a cab to the Bath Hotel and found that Mummy had come through from Edinburgh but had taken off for the bus terminal with Cousin George who was on the phone to the front desk almost as soon as I arrived there.

"Please bring me some black coffee," I begged the hall porter. It was one of my lowest moments in that traumatic trip. I was empty, both physically and emotionally.

"But, madam, you'll be having your lunch when Mrs. Lillie gets back and she's on her way the now!"

"Look," said I, "I haven't had any breakfast. If there's no coffee, surely you can find some orange juice?"

He did, and my blood sugar was starting to rise by the time

Mummy showed up with George who swept us firmly into the bar.

Instead of succumbing to the cancer within two weeks, Littie lasted over four months, didn't suffer much, and died quietly during a Sunday afternoon nap. By then, I'd gone back to New York. He and I had made peace with each other and Mummy and I had discussed the future. Some of her well-meaning friends so brainwashed me about my duty to her, I finally demanded to know if she wanted me to move back to Scotland?

"Of course not!" she said. "You have your own life and so have I."

I asked her what she planned to do immediately after Littie had gone? Bella Walker wanted her to go to Aberdeen and let herself be cossetted with breakfast in bed and complete rest.

"I'd much rather go to London and see some plays," said Mummy, who had dropped everything when she learned Littie's illness was terminal. She had become an active volunteer in two stimulating Edinburgh projects. One was the Davidson Clinic, the pioneer psychiatric centre started in 1939 by the late Dr. Winifred Rushforth, who became Mummy's friend and mine too. She wrote me a treasured letter about my first novel, *The Listening Silence* praising my characterization of "the poor neurotic minister – so true to life!" Dr. Rushforth also let slip that she was intrigued how such an introverted mother had raised such an outgoing daughter as I.

The Davidson Clinic flourished for thirty-five years, and in 1978 at the age of 93, Dr. Rushforth organised a successor to it named the Wellspring. In 1997, Prince Charles, the Prince of Wales, unveiled a memorial to this indomitable lady in George Square Gardens in Edinburgh.

Mummy also worked hard raising money for Lord MacLeod's Iona Foundation. She especially approved that in the beginning the enthusiastic young clerics who wanted to rebuild the Iona Abbey had to do this with their own hands, taking their orders from professional working men.

She was impressed by the stimulus the Iona-trained divines gave to the Church of Scotland. And so as Uncle Ned's trustee, she guided his money into this Foundation. She was en route to a coffee party with "the Iona ladies" when she had her last fatal stroke.

But this was years ahead. Meanwhile, Littie, I'm glad to say, had become so involved in Church of Scotland affairs, he was visited and prayed over by so many eminent divines Mummy worried about which one she should ask to handle his funeral service. I was quietly amused when two of these gentlemen discreetly alerted me to the best options in crematoriums through some professional gossiping during a pastoral visit.

My two uncles rallied around too, visiting regularly although at the time Uncle Bertie and Mummy were involved in some complicated feud. I was greatly touched when Uncle Jack offered to forego the highlight of his summer, a voyage around the Scottish coast to inspect the lighthouses. Uncle Jack was Sheriff of Fife and Kinross and, as such, a member of the Northern Lighthouse Commission. Every year the Sheriffs spent two weeks aboard the Commission's service vessel, a small ship called the *Pharos*, many of them taking full advantage of the free "waters" set out for daily refreshment.

Littie kept wanting to give me a present. What I really needed was some ready cash because I hadn't brought much with me. But I wouldn't ask him for money, or Mummy either, and towards the end of my stay I was brazenly collecting from women friends for hard-to-find items of clothing they wanted me to buy for them in New York. But, with some nudging from Mummy, I told Littie I needed a wrist watch, bought one downtown and charged it to him. I later lost it, though not by design.

Emotionally, I was in limbo that summer. It was pleasant despite the underlying sadness of Littie lying in bed waited on by nurses who annoyed Mrs. Sanderson. People were unfailingly kind but of course neither Mummy nor I felt free to accept much hospitality or to entertain.

I suspect my father lasted as long as he did because for the first time in his life he was the object of his family's total attention, something he'd never enjoyed before.

After two months, Cappy phoned me from London, where he and Virginia were en route back to Manila. He had hired Bill and Gert was coping well. I told him I didn't plan to stay till the end. There was no point and Mummy didn't seem to want it. As for Littie, I think he deluded himself that my returning to New York meant he'd taken a turn for the better.

Anyway, I left without outbursts of emotion. I'd tried to do the best I could as a loving daughter and I have few regrets.

28

Victoria and the Queen of Siam

Gert, my substitute at the office, stayed around briefly after my return and I asked her what she thought of Bill, our new US manager? She hesitated, then said, "He's pretty mixed up."

"In what way?" I queried.

"You'll see," she answered. All too soon I did.

He was used to being part of a large company where someone was always available to cover for him if necessary and do the little chores, like turning off lights at the end of the day and locking the office, which are indigenous to a small business. Although he made innumerable calls and presumably stimulated interest in the Far Eastern market, as a salesman, he couldn't nail down a contract. But our Filipino clients liked dealing with him because he was a man. They never seemed to realise I was the one who did all the extra-curricular jobs they requested. Bill got a trip to Manila and I never did. Maybe I would in the career climate of the 1990s. Certainly, today, I'd ask for it.

Bill was a pleasant guy, but though it wasn't immediately apparent, he was an alcoholic. Our pragmatic accountant had him sign a bunch of blank cheques, ostensibly because he might be out of town when bills and salaries had to be paid. "And he mightn't be sober enough to write his name," Leo remarked privately to me.

Bill and I got along all right at first, and I had a certain sympathy for him because I was so much closer to Cappy who obviously trusted my opinions over his.

But my professional life settled down reasonably well on return from Scotland and socially it improved.

At Jones Street I'd found cockroaches literally climbing the walls. Fortunately I had a realistic Jewish landlord who made no problems when I told him I had to move. I'd found a small but well-maintained apartment on York Avenue in the East 80s with a short enough stair so that Mummy could come for a visit. The wonderful Giraldi sisters helped me organise this apartment located in "Gracie Square on the wrong side of the tracks," as the previous tenant put it. When Mummy arrived, she had a good stimulating visit and adjusted amazingly to my life style. One Friday night I came home and started cleaning the bathroom after dinner. "Why don't you leave that job to the morning?" she asked.

"Because I'm in the mood," said I. "Tomorrow we're going out to Long Island and Sunday we're entertaining here!"

We also made a brief trip to Washington, DC, and toured it extensively. I've always been glad that she saw so much of the city where I later lived. It was a good visit, and I promised to make one to Edinburgh soon after.

While in Scotland, I'd read in Glasgow's tabloid the *Bulletin* some entertaining features about American life contributed by my university teacher, Dr. Catherine Gavin. She had married an American and moved to New York City where she worked for *Time*. I disagreed with one of her columns which I felt was unkind to the country for which I was homesick, so hunted out my old typewriter and sent a lengthy rebuttal to Alison Downie, her editor at the paper. A few weeks later, Dr. Gavin responded to this letter point by point in print and with her usual bite.

Back in New York, I wrote to her at *Time*, reminding her that I'd once been her student, and suggesting that after our "flyting" in print we should have a drink together. My phone rang early next day. "Helen!" said a well-remembered voice. "It's Catherine Gavin. When are you free for lunch?"

Like me, Catherine was divorced from a first husband. After a distinguished career as a war correspondent, she had married a handsome American from the Philadelphia Main Line called John Ashcraft, a publisher's rep, like Cappy, but with Europe as his territory. They lived in the East 70s not far from me.

"Teach" was determined I'd marry again. So to activate the available prospects, I gave another New Year's Eve party, at the York Avenue apartment. Mike was invited, so was Jere Faison and as something of an afterthought I included Charlie Marwick,

204

now in New York at Columbia University.

Most of the male guests showed up clutching brown bags which held as often as not, a pint of Imperial rye whisky. Close to midnight, however, my Scotsman arrived with a briefcase. He set it down at the door, opened it and as he produced the inevitable paper sack, told me,"Put that aside and we'll drink it later."

He had brought a bottle of Drambuie, small but authentic! And I'd just time to note that this man had some style when the radio announced the New Year and up the stair came John Ashcraft, who as a tall darkish man, had been promenaded up and down the street by his Scottish spouse until it was time to first foot me.

My other recollection of that party is that Mike O'Brien liked Charlie and rashly offered to give him a lift home in his cab. But by the end of the evening my Irish pal had drunk enough to get other ideas and started trying to outstay everyone. Finally we were down to himself and Charlie, who was starting to mutter about leaving when my foot came down on his and he got the message. Eventually Mike gave up, and when they left together I collapsed thankfully onto my small studio couch and slept out what was left of the night by myself.

That summer, the Ashcrafts moved into a charming little house in Old Greenwich, Connecticut, and one Saturday I took Charlie out to visit them. John made a mean dry martini and Catherine was a fine cook. At one point, she hauled me into the kitchen and said, "Now look, Helen! Here's a man who's smart and intelligent and nice and he's not neurotic! Go after him!"

"But he's so much younger than me!"

"John's younger than I am too. Age doesn't matter. This chap's attracted to you."

"Well, he's a good cat sitter," said I, hedging.

"And how many men are prepared to take on a woman with two cats?"asked Teach. When I'd acquired my second feline, she'd asked me over the phone, "Don't you ever want to get married again?"

For shortly after I moved to York Avenue, Grace had told me I should get myself a pet, pointing out that I was always talking about Dennis, and missed Topsy who, alas, had had to be despatched to the Great Cattery in the Sky after coming too early to motherhood.

Grace had friends with kittens available for adoption. Their mother was a handsome animal. When I asked her name I was told, "Caroline. You know. Caroline Chapman Catt." An emiment nineteenth century feminist no less!

They also had a toddler who, throughout my visit, was constantly trying to grab the tiny furry objects scampering around the floor. One was a calico with big green eyes in a white face. She was so small she could sit on my preferred hand. During the sixteen years we shared, she always hated to be picked up and hid whenever children were around. I knew why.

I called her Victoria Regina MacArthur because the day we met, Bill and I had closed the office early to join the crowds of New Yorkers lining Fifth Avenue to welcome of the saviour of the Philippines, newly fired by President Truman. All I saw of General Douglas MacArthur was a huge hand raised in a victorious gesture as the parade passed me by, but it was a memorable moment!

Shortly after Victoria joined me at York Avenue, the editor of the *Manila Times* came to town. David Boguslav was Russian by birth though he'd grown up in America and once worked for the *Chicago Tribune*. His adored wife had died from privation in a Japanese concentration camp during the occupation of the Philippines so he hated all "Nips." He was a lonely man with only cats for company at home where he spent his time listening to music, reading and drinking.

He was a great newspaperman. Each day, according to Vicente Guzman, the political reporter, when Dave arrived at the Manila office armed with a pint of whisky to sustain him through putting the paper to bed, word would get around that he was in the building and everyone would start pulling together.

When in New York he took me to many theatres. It was the great era of the musical, like *Carousel* and *Moulin Rouge*. Dave drank far too much but credited alcohol with saving his life. Once, he told me, he'd come to work feeling so ill he brought a quart of whisky with him instead of the usual pint but even that hadn't doused the pain which made him quit early, to the consternation of his staff. When he reached home, he found the publisher's sister, a formidable lady, waiting for him with a prominent local doctor in tow. "Examine him!" she ordered. Despite protests, Dave then found himself rushed to a hospital and when he came out of the anaesthetic learned he'd had a ruptured appendix and should have been dead.

"But there was so much hooch in your system, you were disinfecting yourself," the surgeon told him.

Dave fell in love with Victoria. One night he phoned me at home and informed me I was going to have to cope with problems of racial integration. "What d'you mean?" I asked. He'd obviously had a few.

"I'm down in Macy's and I've just bought Vicky a little sister. She's Siamese. I'll bring her into the office tomorrow."

Next morning, he turned up with a squawking bundle under one arm. The kitten had huge crossed blue eyes and beautiful buttery fur which turned dark brown around her face and legs.

"What should I call her?" I asked.

"Why don't you call her after the mother of the King of Siam? I met her once – danced with her. She was a nice lady."

"And her name?"

"Geez, I've no idea."

I phoned the *New York Times* Information Services and after a remarkably brief wait, was told the Queen Mother of Thailand was called Sgi Wag Wan. When this lady died in 1996, I discovered her name was more properly spelt Sangwal. Too late for my wee pussycat who only lived till 1966. The researcher spelled it out for me but didn't say how to pronounce it. I just called her See Wah Wan.

Sig Wag Wan was man crazy and would complain to me if there was no male company at a weekend. If a date showed up, she'd unabashedly study him and if she felt he was worth the effort, she'd introduce herself. Mike O'Brien couldn't stand her, referred to her as "that little weasel." He professed to dislike cats although he made an exception of "your charmin' Victoria."

Jere Faison was once sounding off in his mellifulous voice about some obstetrical problem to an admiring audience of my female friends when he looked down and found Sgi Wag Wan rolling sensuously on her back at his feet, her paws hovering in midair, her eyes half-closed. "You depraved cat!" he exclaimed, laughing so hard he lost the thread of his lecture.

Long before I did, Sgi Wag Wan had narrowed down her choice of a permanent male room-mate to Charlie Marwick. Several times when I went to Scotland he stayed in my apartment, and after our marriage, she made it plain that she was now his cat. I'm quite sure she believed he moved in permanently on her account.

"Vicky-My-Pet" liked Charlie too but she and I had been single together and we always remained close. Indeed, she took such good care of me I can't understand how people can claim that cats are insensitive? Even Mummy, who professed not to like cats ("because they kill the birds") was charmed by Vicky, in whom she recognised another lady. Once I had such bad flu I stayed in bed all day, waves of fever rolling through me. Vicky never left my side, prodding me now and again so I'd open my eyes and reassure her I was all right.

A few years after Charlie and I were married, when we were living in the last and nicest of our New York apartments, 413 Bleeker Street, there came a weekend when we thought we could sleep late. But at 6 o'clock that Saturday morning Victoria had other ideas for us. She jumped up onto the bed and started prodding me with her paws. I regret to say I pushed her away and pulled the sheet over my head.

She then went to work on Charlie who got up to find out what was bothering her? She escorted him to a small back room overlooking a roof area we shared with the building next door.

Charlie took one look out of our window then hurried back and told me to get some clothes on because smoke was belching out of the adjacent apartment! I was pulling on a sweater and pants when a fireman knocked on our door and told us to be ready to get out at short notice. In the end we didn't need to but I never ignored Vicky's warnings again.

Once Bill rang me at home and started yelling at me in a drunken rage. I hung up on him and was in tears when Mike phoned. He told me to mix myself a drink, and when he'd done the same he'd analysed the situation "like a hard-headed banker." His opinion was that the outburst was a guilty transference on Bill's part. Mike urged me to cable Cappy, which I did, from my home telephone.

I then relaxed enough to go to sleep but throughout the night, was wakened by little gentle kneadings. I'd open my eyes to find Vicky's concerned little cat face peering into mine. She never left my side until I went to work next morning, arriving ahead of Bill.

I found a cable marked personal from Cappy telling me to "unworry repeat unworry" myself, and to "put everything on hold until Poppa gets back" to New York, on a planned trip.

The day he arrived, Cappy contrived to take me out to lunch without Bill, sat me up at a bar and said, "Now talk!" I did, trying hard to be charitable.

Next morning, Bill wasn't at work by 9.45 which wasn't very smart.

"Is he always this late?" Cappy asked, pacing the floor.

"When he misses the earlier train from Long Island," I said.

"Well, look, when he does show up, get lost and leave me alone with him."

I had cleaned out a huge cupboard stacked with old newspapers by the time Cappy sounded an all clear.

"I fired him," he told me. "We had quite a showdown. Of course when I raised the business of his drinking, he accused you of telling on him. I said that wasn't the case, I'd heard it from one of his best buddies on Madison Avenue."

We then hired a brilliant, crazy guy called Talcott. He was allegedly completing a PhD at Columbia but wanted a part-time job. Part of that part time he too was drunk but even so, he could accomplish things and though he often infuriated me, I adored him!

Periodically he'd decide to straighten himself out and once went for psychological testing, at considerable expense to his family. The day after, he came in obviously anxious to talk about it so I suggested we go out for coffee. "They told me," said Talcott, as soon as we were alone, "that I had an IQ close to genius." I nodded in full agreement. "But – I scored the highest marks they'd ever had for sheer confusion."

I asked him what else was new and what else?

He looked sheepish. "They also told me I had a breast fixation."

"You mean to say you spent all that money to find that out!" I exclaimed. "Just look at your girl friends! They're all incredibly stacked!"

One weekend he made love to a girl on a patch of poison ivy and phoned on Monday to say his doctor didn't think he'd be back at work for three weeks. "Call Phyllis Lintott." I advised. "She takes some homœopathic stuff for that kind of rash."

Before the end of the week, he walked into the office, beaming. "The Rhus Tox did it," he said.

One Saturday, Talcott took me to lunch at the White Horse Tavern on Eighth Avenue. At a table, staring into a mug of beer, was the most hungover man I'd ever seen. "Hi," said Talcott, and as we sat down beside him he added, "Helen, this is . . . mumble mumble." It started with a D. Another man joined us, and introduced himself as Oscar Williams, an anthologist. We were half way through our meal before I realised that the miserable individual was the great Welsh poet Dylan Thomas!

He didn't say a word until the conversation turned to a sensational murder case then going through the British courts. Then he began to talk, telling us some fascinating things that hadn't been in the papers. As he warmed to the subject, he started sipping his beer, and Oscar Williams immediately signed to the bartender who set a nice healthy sandwich down in front of him. Without apparently noticing Thomas ate it and looked a lot better.

When we left, I castigated my co-worker for not telling me who the celebrity was! "I wanted to watch it dawning on you," said Talcott.

I still have the paperback anthology of poetry Mr. Williams gave me, autographed by the poet and himself.

If I seem to have dwelt a long time on these happenings, it's because they were typical of New York in the 1950s and of the relaxed way women were becoming accepted as business equals.

It was also the era of Christian Dior's New Look, the most

elegant and becoming feminine clothes in many a year. I achieved my first New Look dress a few months after I went to work for Cappy. Then I bought a long black winter coat which covered all my short skirted suits and felt fashionable again.

Most of the space buyers in the advertising agencies were female – although the account executives were still predominantly male. And I well remember a speech made to the Advertising Women of New York by Harriett Raymond Stemmler, then one of the highest ranking women on Madison Avenue. "If I'd been a man, I'd probably have been vice president of my agency," she concluded.

29

Changes, Changes

Cappy thought I was paying too much money for too little space on York Avenue and said I ought to look for a place in the Village. His ex-wife, Jane, still stayed in his Minetta Street apartment during his absences in Manila but there had been a sticky incident when a woman in the real estate company handling the property began suspecting the occupancy was illegal and threatened eviction unless Jane handed over $200, a lot of money in those days.

She asked me if Cappy would pay this? Incensed, I went to the New York rent control authorities and told them (nearly) everything. I didn't mention Jane was paying for the convenience of staying in her ex-husband's apartment while he was out of the country, but the sympathetic City employee I consulted probably figured this out. However, he instructed me how to write a letter stating she was there "dusting the furniture" and he'd notify the rental people to lay off.

A few days later, the manager of that company, a Mr. Tara, phoned me at the office and said Jane's occupancy was secure but he'd incurred some legal fees in the process of arranging this and would be sending me the bill. I told him I had no authority to pay it and hung up. ·

"So Cappy should pay for his own eviction?" commented Leo the accountant who was in the office at the time.

I wrote to my boss in Manila, and he responded with a marvellously polite letter to Mr. Tara, telling him, in essence, what he could do. Then, on his next trip to New York, Cappy went to see him and offered to increase his rental payments. Back at the office he asked me, "Why don't you get Tara to find you a reasonable place in the Village?"

"He'd see me in Hell first," said I.

"You're wrong. He has considerable respect for you. You called his bluff and beat him hands down. He asked me about you and sent you his regards. Call him up right now, sweetie."

Again, only in New York! Mr. Tara found me my all-time favourite apartment, half of the third floor at 224 West 11th Street off Seventh Avenue at the corner where West 4th illogically intersects itself twice. The property belonged to an Episcopal church, St. John's-in-the-Village, and the pastor, the Reverend Charles Howard Graf, lived downstairs with his wife and dog. The dark stairs had an ancient musty smell I presumed was the odour of sanctity.

I had a big living room with a functional fireplace and two sunny windows looking down on an enclosed garden, built by a nineteenth century pastor with a private income. There was a small bedroom, an even smaller kitchen and a bathroom with a skylight. The whole place needed painting but the shabbiness increased its charm.

My first misgiving about my landlord came when he learned I had two cats. They might smell, he told me, so he couldn't have us as tenants. I responded that he'd already accepted my down payment so couldn't renege on the lease. I added that altered felines were odourless and supplied the name of the veterinarian who'd operated on Vicky. After checking with him, Father Graf dropped his objections, and I moved in, but I was always suspicious of him and with good reason.

For some inexplicable reason, while I was unpacking, I kept humming, "By the waters of Babylon, we sat down and wept." Maybe it was because I'd just joined the Madison Avenue Presbyterian Church on East 73rd Street, and the Reverend George Arthur Butterick, a very different pastor from Father Graf, had encouraged me to join the choir there. Francis and I had occasionally gone to services at this church though I'd never belonged to it or indeed to any religious establishment. Curiously, this had been omitted during my upbringing. I was also suspicious of organised religion, believing the old Scots saying that "you should never see the legs of a minister."

But my friend Grace had had a nervous breakdown, tried to commit suicide, and wound up in Bellevue Hospital. Her

213

psychoanalyst said she didn't want people to know, but I felt someone should visit her. That Sunday after the church service I asked Dr. Butterick if I could talk to him? He'd never met me before but that made no difference to his warm response. He told me to follow my heart and go to see her, adding he'd visit her himself if I thought it would help. Later, alas, she succeeded in ending her troubled life. As I grieved, I was so impressed and sustained by Dr. Butterick's practical Christianity, I joined his church. He was one of the greatest preachers of his generation and a much-loved man, who also had a wonderful sense of humour.

The choir was both an educational and a fascinating social outlet for me, and I made several friends with whom I'm still in touch. I discovered some magnificent music, notably the Mozart *Requiem*. Charlie Marwick often picked me up and escorted me downtown on the subway after rehearsals and several times we ran into an overweight tenor who for a while was a soloist. This man asked me once, "Are you involved with that little guy who sees you home?" I looked straight at his midriff and said, "Yes. I prefer quality to quantity."

A woman friend once asked me if I was religious and off the top of my head I replied, "No, except in foxholes." The time spent in these seems to increase with age. On balance, I have more belief than unbelief in the teachings of the Bible.

When Dr. Butterick retired, the Madison Avenue church imported a tall, handsome war hero, the Reverend David H.C.Read. He had been pastor to the Royal Family in Scotland and on religious holidays wore a dramatic red robe. "Just playing Father Christmas," he remarked to us before his first Yuletide service.

So, between the Kirk, and new friends like the Ashcrafts, my life was widening out. I was also involved after hours with business groups like the Advertising Women of New York. I was also active in the Export Advertising Association and I wrote an article on the Philippines for their trade organ. Talcott remarked that my clichés were chosen with more discrimination that those in the rest of the magazine.

During its seven years' existence, Media Reps sold the Far Eastern market so successfully that the centre of business moved out to Manila where Cappy and Virginia were well settled. The New York office had become redundant.

In other words, I was going to be unemployed again but, I hoped, in different circumstances from 1947. I was fancy free in my private life and now believed in myself and my ability. I also had good, though off-beat expertise to offer prospective hirers. The snag about that was, of course, that to personnel people I'd been a glorified secretary. The title of Administrative Assistant wasn't around in those days. However, by the late 1950s, women were acceptable in middle management even if few made it through the glass ceiling to the top. But I had hopes for job leads through the Advertising Women of New York and I had many contacts for inside information on companies.

Louise Giraldi had also put me in touch with a pioneer career counsellor, Anne Heywood, author of a book called *There's a Right Job for Every Woman*. She lived in New York and acted as adviser and sometimes wailing wall for people like me who wanted to break through the secretarial barrier. The art of making career changes was relatively new then and there were few of the support groups and networks that, today, help to reinforce morale in the jobless.

The break with Cappy was painful for both of us. He so agonised about my future I finally blew up at him and for the first and only time burst into floods of tears in the office, screaming at him that I couldn't get my mind onto job-hunting when he was so busy worrying about me.

The last day we were together at 270 Park Avenue, clearing out files and cupboards, was a Saturday. No one else was around until, of all people, my ex-husband Francis Leary, briefly returned from France, walked in looking for me. I got rid of him by suggesting a drink later in the day.

"What was the matter with Capotosto?" he asked me that evening. "He acted as though I wasn't there!"

As I went down in the elevator from the seventh floor that afternoon, I couldn't help but think of all the farewell parties I'd put on for other people and felt, like T.S. Elliot that,

> This is the way the world ends
> Not with a bang but a whimper.

215

30

Avon Calling!

Self-pity is a negative and unattractive emotion, destructive to any self-promotional campaign. Besides, with hindsight it is usually uncalled for. In my own case, Cappy was instrumental in getting me one really good job and it had been time for me to move on anyway.

The best way to start a job search is to stimulate one's natural curiosity about both people and companies. You never know what this may lead into. One of the first large corporations I approached was Avon Products, then the world's biggest cosmetic company, selling its merchandise exclusively through representatives. Avon Ladies traditionally rang doorbells to locate customers, a sales technique better suited to small towns that to cities. Several months into my job search, an employment agency sent me on an interview to Avon, then about to introduce its cosmetics into Manhattan.

I knew a lot about the company's history because I'd researched it with a friend from ANWY. Avon in those days had no international advertising division and we thought we could set one up for them. This pipedream never materialised but what I'd learned while working on it gave me an edge on the competition for the position now available. I made a confident pitch, and was downcast when they hired someone else.

But in career-hunting you never know what may happen next. After all, I found my longest-lasting and most rewarding job by sweeping into the wrong office. So I shouldn't have been surprised when, three weeks after turning me down, Avon's Manhattan manager phoned, all sweetness and light, and invited me to join her staff. The woman she'd hired, I learned later, had walked out in a frustrated rage and I soon appreciated why!

Becoming a cog in the wheels of a huge stratified corporation was a cultural shock for me after running an office on my own. I was now an organisation woman and not expected to show initiative. I discovered this when Patricia, my boss was on holiday, there was some hitch in deliveries and I phoned headquarters upstairs for the names of people to pressure.

"Field Managers Don't Call the Factory!" a prune-voiced secretary told me.

"But the reps need their orders filled!" I protested.

"It's the Manager's job to investigate."

"She's out of town until the end of the month."

Eventually I got the information I needed but after much time had been wasted.

However, if sales fell off as they did in early summer, it was my fault. Pat called me in and censured me before going off to lunch with some top brass. I did some checking and found half my reps had been on holiday. But the others

> "I admired the Puerto Rican women who held full-time jobs in sweat shops, kept house for large families and still sold lots of cosmetics – they were colourful and pretty, like their tiny apartments where there was often an idle man watching television and drinking beer."

had all increased the size of their orders. I wrote Pat a memo on this and she used my information to protect her own beautiful skin upstairs.

I spent a year as an Avon field manager, working strenuously but having fun too. I gave a standard sales interview, keeping up my own interest by tailoring it to my prospects. When my recruits needed money for something specific, like a move to the suburbs, they did well, selling Avon Products as a secondary career to their job. But bored housewives, widows or individuals who distrusted people or weren't interested in cosmetics seldom applied themselves. They just wanted a manager who'd listen to their complaints until they dropped out.

I made field trips to offices and demonstrated the products.

And upon request I'd visit prospects at home which took me to New York neighbourhoods like the Lower East side I'd never seen before and wouldn't dare visit nowadays. In the late 1950s, it didn't occur to me to be apprehensive and only once did I hesitate to go into a building, past a drunk sitting on the dark stair.

I admired the Puerto Rican women who held full-time jobs in sweat shops, kept house for large families and still sold lots of cosmetics ("But only to Spanish people, please!"). They were colourful and pretty, like their tiny apartments where there was often an idle man watching television and drinking beer.

As part of my training I'd had to ring door bells and did so at my old apartment house, 6 Jones Street where I knew the superintendent. In mid-morning, the only tenants home were scruffy young men who reported that "the lady of the house" wouldn't be home until after six.

One Friday, when I had a dinner date, I scheduled an early afternoon home interview on West 11th Street near my apartment. My prospect was a depressed woman who kept talking about "my group." When I asked its name, she said, "Alcoholics Anonymous. I hope you don't hold it against me that I'm an alcoholic." I didn't, and she then gave me such an inspirational harangue that when I left, at 4.30, I was so uplifted I decided to make another call.

Thumbing through my notebook, I found a good, steady rep who'd always come to the Avon office for follow-up. She'd described herself as the manageress of a restuarant, which turned out to be a waterfront bar and grill.

As I came through the door, she set two bottles of booze on the counter and greeted me with, "Great to see you, Mrs. Leary! Whisky or gin? It's on the house!"

So, straight from my AA prospect, I sipped Scotch throughout our sales briefing which intrigued the longshoremen at the bar. My rep did her Avon business when she delivered lunches to business girls working near by.

Our Manhattan Sales Office had an efficient administrative assistant and, by the time I left, four field managers, one of whom spoke Spanish. Pat ran training courses and was our liaison with company headquarters upstairs. Eventually she promoted herself into a vice presidency. We were a congenial group but I didn't want to make a long-term career with Avon, so quit after a year, saying I had to visit my mother in Scotland. Pat wanted to hold my job open for me, but I was relieved when the higher-ups vetoed this idea.

I came back from Edinburgh full of confidence. Mummy was enjoying her widowhood, busy with many worthwhile projects. I had met the Marwick family across the street and liked them.

But, in New York, the job market was tight again. I eventually found work selling space on commission for an elegant little publication put out by a society organisation, the Junior League, and with some nice advertisers. Unfortunately, I wasn't told they'd only pay me commissions on new business so I had a lean winter.

Charlie, now gainfully employed, came in one Friday evening and handed me fifty dollars. "You must be a bit short of cash," he said. "This is a loan and I don't want it repaid until you find a better job."

That kind of thoughtfulness increased my fondness for him. After graduating from the Columbia Journalism School, he'd gone to work for a theatrical press agent so got free tickets to Broadway shows. The one I best remember was *The Crucible*, Arthur Miller's version of the Salem witch trials. Charlie liked me to dress up for these performances. He himself was now well-dressed too.

I was still dating Mike and Jere and a few stray males but after Charlie moved into an apartment round the corner from me on Bank Street, he become my regular escort. One Friday we went to a movie straight after work, ate, then returned to West 11th Street for a nightcap.

The key my elderly cleaning lady left under the doormat wasn't there, my apartment door was unlocked and some clothing, jewellery and my typewriter were gone!

The burglars had drunk – and spilled – some orange juice but left a bottle of gin untouched. They'd turned out some drawers and left my underwear all over the floor but though they'd taken three newly-ironed summer dresses hanging up in the bathroom, they hadn't touched anything in the closets, like my Scottish suits and a fur coat.

Amateurs, probably teenagers, but to find that strangers have been in your home pawing through your intimate possessions is almost like rape. Father Graf wasn't in but his assistant came up and helped me cope with the police. A young couple next door came came by and we wound up drinking the gin and having quite a pleasant evening. But as everyone started to leave, I realised some unknowns had access to my apartment. I couldn't get my locks changed so late even in the Village.

"Would you like me to spend the night?" Charlie asked. "I'd sleep in the small room."

I thought that unlikely. One of the charms of our relationship was that, though we were attracted to each other, he'd never tried to go beyond some affectionate kisses.

But I was so frightened, I agreed to his suggestion and he collected his shaving gear and pyjamas from nearby Bank Street while I made up the single bed.

To my amazement, he spent the whole night in it, leaving me alone in my usual sleeping place, the livingroom couch adjacent to the radio. No other man of my acquaintance would have been such a gentleman! I was enormously relieved. Our pleasantly uncomplicated friendship hadn't been disturbed. My liking and respect for Charlie doubled. Too bad he was so much younger than me.

Next morning, I made us breakfast and, as he headed downstairs en route to his own place, he met my landlord. To the pure all things may be pure, but when, at a later date, we called upon the Reverend Charles Howard Graf to tell him we were getting married his comment was, "Well. It's about time."

31

Even the Hudson River
Couldn't Quench Love

I wasn't making any money at the *Junior League Magazine* selling advertising on commission only, so I resumed reading the Help Wanted advertisements and studying business publications for possible job openings. When I read that *Family Circle* had promoted its Chicago sales manager to be a vice president in New York. I wrote to congratulate him and added that if he wished to hire his own staff, I was available.

In a prompt reply, he invited me to phone for an appointment. A pleasant guy, he looked over my magazine and said, "This is a nice little book. Why d'you want to leave it?"

"Because," said I, "I could make more money for the same amount of effort working for you."

He then told me the editor of the mail order section, known professionally as Evelyn Kent, wanted to replace her male salesman with a woman who'd be more knowledgeable about household items and gadgetry. He sent us two "girls" off to lunch to get acquainted. In other words, he let her do the hiring.

'Evelyn' and I liked each other. She said she "hoped to have a baby" and wanted to be sure she could leave her department in more concerned hands than those of her current salesman who considered his job a mere stepping stone to better things. I thought her pregnancy was still in the planning stage, but the Monday I started work, she showed up in a smart maternity dress!

Cappy was in town, on a quick trip from Manila. He still had desk space at 270 Park, and after my lunch on *Family Circle*, I called him from the lobby of the Waldorf Astoria, where the *Junior League* had its office.

"Look, Cappy," said I, "I'm in line for a job I want. I gave you

221

as a reference and the man who'll hire me is in his office right now. Please give him a call. You can make the excuse that you're only in town for a few days."

"Sure, sweetie," said my former boss. "Just tell me what you want me to say."

I filled him in, gave him the number, then, remembering his procrastinating habits, I added, "Phone right now, then call me back. I'm in a booth but I'll wait."

I gave him the two numbers then hung up, and sat there crossing my fingers. After an interminable time and many dirty looks from people who wanted to use that telephone, it rang and Cappy said, "I told the guy you were a super saleswoman ... added that if we hadn't closed up here, you'd still be working for me and if I ever opened an office in New York again, I'd rehire you. Let me know what happens."

By the time I'd made it up to the *Junior League* on the fiftieth floor, there was a message for me to call the *Family Circle* number. Back downstairs I went, and then returned and handed in my resignation.

My only regret was that I no longer worked in one of New York's nicest hotels. The Waldorf Astoria had a comfortable and reasonably priced café where I and a fellow-saleswoman on the magazine had business conversations we didn't want the snoopy secretary to overhear. We got to know the elevator operators and the doormen too.

For several years, my second cousin, Nancy Donaldson, had come down from Canada for an Easter visit. We'd been pen pals as children and met in Montreal where she was studying dietetics during my first year in North America. Nancy's first trip to New York came soon after I moved to York Avenue. One of her Scottish aunts was a militant teetotaller and Mike O'Brien wanted to take us out, so one of the first things I had to find out about the adult Nancy was her attitude to alcohol? "I'm all for it," said she, "I hope you are too." Then, and in later years, we'd shop for summer clothes at discount houses like S.Klein on the Square, boosting our energy with Daiquiri breaks.

The year I worked at the *Junior League Magazine*, Nancy arrived mid-morning on Good Friday. She left her suitcase at my office, collected a key to my apartment, and took off sightseeing. After work, I lugged her bag to the elevator where it was promptly picked up by a Waldorf employee who asked if I needed a cab? I did, and he offered to find one for me. It was a rush hour on a holiday weekend and it took him a good twenty minutes. Meanwhile, I'd been checking my change and found I'd nothing smaller than a twenty dollar bill. Honesty seemed the best policy so, as he escorted me to the taxi, I opened my purse, showed him all I had, and asked him – please, please! – to come see me on Monday in my office.

He just laughed. "My dear, I wouldn't accept a tip from you. You work in the Waldorf and so do I. It's on the house." And every time we ran into each other after that, he'd give me a wonderful smile.

Back in the 1960s, there were few female space salesmen. *Family Circle* had had one in Chicago, but I was the pioneer on the New York staff. After my first sales meeting a male co-worker took me out for coffee and gave me a pep talk. Its thrust was that I mustn't let the side down when making up my expense accounts. I'd already been told this by Evelyn Kent. "The boys," she said, "are quite generous with themselves."

I had an allowance for a car which I neither owned nor needed and this money I used for taxis to which I became more accustomed than the frugal Charlie Marwick who was so intrigued by New York's public transportation he once travelled around the grotty Astoria subway line "just to see where it went."

He hadn't stayed long with the press agent, having found a better job as an assistant publications editor at the New York Academy of Sciences. From there he went to work as a science reporter on a publication directed at the medical profession called *Medical News*. Later he joined *Medical World News* and eventually moved to be the Washington representive for the news section of the prestigious *Journal of the American Medical Association*. His career in other words followed a consistent and upward pattern.

When I joined *Family Circle*, he was at the Academy where he'd made friends with an old bachelor called Frank Furness who loved to listen to music and sail on the Hudson River. Frank had a long canoe with a sail and an outboard engine, which he kept at a rundown boathouse off Dyckman Street above the George Washington Bridge. Charlie started going out with Frank on weekends and in due course I was invited to join them.

I had never learned to swim but I reasoned that Frank was an old pro in the water and Charlie had studied sailing in school at Gordonstoun so could be trusted to save me in an emergency.

"Wait till you see the boat!" he'd warned me. But once I got in, I found that being seated so close to the water, even though it was obviously filthy, gave me confidence. We sailed across the Hudson River and picnicked in beautiful woodlands on a little beach called Lambiers. Frank called it Lambs' Beers. He was a vegetarian and didn't drink but Charlie brought plenty of cold cuts and beer.

Frank ceased to be teetotal after a narrow escape from drowning during a midwinter sail. His canoe overturned upon hitting a block of floating ice. The New Jersey park police managed to drag him out of the river, salvaging his boat and much of his gear too. But after thawing out in a hospital, Frank went home, and couldn't sleep or get warm. Someone suggested he try taking a drink. He bought some Drambuie which worked so well he decided to investigate the effect of other liquors. From that time on, he always had some booze stashed away on his boat and sipped beer while he sailed.

We had one really scary experience on that canoe. During an autumn weekend, a thunderstorm blew up unexpectedly while we were having lunch on the New Jersey shore. We packed up fast and took off. The waves were enormous. All I could see if I opened my eyes was Charlie moving back and forth using his weight to balance the boat while Frank, thoroughly enjoying himself and looking like the Old Man of the Sea, handled the sail. We went straight across the river into calm waters some distance from the boathouse. At that point, I found my voice and asked to be put ashore.

In the early Spring of 1956, I had a dinner party at 224 West 11th Street. Charlie came, and so did Carl and Conchita Messinger who brought with them her pre-teen son Michael, now arrived from the Philippines. Since they were such gourmets and had shown me so much hospitality, I cooked an elegant meal. We had dry martinis to start, white wine with the chicken, and for dessert the fashionable Irish Coffee. Michael of course wasn't allowed to sample this so amused himself trying to play with my two cats, neither of whom trusted children. The Messinger family then went home, but Charlie stayed behind to help me clear up.

Neither one of us was entirely sober and as we were stacking the dishes in my tiny kitchen, I suddenly cried out, "Where's Vicky?"

My favourite feline sometimes ran out of the door onto the landing and had to be caught or chased back home. I was always terrified she'd go down the stairs and outside onto the street where she'd get lost or be killed by a car. She was also good at hiding herself in the apartment, so I was frantically pulling out chairs and the couch when Charlie called from the other room, "She's here!"

I rushed in and found him lying on his stomach on the floor peering under the bed. Dropping down beside him, I looked too, and there, in the farthest back corner, sat Victoria Regina. Her paws were tucked neatly under her and she was eyeing us challengingly.

All of a sudden Charlie turned to me and asked, "Will you marry me?"

I've no idea what I said. I had a confused idea that he must have had too much to drink. I knew I had. Somehow I got it across that we'd have to talk about it later and he went home to Bank Street. Next morning, tired and hungover, I wondered if I'd dreamed the whole thing, but during the days that followed, I realised I had to know my own mind by the next time we met.

He had other girlfriends. I'd met some of them and they were very chic and also nice. If I turned down his proposal, the chances were we'd start seeing less of each other and in time he'd move out of my life. Could I get along without him?

The answer was a resounding no, and not because, like previous generations of women, I needed a man for security and prestige. I enjoyed his company and the things we did together, like sailing. But it was more than that. I must be in love with him although the way I felt was quite different from past experiences.

And although he was far more mature than other men I'd known, he was still eight years younger than me, which hadn't fazed Catherine Gavin but bothered me a lot.

The following Friday evening, he came round to my apartment and after we'd had the first sip of a drink he said, "Well. Have you thought over what we talked about last week?"

I had. By way of token hesitation because of the age factor, I pointed out we mightn't have children . . . "Don't worry," said Charlie, "my brother's got six."

32

Happy, With Problems

Before that momentous evening, I'd made plans to take my vacation early and join Mummy for a trip to Italy. My most hectic season as a space salesman came during the summer selling the November issue of the magazine with all the Christmas advertising. The thinnest month was always July and that year I made more fruitless calls on prospects than ever before.

Mail order clients in Manhattan were frequently small companies and their businesses were scattered throughout the Lower East Side. The week before I was due to take off I was so depressed that, late one afternoon I called on a firm run by two brothers of Italian descent who'd always been so courteous I knew that at least I wouldn't get a brushoff.

After I'd told him about my upcoming trip, the one who saw me asked, "Which issue of your magazine are you selling now?" When I told him July he inquired, "Do you have any space left?"

I'd nearly all my space but of course wouldn't admit this so just said, "I could still work something in for you."

"Let me talk to my brother," said he, and disappeared into a backroom. A few minutes later he came back and handed me a contract for nearly a whole page in our national edition!

So I took off for Italy in good spirits, planning to tell Mummy about my forthcoming marriage at the proper moment. I didn't know how she'd react. She wanted me to be happy, of course, but she was ambivalent about marriage as an institution and I knew she'd think Charlie was too young. But at least she knew and liked his family. He'd bought me a pretty little silver ring set with a moonstone as a token engagement present. Mummy admired it and I got as far as telling her he'd given it to me but that was all. We were having such a good time, seeing Florence, Naples, Capri and Rome, where every handsome man reminded me of

Cappy, I didn't want to introduce anything potentially controversial.

Charlie had dovetailed his holiday with mine so that he could take care of my cats during my absence. Then he, in turn, took off for Scotland. One evening when he told his parents he was going to see Mrs. Lillie, just returned from Italy and his father remarked he should be spending his time with pretty girls not visiting old ladies, Charlie said nothing. He crossed the street, wearing his best suit, and formally asked my mother for my hand. She was delighted, and wrote to me that he really loved me. She arranged for him to meet Uncle Jack whom she considered the head of the family. Charlie went back across the street and gave them his news. His mother immediately wrote me a lovely letter welcoming me into the family.

So, when he came back from Scotland, we told our American friends we were getting married. Inadvertently I gave a mild shock to one of Charlie's girlfriends who phoned me to ask what was new? When I told her, there was a thunderstruck pause at the other end of the line – then she made some comment to the effect that he'd been sure to be snapped up by someone. One of my own closest female confidants, a divorcee, asked me point blank if he was good in bed? I'd never sampled him there but lied confidently and said he was thoroughly satisfying. "Sex is important," she remarked. "That was something we didn't realise, the first time around."

We also set about planning our wedding. I wrote to my old boss, Stewart Wark at his advertising agency in Vermont. He had several hotels as clients and sent me a delightful collection of folders with notes identifying those that were overpriced or old ladies' homes. We settled on the Woodstock Inn and wrote for reservations.

Then I phoned Bob Lee, Madison Avenue Presbyterian's musical director and newly ordained. When he asked me which of the ministers I wanted to perform the marriage ceremony, I told him, "You of course. You're the one I know best."

He gulped and said, "I suppose I could."

"Sure you could. When our alto soloist had a baby, you christened it."

We kept the information that this was Bob's first marriage

228

ceremony from Catherine's husband who was nervous enough already about being a best man. His wife had no such qualms as my matron of honour.

The Giraldis, who'd so often included me in family parties, said they'd put on a wedding reception for me. Louise asked me why I hadn't invited her to be my bridesmaid? I explained that as a Catholic she couldn't be part of a Presbyterian ceremony. Nowadays,this isn't so, but it certainly was the case back in 1956. I had been in the bridal party when a mutual friend we called "Irish Helen" got married but I hadn't joined in the communion.

My wedding dress was a street length greyish blue taffeta with straight 'Empire' lines and I had a tiny hat made to match by a wonderful wacky milliner on East 8th Street called Lucy Stander. She was divorced from the actor Lionel Stander and puffed constantly on cigarettes. Louise and I would go into her little shop and describe the kind of hat we had in mind. She'd listen, disappear into the back and return with a couple of totally different bonnets. When we said these mightn't be what we wanted, she'd haul out a lot of headgear for us to try on and of course eventually we'd pick her own first choice. It was always just right, too.

"Water leaves spots on taffeta so keep it out of the rain," warned 'the Lucy' when she handed me the lovely little cap she'd made me for a rockbottom price.

But September 26, 1956 dawned damp and misty. Leaving my apartment, I put on my going away outfit, a blue wool dress and a tweed coat, and carefully swaddled my ceremonial dress and hat in plastic for the cab ride across town to where the Giraldis lived. There I changed into my blue taffeta ensemble. I had pale beige gloves and carried a little sealskin muff which my bridegroom had given me the Christmas before. To this I pinned a corsage of yellow roses. Our families in Scotland had sent flowers for the apartment.

Mrs. Giraldi, Aline and Louise and I got into a taxi for the long ride uptown to Madison Avenue and East 73rd Street. We were excited but on edge. The rain had stopped, but it wasn't far away. To avoid the midday traffic we took the East Side Highway on the fringe of Manhattan Island.

At East 34th Street the cab stopped. The large taciturn driver got out, walked slowly around his vehicle, stuck a cigarette in his mouth, lit and drew on it, then opened the back door. "Everyone out," he ordered. "I've got a flat."

"But I'm on my way to my wedding!" I protested.

"Sorry, lady. I gotta go find a phone and call a repair service." He ushered us out, locked his cab and shambled off.

Aline jumped purposefully onto the road and by some miracle flagged down another taxi. By that time, we were all shaking.

And then, at East 68th Street and Lexington Avenue, our driver, a much nicer man, turned and said, "Ladies, you're not having much luck today. I've got a flat too!"

In all my years of constant taxi travel, I'd never had a single taxi break down and now on my way to my wedding, I got two in a row. I wondered fleetingly if it was a bad omen.

That second incident, however, didn't increase our panic, it started us laughing. We were within walking distance of the Church, the rain had stopped, there were so many empty cabs around, we found one immediately.

Even so, we arrived just in time for the ceremony, scheduled for 11.00 because there was a funeral at 2 o'clock. Dorothy Lee, Bob's wife, was to play the organ for that, leaving him free to marry us in the chapel. This meant we had no music – except in our hearts.

Waiting for me at the door of the church, Catherine greeted me with, "Charlie looks very nervous."

"What's made him nervous?" I asked. "Did he have two flats on the way up here like me?"

Bob had always said a brief prayer before the choir processed into the church. Now he gathered Charlie, the Ashcrafts and me around him, and blessed us before we entered the chapel. There were about twenty people there, including Dorothy Lee and one of her children. My old pal, the Englishman Bill Farrell, acted as usher.

And then the sun came out and shone! I have a collection of photographs snapped on the side steps of the church including a sweet one of Charlie and me gazing into each other's eyes. Since it was a weekday, people had to get back to work, but the

President of the Advertising Women and several members of that group were there and so was the editor of *Medical News*. "You should give Charlie more time off!" my BIS pal Dorothy Harmshaw informed him, after some champagne, and he good-naturedly agreed.

It was a happy party and on a late afternoon train to Vermont we slept off the champagne, emerging at White River Junction into sharp clear cold air that completed our sobering up. We took a taxi to the Woodstock Inn, and arrived close to midnight.

Upstairs, in the bedroom, Charlie's first question was, "Did you remember to pack that Johnny Walker I brought you from Edinburgh?"

"It's right on the top in my suitcase," said I, the perfect wife.

Scots don't need ice in their whisky. He mixed us a couple of healthy drinks in the toothbrush mugs and, still fully dressed, we sat down side by side on the bed and toasted one another. We then started replaying the day, starting with the two failed taxis.

"How did *you* get to the kirk?" I asked.

"I took the subway," said Charlie and we began to laugh.

The bedside telephone peeled. It couldn't be Stewart Wark. He'd left a note saying he'd pick us up at noon next day and take us out to his home for lunch.

"The lady in the next room," said the desk clerk, "just called to complain about all the noise you're making. Please, Mr. and Mrs. Marwick, be more quiet."

So we muffled our merriment and in due course consumated our marriage as quietly as we could. My hypothesis that a man is the same in bed as he is out of it proved correct and I can honestly state that never thereafter did I have the slightest inclination to sleep with anyone else but Charlie.

We had a delightful honeymoon and returned to West 11th Street where Bill Farrell had been feeding the cats and taking messages. It seemed to me that every man I hadn't seen in ages phoned me for a date that weekend and got news of my marriage from a male voice with a British accent.

33

A New Kind of Life

We had planned our wedding for late September, after the November issue of my magazine had, as the saying goes, gone to bed. I was reasonably happy on *Family Circle* and been given a raise in pay because my sales had increased. But Evelyn Kent lost her baby in late pregnancy then resigned and I found her successor, Florence, less compatible. She was unfriendly, possibly suspicious of other women in business, and she considered me a bit flaky.

While I was working flat out on the November book, a pleasant young space salesman walked in looking for work. The magazine, although in financial trouble, hired him, assigned him to the mail order section, and told me to orient him. I said I was glad of extra help but didn't have much time for briefings. He was a nice chap and we got along well. Florence and our secretary adored him.

The week before my wedding, the advertising manager called me in and asked if I planned to keep on working as a married woman? I said I did. He then told me that the magazine couldn't afford me. They were replacing me with the young man, presumably at a smaller salary. "Because, honey, he has a future with us and you haven't," he added, leaving unsaid that, like Evelyn Kent, I'd probably get pregnant and want time off the job.

He couldn't have fired me on these grounds today. If he had I could have sued the magazine for gender discrimination.

At the time, it came as a shock but I kept my cool, since it wasn't this man's fault and he was so obviously embarrassed by what he had to do. I parted on good terms with him, and walked out, after making a date for lunch later that week with Carole, the junior secretary in the mail order section.

That morning she phoned me at 9.15. "Helen, I couldn't wait till noon to tell you the news. The whole office is in an uproar. Guess who else got the axe!" The list included the vice president, everyone he'd hired and all the better-paid salesmen.

I found something else before long and during that job search remember only one interview – with a public relations man, a real Madison Avenue type, who asked me why I'd left *Family Circle*?

I told him, "I was fired."

He gulped, then said, "Well, that's an honest answer anyway."

I explained, "The way they put it was that they were letting me go for reasons of economy. To me there was no distinction between that and being fired."

"They were replacing me with the young man, presumably at a smaller salary. 'Because, honey, he has a future with us and you haven't,' he added, leaving unsaid that I'd probably get pregnant and want time off."

On my resumé I'd always listed Lennox Personnel as my first job because "So you worked for Maud!" was invariably the opening comment from interviewers many of whom had either done the same or knew people who had. This made me an unemployed co-worker rather than an applicant.

I developed a good rapport with one woman who was building up a nice employment business. She'd found me the *Junior League* job and been embarrassed when the reumuneration turned out to be so thin. Now she referred me to a management consultant whose female vice president, a retired US government executive, was a specialist in streamlining correspondence. "Dress yourself up for the interview," recommended my friend.

And so I met my best boss after Capotosto. Her name was Mona Sheppard and she was born in Alabama. She was sixtyish, handsome, forthright and always stylishly turned out. We got along famously and she hired me. As I left that first meeting, she remarked in her Southern accent, "Honey, that's the cutest little hat you're wearing!"

We had some wonderful times working together. She liked me because I spoke my mind and joked with her, to the horror of one young male executive in the company whom she scared to death. Once I remarked on this to Mona. "But, honey, whyever would he be scared of me?" she asked, genuinely surprised.

"Because you're so much smarter than he is," I told her, "and you don't have three kids to support."

We composed sets of letter for, among others, the New York Stock Exchange. This involved my spending weeks thumbing through files and establishing the commonest queries that could be answered with variations on a form letter. I also had to look out for gobbledygook and verbose writing. "Find me some horrible examples, honey!" Mona would beg. It wasn't hard. In our final presentation for the Stock Exchange executives, we included these communications, transcribed without identification by a temporary helper, a beautiful eighteen-year unemployed model.

As she was typing up the portfolio, her machine suddenly fell silent and a little voice inquired if she could ask me something?

"What's the problem?" said I.

"This paragraph doesn't make any sense!" exclaimed this kid who hadn't even gone to college, pointing a red-tipped fingernail at a letter signed by a man earning many, many times her daily wage.

"That's what this job's all about," I explained. She loved it.

At one seminar, Mona assigned the men (I don't remember any women executives!) to rewrite some of the horrible examples, and one of these came out even longer than the original, causing my boss to groan, as we packed up at the end of the session, "Honey, let's go find us a martini!"

We spent a week in Massachusetts trying to move the Boston and Maine Railroad into the twentieth century. The managerial floors were freshly painted and modern, staffed by beautiful young women under twenty-five. Downstairs there were Ediphone Operators, some of whom had done whatever they did for over half a century. "I hate to ask those old ladies for anything, it causes them such physical pain just to stand up," sighed Mona.

We had desk space in a big office where elderly males wearing eyeshades and with metal clips around their shirtsleeves fiddled with strange outmoded instruments until Mona or I got up to walk around. Then all their heads would lift up and dim but lecherous eyes would follow our every move. "Helen, I swear those old men never saw a woman before," remarked my boss.

In every firm, I noticed, there was someone, usually in middle management, who resented changes and subtly fought our efforts to streamline the systems. At the B & M, it was a Mr. Carroll. He had a pronounced Baaast'n accent, and Mona, when the chips were down, would revert into a Southern belle to achieve her ends. I spent one morning listening to her debate some procedure with this Yankee and by the time she got up to leave, they were talking two totally different languages.

A nationwide recession hit management consultancy and I was let go. I was the company's most recently hired employee and also, of course, female. Mona returned to her home in Bethesda and went into business for herself. A few years later, when Charlie and I moved to Washington, DC, I worked for her again, met her sister and her elderly mother, and loved them all.

Having lost three jobs through no fault of my own, I got the message and concentrated on my own writing. By then Catherine Gavin had published the first of a long line of successful historical novels and she had had enough of her weekly column in the *Bulletin*. With her connivance I wrote to Alison Downie, still the women's editor, offering my services and enclosing a couple of articles.

From then on, I wrote regularly for the George Outram Company, moving my weekly Inside USA column (later entitled Helen Lillie's Washington Letter) into the *Glasgow Herald*. I also recycled a lot of Charlie's stories for overseas medical publications.

And I also completed my novel, *The Listening Silence*, with encouragement from Elizabeth Byrd whom I'd met in 1948 when I moved to Gay Street. She was as wonderful as a friend as she was as a historical novelist. She is now dead and I miss her greatly.

By 1964, Charlie had grown frustrated with *Medical World News* and a friend who was resigning from the *Detroit News* recommended him as a replacement to cover science and medicine. So we moved to the Midwest, leaving behind a charming apartment at 413 Bleeker Street, much bigger than the one on West 11th.

This move was our only major disagreement in over forty years of marriage, although with hindsight I know he was right to act as he did. But I hated Detroit although I made several long-lasting friendships there. We stayed less than a year for Charlie was no happier than I was. Besides, his previous employers at *Medical World News* realised his value once he was gone and offered him an opening in their Washington bureau.

So, with all expenses paid, we moved to the District of Columbia, first into an apartment in Georgetown, then into the first of two small houses in the same lovely neighbourhood.

I like books to have happy endings, so I'll leave us there, still reasonably young and healthy and ready to enjoy many years of good life in a lovely city where we made many friends. Most of the public happenings I wrote up in my column for the *Herald*, from which I fired myself in 1994, burned out and ready to switch – finally! – to writing books.

Postscript

A Long Way, but it's Only the Start

The question underlying these memoirs, and indeed much of my life, is what my generation of women have achieved in bettering their way of life? Women *have* made progress. But we've still a long way to go and God forbid that future generations should take our little bit of progress for granted. So please, Gentle Younger Readers, read on!

Today's young careerists complain that their generation suffers from "option overload." There are too many places a girl can go, and too many ways to get whatever she thinks she wants in life, like a career, motherhood, or both, either simultaneously or at different times.

Even in wartime, her grandmother's contemporaries seldom had that problem, and while in no way disparaging its seriousness, having it to make shows how far women have progressed during the twentieth century.

They now start even with their brothers in the job market. In 1939, when Francis and I came to New York, he was a candidate for trainee positions in publishing firms while I was being offered receptionist or junior office jobs like filing and typing. I wasted years doing secretarial work for which I wasn't suited, physically or psychologically. But few firms would consider me for anything else. One possible lost opportunity that I sometimes regret came when I was a candidate for secretary to Mrs. Blanche Knopf, whose husband Alfred owned the prestigious publishing firm. Among the requirements for the job was a willingness to work late and sometimes on weekends and for that reason I told the employment agency I wasn't interested because I had to cook for my husband. Today I wouldn't have had that problem because Charlie can if necessary feed himself and wouldn't have minded in the circumstances.

Nowadays, young women professionals, such as lawyers, protest that early on in their careers they get the dullest projects to handle but this is probably also true for their male counterparts. And today, newspapers would be unlikely to tell an experienced journalism applicant (as they told me in 1947) that women had to be secretaries for five years before they became staff writers. That was the standard attitude. Mary McGrory, now a respected columnist on the *Washington Post*, was once told when applying for a job on another newspaper, that in addition to being a reporter, she'd have to work part-time on the switchboard!

Though women are still the first to be let go when the economy is tight, they have more legal safeguards nowadays. Looking back over my own career, I'm sure that nowadays, the Scarsdale Country Day School couldn't have used instructors' wives as full-time teachers without paying them, nor would modern women accept such exploitation. And, today, I couldn't have been so easily exchanged for a less expensive male salesman by *Family Circle*, a magazine, incidentally, with a predominantly female readership.

Nor might I have been ousted so easily from my job in the advertising agency. I could have demanded proof of my alleged inadequancies, and I mightn't have hesitated, as I did, to point out the underlying issue, i.e. that one man wanted me gone because he was afraid of what I knew.

"But women do get eased out!" a handsome, successful, fiftyish female friend, an editor, told me recently. "My company just hired a pretty twenty-five year old for more money than they're paying me and put her in a job where I have to report to her. I get the message so I'm looking around. I'm also hiring a woman lawyer who's specialised in this kind of case."

In my day and even as late as the 1980s, men thought women who sued their employers were wasting time and energy. The male attitude was, "Why don't they just look for other jobs?" But a growing percentage of these women are heads of households with children or ageing parents to support, just like their bosses.

The British Information Services, because they relied on experts who came in both sexes, didn't obviously discriminate, at least in the Information Division. We were a team of friends and equals. But at the predominantly Canadian British Security Coordination, women were second class citizens though they could head up a files division or a secretarial department. Even although what I produced was properly considered important and rewarded by small pay raises, I was always just an assistant in the communications department. I was never included in the policy meetings, and I'm quite sure I didn't draw as high a salary as Roald Dahl.

Cappy always treated me as a valued partner and once pointed out to me the number of powerful females who were media buyers in advertising agencies. But from daily experience, I knew that few of the people we dealt with, starting with our Filipino clients, considered me more than a glorified secretary, and "breaking the secretarial barrier" was one of the commonest problems job counsellors in those days advised on.

Today any secretary worth her salt is properly known as an administrative assistant and women in the kind of job I had at Media Representatives ask for titles like Assistant Director. As for the way my efforts were interfered with by people like the alcoholic Bill, I suspect that, today, one good threat from me might have given him pause. And the legal weapon of sexual harassment would have brought into line some of the characters with whom I had to do business while Cappy was overseas.

When Charlie and I moved to Detroit, I had introductions from ANWY to the local Womens' Advertising Club. Nevertheless, at my first meeting I was identified as "the wife of the new medical editor on the *Detroit News*." I stood up and pointed out that, as myself, i.e. Helen Lillie, I had been active in New York in sales and public relations. Moreover, I was already contributing to the city's other major newspaper! I wrote features and reviewed books for that publication and the *News*, which had ignored my existence during my husband's hiring, didn't like this. Today, they would probably have had to offer to find me work when persuading him to take the job. Relocation of career couples is an area in which married women have made genuine progress.

It seems incredible that only at BSC did I have any health insurance through my job, a problem shared by male co-workers. And never did I even think of claiming overtime from any firm I worked for. I wish I had! As late as the 1960s I went on a job interview spying for my employment agency pal. The position involved contract work in a major publishing firm. When the pleasant (male) executive who interviewed me brought up salary, I commented that what he offered was remarkably low for the amount of responsibility. "Yes!" he answered off the top of his head, then backtracked quickly to point out the advantages, like security of tenure and that old cliché about "meeting interesting people." I reported to my friend that the company was looking for a female replacement for a man because they could offer her less money.

Corporations wouldn't dare try that today because women applicants would have researched the job and through minimum wage scales they are protected by equal opportunity legislation. That they sometimes don't invoke this may be due to ignorance or fear. We still have to overcome the victim psychology that leads to battered wives at home and exploitation in the workplace.

I hope that by now we've gone beyond the kind of sexist regulations that made me enter through a special door of the Princeton Club when I was President of the Glasgow University Club of America on the single occasion we held a meeting there.

Obviously, women keep moving up in every profession, despite the widely publicised "glass ceiling". In America, many ambitious women start their own companies rather than waste time battling a male establishment in their professional area.

So I've lived to see a partial breakthrough in one of the two biggest career problems for my generation of women.

The other was sexual harassment and according to a recent *Wall Street Journal* article, accusations from female workers are now greatly feared by large corporations. Though many of the cases are ludicrous, and the machinery for redressing grievances often so legally clumsy it's easy to criticise, at least the situation is now recognised as a legitimate problem and not something to be laughed off by male management, as it certainly would have been in my father's day. ("Stop it! I like it fine!" was his interpretation of any young girl's refusal to be tickled.)

As a very young girl, when British women won the right to

vote, I overheard a group of my father's business friends making light of this momentous happening. They chuckled that there would now be toasts to "The Ladies. Once our superiors. Now our equals." I never forgot this and I'm sure my mother, who was present, didn't either.

Such snide, defensive denigration is still around. As I write, in America there's a male backlash directed against Hillary Rodham Clinton, who is strong, capable, charming and, as First Lady, extremely powerful. I can remember how, over fifty years ago, Eleanor Roosevelt was similarly attacked.

At least modern women can fight back with support from organisations like the National Organisation for Women (NOW) which command good financial support from their own members. Money supplies what Henry Kissinger described as the strongest of aphrodisiacs, namely power. Today women can earn it and many of them are millionaires.

Unfortunately, however, special interest groups can abuse the prospect of money and notoriety to lure young women like Paula Jones and Monica Lewinsky into attacking effective though oversexed public figures like President Clinton. But, viewed in historical perspective, the current deplorable exploitation of unwary women by male extremists implies an acceptance of equality between the sexes in the workplace and, to that extent, it's healthy. Also, it may lead to better legislation on sexual harassment. Certainly it has brought the whole subject well out of the closet, even more so than Anita Hill's accusations against Clarence Thomas a few years earlier.

> "As a very young girl, when British women won the right to vote, I overheard a group of my father's business friends making light of this momentous happening. They chuckled that there would now be toasts to 'The Ladies. Once our superiors. Now our equals.' I never forgot this and I'm sure my mother, who was present, didn't either."

I admire women who achieve power and a definitive lifestyle through their own endeavours, but riches, especially the inherited kind, don't impress me at all, something many of my friends find incomprehensible. I have observed that making money is a special talent and has little to do with intellectual qualities or superior intelligence. Some people have it and others haven't. If you don't believe me, Gentle Readers, just look around you at the self-made millionaires you know or have read about.

As long as they have money and political clout, women can keep their hard-won control over their own bodies, a right the erroneously named Pro-Life movement would deny them. How much of the anti-abortionist platform is a sincere desire to save babies and how much is it just plain anti-feminism? Though I was never faced with the prospect of an illegal abortion I knew women who were and I am proud to have participated in feminist demonstrations to keep the procedure legal in the United States.

Having lived long enough to read the life stories of contemporaries, I find that a lot of my less chaste behaviour was typical of my time. Many of my female contemporaries still lacked professional training, and their only way to achieve security was the time-honoured finding of a man. The career of Pamela Digby Churchill Hayward Harriman is an example of how the right marriages (and some less formal arrangements) led eventually into such a successful career of fundraising she was rewarded by being appointed Ambassador to France, a post she filled admirably until her untimely death in 1997.

There was a lot of sleeping around during the 1940s and 1950s. Some was reaction to World War II and the male argument that, "I'm off to the front line tomorrow and may never come back." But I think it also demonstrated that women felt they were entitled to equal pleasure when doing men's work. In those days we didn't have the Pill or legal abortion to protect us but these followed.

We're starting to appreciate how political pressure can speed up research into diseases like AIDS and breast cancer so maybe women having the vote led to the so-called sexual revolution with its progress in contraception measures.

World War I used women for many jobs and some of them never returned to the home front, they kept on with their careers. But when peace came in 1918, the majority of that generation of girls returned to being "flappers" or daughters at home because they didn't have enough education or experience to compete in a male society.

In World War II, with their usefulness in the workforce already established, women were able to move up fast into good jobs. But then the troops returned and their female substitutes were eased out and, perforce, many became housewives and mothers in suburbia.

But it was a case of "How you gonna keep 'em down on the farm, After they've seen Paree?" In 1963, Betty Friedan articulated this in her book *The Feminine Mystique* and we know the rest.

There will be periods of retrogression – and we may be moving into one at present – but as long as women keep their right to vote, to keep their earnings and control their bodies, the enterprising ones will still be able to have the kind of lives they want.

In one area at least they've already accomplished a revolution which has had far-flung consequences. Undereducated or so-called 'working class' women don't necessarily have to settle for life-long domestic service. And well-educated but impoverished spinsters don't perforce become nannies or governesses. If they do go into these professions, they no longer work around the clock like their Victorian and Edwardian predecessors.

Today, the Brontë sisters and their fictional counterparts would command good salaries and be less dependent on finding dubious male employers like Mr. Rochester. And if, Reader, the modern Jane Eyre married him, her action, today, would be seen as doing him a favour.

This domestic revolution – for such indeed it is – means that many affluent women householders are having to participate actively in many more domestic duties, even when they have regular help. This has led to a new approach to home and kitchen design which in turn has had major repercussions on many corporations.

I own two copies of Mrs. Beeton's classic *Book of Household*

Management, one published in 1888 (and inscribed by Uncle Ned, "To a good and kind Housewife," probably Auntie), and a revised edition Mummy sent me in 1960. In the second book, the print is larger, recipes are easier to read and far more calorie conscious, and the chapters on training staff like footmen and scullery maids have been replaced by guidelines on hiring part-time employees for parties.

The chapters on equipment have also been totally replaced, for a buyer who is going to use the product herself has a different approach from her grandmother who invested in major culinary items like stoves and freezers for her servants to use. The same is true of pots and pans, casseroles and kitchen gadgetry. And would the use of labour-saving electricity in homes have developed so fast without women's influence?

The time it takes to produce meals is, today, such a major factor in home life that it has created whole new industries – of canned and frozen food products to say nothing of the ubiquitous carry-outs. All these have revolutionised the marketing of food items. I wonder if the management of companies selling TV dinners ever consider how much they owe to Women's Lib?

As for maintainance, my old employer the Cleanliness Bureau, which encouraged people to use soap for just about everything, wouldn't have been needed at the turn of the century when a bestseller in Britain was a comprehensive collection of *Tried Favourites* by Mrs. E.W. Kirk, a Scottish minister's wife. Her opus went through twenty-six editions before 1947, the date of the copy I inherited from my mother. In addition to recipes Mrs. Kirk offered directions to housewives on how to make their soap, ammonia too, polish for furniture, brass and steel, boot and shoe cleaner, even waterproofing for coats and shawls! Thrifty middle class women didn't go to a supermarket to buy their cleaners in her day.

Womens' ability to earn money has also led to changed guidelines within the home. In biographies of the Brontë family there's no mention of Bramwell having domestic duties like his brilliant sisters. In today's household who does the cooking and cleaning is not so clearly defined. And when both partners work,

246

does the husband or wife stay home when a child or parent is sick?

Recent (1998) studies of working couples have found that, today, women with jobs spend only 45 minutes a day more time on domestic matters than their male housemates. Home and career priorities are also becoming increasingly similar for both sexes with men less anxious to work overtime because they want to be with their families.

I can't speak from personal experience about allocating responsibilities in households with children, but I've always been considered responsible for keeping my home clean, though I seldom accomplished this. One of my first actions after leaving Francis was to hire a cleaning woman, nudged by Phyllis Lintott whose 'lady' had a free day. Since then, I've never been without one, and have learned that there are many intelligent people who genuinely enjoy coping with domestic dirt and disorder.

But the preparation of food remains a grey area for men and women who live togther. "I never realised marriage meant cooking a dinner every night!" wailed a successful careerist who married in her thirties. "I like making meals but – every night!"

Every night, Josephine, unless there's a convenient carry-out near the office or the male of the household fancies himself at the stove – as many do, unlike my father's generation who could barely make a cup of tea. My first husband, who expected me to make cooking his dinner my first priority at the end of my working day would now find himself an anachronism in the modern marriage mart despite his charm. Today I could have divorced him because he gave me no help in the kitchen. One reads of such cases. And men who elect to be "house husbands" because their wives have better career and earning potential are becoming increasingly common and socially acceptable.

Between marriages I used to joke that if I ever took another spouse he'd be a good cook – and this I achieved with Charlie Marwick, whose far-sighted mother trained her two sons and two daughters to handle the same domestic duties, both cleaning and culinary. She was away ahead of her time.

As I grow older, my husband takes on an increasing amount of the catering, a job I'd love to retire from. I hope one of the next steps in Women's Liberation will be recognition that preparing meals is a demanding job which must be done at times of day when blood sugar is low, like first thing in the morning or after a day's work. It also involves a lot of advance planning and time-consuming shopping.

I am not speaking lightly when I say that the apprehensions I, like others, have about the Hereafter, decrease when I consider the unlikelihood of having to prepare meals in Eternity! That for me is a future devoutly to be wished for. I do enjoy good food properly served. But I grew up expecting it to be put before me and getting a meal together has always been stressful to me. At the Swiss school, there was the fear that spoiling a dish would leave my classmates hungry. With my first husband, anything he didn't like was a cause for complaint. Nowadays because I love Charlie I want him to have a proper evening meal but alas! I bitch while preparing it because I too have been working hard enough to be tired and am also growing old.

The American columnist Ellen Goodman has pointed out that when men cook women lose some domestic power. Problems can arise, too, when couples share the catering. "My husband cooked himself out of his first wife," a woman friend told me. "He'd rearrange things and keep the place cold to marinate meat. When we revamped our kitchen, I positioned the stove at right angles to the wall so that he could work on one set of burners and I on another, and we could both have our own equipment."

Two in the Kitchen, (Acropolis Press, 1974) written by a couple of Washington journalists, Joe and Jeanne Anderson, addresses wittily, the problems of dual activity at the stove. They spell out guidelines for amicable partnerships but also make the excellent point that cooking together gave them more time to enjoy each others' company. They also emphasise that "love" is the most necessary ingredient in the preparation of food.

I think it's the most necessary ingredient in everything!

Envoi

My Yale Drama School contemporary Alladean Bell once told me how she and some contemporaries had made lists of what they had wanted early in their careers and upon going through these in later life, found nearly 90 percent of their objectives had been achieved. I'd agree with this result. In my own case I've written some novels that have a small but dedicated readership, and I have a happy marriage. So I've done what I most wanted to do.

My mother subtly influenced me against having children, on the grounds that diseases like otosclerosis (the type of deafness afflicting the Lillies) and manic depression were hereditary. My first husband, Francis, didn't want any offspring. Charlie didn't care. My books and the characters in them have been my offspring, as is the case with many writers.

I've enjoyed my long life and currently live in "the best of all possible worlds," Washington's Georgetown, where I have a small garden with flowers, trees and many birds, yet within walking distance of parks, shops, good restaurants, churches and libraries. And the Kennedy Center with its concert halls and theatres is a short taxi ride away. My husband takes a bus to work and when we need a car, we hire one. We have nice neighbours and a variety of interesting friends whom we've met through our profession of journalism or through associations like the Society of Woman Geographers, the American News Womens' Club and various science writers' groups.

I believe that, as Professor Bowman told his students at Glasgow University, the most important aspect of life is the inter-relation of spirit with spirit, i.e. friendship and love. But I've learned that individuals with mental illness can only be helped by professionals. However much they care, friends can't do it.

Profesor Bowman emphasized to his students that Plato's definition of justice and a just society in *The Republic* boiled

249

down to people minding their own business, concentrating on doing the best they could in their own areas of expertise and leaving others to do the same.

To me the most subtly destructive pronouncements start with the words "You should . . ." It's presumptuous to tell other people how to run their lives when our own are so imperfect. I've also noticed that when individuals sound off on what the rest of the world ought to be doing, they themselves are usually in the midst of some demeaning crisis of their own.

That's why I don't listen to unsolicited advice and try not to offer it. It's just opinion. Only when someone asks you for help or information are suggestions potentially useful, and then they should be given unjudgmentally.

I base this on many years of involvement with career counselling, most recently as a volunteer with a pioneer Employment Support Centre in Washington which holds regular open meetings for laid-off white collar workers. Over a brown bag lunch and free coffee, participants are offered programmes on interview techniques and the like. But mostly they just talk, swapping job leads, "letting it all hang out" among their peers, and improving morale by listening with understanding to problems and complaints. One of our graduates, a banker, described these exchanges as "love" (that word again!) in the letter of appreciation he wrote to us when, after a long eight months, he found a job.

In her late eighties and still in reasonably good health, Mummy got up and dressed one December morning in 1970, then suffered a massive stroke. Mrs. Sanderson found her unconscious at the foot of the stairs, with a broken hip. Mercifully she never recovered her senses before the end came.

"She doesn't want someone living in the house," my sensible cousin Morag had told me not long before, "so if she's found dead some morning, that's the way she wanted it and you mustn't feel guilty." I never did.

Two weeks earlier Mummy had written to an old friend that, "Death must be like wakening from a bad dream into a glorious summer morning."

250

She'd been en route to a coffee party downtown. In her purse, tucked in beside a transcript she'd made of Emily Brontë's poem, 'No coward soul is mine' she had a ticket for a ballet performance. After the funeral, one of her friends, a salty old lady whose husband was then professor of Moral Philosophy at Glasgow University, phoned me and said, "It was such a shame your mother died when she did. She was planning a trip to Glasgow for the following week. She and I were going to see *Hair*."

Not bad to depart this life while you're still able to enjoy yourself. And, although I don't think she altogether liked it, I'm glad she lived to see me publish *The Listening Silence*.

Uncle Jack lived to be almost a hundred and appointed me his residuary legatee. While clearing out his flat at 85 Great King Street in Edinburgh, I stayed in the Robert Louis Stevenson House at 17, Heriot Row, with Kathleen Macfie (now Lady Dunpark) whom I'd met through Uncle Bertie soon after Mummy died. Kathleen was invaluable in finding appropriate charitable outlets for all the odds and ends I needed to dispose of, and she remains a valued friend.

I kept little 2B Church Hill, for my husband liked it as much as I did. We built on another room and rent it furnished, usually to Americans who appreciate the good central heating. Once, when spending a night there, Betty Byrd wakened and saw the word LOVE repeated all over the bedroom walls. "You're surrounded by love in that house," she told me.

In 1999 I received a letter, out of the blue, from a former tenant who'd met his wife while living at 2B and he claimed the same thing!

THE END

Other Books from Argyll Publishing

The Strathblane novels Helen Lillie
Home to Strathblane 1 874640 40 8 352pp £5.99
Beginning in the years of the French Revolution and Enlightenment
Edinburgh, Lillie's characters live out their lives in and around the
Stirlingshire village of Strathblane.
Strathblane and Away 1874640 47 5 240pp £6.99
Douglas Stewart, headstong yet principled local doctor and son of
a Borders manse, continues to question the existing order. Yet
whether trying to make peace with his conservative Melrose
father, mixing with company in Enlightenment Edinburgh, or even
happily living at his Strathblane home with his new wife, Jean, he
yearns for new challenges.
The Rocky Island 1 874640 79 3 208pp £6.99
The third novel in the trilogy sees the Stewarts complete their
voyage to America and set up home in New York. Just as she
captured the spirit and detail of late eighteenth century Scotland,
Helen Lillie brings her historian's eye and her story teller's craft to
her characters' lives in the new United States.

The set of three Strathblane novels *Home to Strathblane*,
Strathblane and Away and *The Rocky Island* in a slip case. only £9.99
> "recreates 18th century life in her native parish with a
> sympathetic pen" *Scots Magazine*
> "a sound, gripping piece of story telling. Lillie knows her Scott
> and his tradition" *Books in Scotland*
> "a fluidity of style, convincing and authentic" *Scottish Field*
> "a gifted storyteller" *Scottish Home & Country*

Argyll Publishing Glendaruel Argyll PA22 3AE
tel 01369 820229